Effective Peer Learning

Peer learning allows a positive use of differences between pupils, turning them into learning opportunities. Yet education professionals often remain unfamiliar with the principles necessary to guarantee its effectiveness.

The aim of this book is to help practitioners establish well-structured and effective peer learning projects using a variety of methods. It introduces and defines cooperative learning (mutual peer interaction) and peer tutoring (directional peer interaction) – outlining general organisational principles that will help practitioners implement peer learning in either of these forms. The authors consider how to prepare and train learners to undertake their roles effectively, and how to organise and monitor the process of interaction as it is happening. They then look at how these systems actually operate in the classroom, exploring how the organisational principles work in practice and giving many practical examples. Subsequently three successive chapters consider how to structure peer interactions in cooperative learning, same-age peer tutoring and cross-age peer tutoring. Finally, the advantages and problems, and the potential and challenges, of peer learning are examined.

The book should be read in stages, with each part being able to be read on its own – thus providing time for reflection. Within each part, readers can choose to focus on cooperative learning or peer tutoring. The successive focuses on definitions, general principles of implementation and practical issues of implementation should help practitioners build their skills and confidence. Many choices between methods are described, and when teachers are confident in one method they may then consider trying a new method. It is the authors' hope that the book will become a model for peer learning by sharing with readers the skills of other practitioners, and thereby helping all children to develop to their full potential.

Keith Topping, School of Education, University of Dundee, UK.

Céline Buchs, University of Geneva, Switzerland.

David Duran, Department of Psychology of Education, Universitat Autònoma de Barcelona, Spain.

Hilde van Keer, Department of Educational Studies, Ghent University, Belgium.

Effective Peer Learning

From Principles to Practical Implementation

Keith Topping, Céline Buchs,
David Duran and Hilde van Keer

Routledge
Taylor & Francis Group
LONDON AND NEW YORK

First published 2017
by Routledge
2 Park Square, Milton Park, Abingdon, Oxon OX14 4RN

and by Routledge
711 Third Avenue, New York, NY 10017

Routledge is an imprint of the Taylor & Francis Group, an informa business

© 2017 Keith Topping, Céline Buchs, David Duran and Hilde van Keer

The right of Keith Topping, Céline Buchs, David Duran and Hilde van Keer to be identified as the authors of this work has been asserted by them in accordance with sections 77 and 78 of the Copyright, Designs and Patents Act 1988.

All rights reserved. No part of this book may be reprinted or reproduced or utilised in any form or by any electronic, mechanical, or other means, now known or hereafter invented, including photocopying and recording, or in any information storage or retrieval system, without permission in writing from the publishers.

Trademark notice: Product or corporate names may be trademarks or registered trademarks, and are used only for identification and explanation without intent to infringe.

British Library Cataloguing in Publication Data
A catalogue record for this book is available from the British Library

Library of Congress Cataloging in Publication Data
Names: Topping, Keith J., author.
Title: Effective peer learning : from principles to practical implementation / Keith Topping, Céline Buchs, David Duran and Hilde van Keer.
Description: New York : Routledge, 2017. | Includes bibliographical references.
Identifiers: LCCN 2016044331| ISBN 9781138906488 (hardback) | ISBN 9781138906495 (pbk.) | ISBN 9781315695471 (ebook)
Subjects: LCSH: Peer teaching. | Tutors and tutoring.
Classification: LCC LB1031.5 .T664 2017 | DDC 371.39/4—dc23
LC record available at https://lccn.loc.gov/2016044331

ISBN: 978-1-138-90648-8 (hbk)
ISBN: 978-1-138-90649-5 (pbk)
ISBN: 978-1-315-69547-1 (ebk)

Typeset in Times
by diacriTech, Chennai

Contents

PART I
Introducing peer learning   1

1   Mutual peer interactions   5
2   Peer learning: directional peer interactions   16

PART II
General principles for peer learning   27

3   Preparing learners for constructive interactions   35
4   Organising peer interactions in academic tasks   57

PART III
Practical propositions for the classroom   79

5   Structuring peer interactions in symmetrical relationships (cooperative learning)   83
6   Structuring directional peer interactions in same-age tutoring   109
7   Structuring directional peer interactions in cross-age tutoring   135

PART IV
Conclusions and onward directions   157

8   Advantages, problems, potential and challenges of peer learning   159

References   167
Index   184

Part I

Introducing peer learning

Welcome to *Effective Peer Learning*. In Part I we introduce the ideas of cooperative learning (mutual peer interaction) and peer tutoring (directional peer interaction), helping the practitioner to clearly establish the difference between them. In Part II we outline general organisational principles for peer learning in a way which will help practitioners implement either form of peer learning. We consider how to prepare and train learners to undertake their roles effectively, and how to organise and monitor the process of interaction as it is happening. In Part III we look at how these systems actually operate in the classroom, exploring how the organisational principles work in practice and giving many practical examples. Three successive chapters consider how to structure peer interactions in cooperative learning, same-age peer tutoring and cross-age peer tutoring. Finally, in Part IV we discuss the advantages and problems, and the potential and challenges, of peer learning, together with overall conclusions and some consideration of where teachers might go next and the options open to them.

We hope that readers will find *Effective Peer Learning* organised in a way that lends itself to reading in stages. Each of its four parts can be read on its own, with time for reflection rather than rushing on to the next part. Within each part, readers can choose to focus on cooperative learning or peer tutoring. The successive focuses on definitions, general principles of implementation and practical issues of implementation are designed to help practitioners build their skills and confidence as they go along.

We assume that most practitioners will have implemented at least one peer-learning project before they look at Part IV. Here we discuss the many choices available to practitioners who have accumulated some practical experience and are asking more complex questions about the best way to do things in their own unique context. Throughout we have tried to refer to the evidence which supports what we suggest, and sometimes the citations and references are rather numerous. Do not be put off by this – just disregard them in your first reading and then go back later to explore them if you are interested. Finally, we hope you will yourself become a model for peer learning by helping other practitioners learn some of the skills you have developed – and thereby of course helping all children develop their full potential.

So where do we start? Traditionally teaching was considered a one-way channel. Information flowed from the expert teacher to the novice pupil. Peer interaction was considered irrelevant, or even as a distraction from the serious business of absorbing knowledge, and therefore to be eliminated. However, more recently teachers and other practitioners have come to regard education as a process of acquiring skills and motivations as well as knowledge – and this cannot be done without opportunities to practice which are engaging.

For some time we have known that interactions between students (peer interactions) can give students the opportunity to practice and lead to learning and consolidation of skills.

However, not all peer interaction (dialogue and joint action) actually does lead to learning. Just as with teacher–student interactions, peer interactions are not always constructive. We outline the conditions required for peer interactions to be effective.

We argue that learning occurs thanks to interaction with other peers, which is in line with Piaget's and Vygotsky's work. Both Piaget and Vygotsky underlined peers as mediators of learning. The former pointed at the importance of cooperative social exchange between equal partners (Piaget, 1928, 1932), and the latter pointed at the importance of peers who have more ability than the apprentice (Vygotsky, 1978). We rely on this general distinction to respectively develop mutual peer interactions (Chapter 1) and directional peer interactions (Chapter 2).

Mutual peer learning represents situations in which students are encouraged to work together in small teams on academic tasks in order to achieve a common goal and to develop mutual knowledge and skills (Topping, 2005a). The relations between students are reciprocal, with all students endorsing responsibilities in the interaction. *Directional peer learning* represents situations in which one student (a tutor) has the responsibility to help another or a limited number of other students (tutees) on academic tasks or schoolwork. Traditionally, in tutoring there is temporary or permanent disparity in information or skills between tutors and tutees.

This distinction between mutual and directional peer learning was refined at the end of the 1980s, based on a continuum regarding the quality of peer engagements or scenarios of the educational peer interactions (Damon & Phelps, 1989). Based on the characteristics of the members, the objectives and the type of interaction, the authors distinguish between *peer tutoring* (relationship and instruction between students presenting different skill levels regarding a specific topic), *cooperative learning* (relationship and acquisition or application of knowledge, established between a group of students with various skills within certain margins) and *peer collaboration* (relationship and focused on the acquisition and/or application of knowledge by two or more students with relatively similar abilities).

With respect to the type of interaction and peer engagement, Damon and Phelps (1989) refer to two elements. The degree of equality or directionality of the interactions determines whether both partners (high degree of equality with bidirectional flow) or mainly one partner (low degree of equality with unidirectional flow) shape(s) the interactions and take(s) the lead. The mutuality refers to the communicative transactions and represents the degree to which partners are connected in an extensive engagement.

Damon and Phelps (1989) proposed that in *peer tutoring* equality is low, derived from the unequal role that each student plays (as tutor or as tutee). It seems clear that this is a kind of peer learning with directional peer interactions, mainly managed by the tutor. However, the closer position of the peer tutor, in comparison with an adult teacher, can improve mutuality. Nonetheless, depending on the tutor's interpersonal skills and/or training, as well as on the tutee's receptiveness to learning, this mutuality in peer tutoring varies from low to moderate.

In *cooperative learning*, the responsibilities developed by the students are supposed to be relatively similar or have an equivalent level, based on students' equal status. Therefore, in general, an equal reciprocal relationship is produced (high equality), although at certain times – throughout the team working – tutorial or directional relations may take place. Any student can act as tutor for the rest of the team members at one moment and as a tutee later. Damon and Phelps (1989) suggested that cooperative learning involves a certain division of responsibilities for mastering the task, which reduces mutuality because each member would work on one part before putting the different parts together. At the same time, however, they underscored that mutuality depends on the subdivision of the task, the competition among teams, the distribution of responsibilities or roles among members and the extrinsic or intrinsic rewards. Therefore, we propose that mutuality in *cooperative learning* varies from moderate to high.

Damon and Phelps (1989) proposed that ideal *peer collaboration* is high on both equality and mutuality. As for cooperative learning, the responsibilities in collaborative learning are supposed to be relatively similar, with partners having the same status, leading to high equality. The mutuality is also supposed to be high, with partners working together on the joint task. The degree of mutuality is supposed to be higher in collaborative learning than in cooperative learning. In line with Dillenbourg, Baker, Blaye and O'Malley (1996), cooperative learning is viewed as requiring division of labour among participants, with each member being responsible for sub-tasks they resolve individually and then the group assembling the different portions into the group task. Coordination would be necessary at the final step for assembling the different parts.

By contrast, collaborative learning would require coordinated efforts to solve a joint problem, with members being mutually engaged in the joint task and working together with high coordination for synchronous activity during the whole process (Dillenbourg, 1999; Dillenbourg et al., 1996). These authors rely on Roschelle and Teasley (1995), stating that collaborative learning involves continued attempts to construct and maintain a shared conception of the problem and requires shared negation and meanings in the group.

Our conception differs from that restricted definition. Indeed, while reviewing the major cooperative methods as proposed in Chapter 1, we will underline that not all cooperative methods require division of labour or sub-tasks. Moreover, even if division is not foreseen in a collaborative scenario, it could happen spontaneously. Therefore, this distinction for mutuality criteria does not seem relevant to us. We will argue in Chapter 1 that a main difference between cooperative and collaborative learning lies in the degree of structuring proposed by teachers. Teachers structure students' interactions to a greater extent in cooperative learning in order to strengthen all students' engagement. But as we will see in Chapter 1, the differentiation is not always very clear between the two mutual peer learning approaches. Table I.1 summarises the argument so far.

Table I.1 Characteristics of the dimensions of peer learning

	Peer tutoring	*Cooperative learning*	*Peer collaboration*
Equality (directionality)	Low: Directional flow, tutors control information and agenda.	High: Bidirectional flow, mutual shared responsibilities.	High: Bidirectional flow, mutual shared responsibilities.
Mutuality	Low–moderate: Favoured by peer relations but can be variable depending on the tutor's qualities and tutee's receptivity.	Moderate–high: Variable depending on cooperative methods (subdivision of the task and reward structure). Can be reinforced with systematic planned sequence.	Variable: Supposed to be high, thanks to joint work on the same problem, but can be variable, depending on social-psychological factors.
Degree of structuring	High: Structured academic task and material.	High: Academic task, material and participation structured by teachers.	Variable: Depends on situations and the organisation endorsed by students.

We argue that it is useful to conceive cooperative/collaborative learning as mutual peer interactions and peer tutoring as a directional peer interaction. It is also useful to identify principles that help teachers to structure scenarios in order to favour students' engagement and constructive social interactions. Part I introduces mutual peer interactions (Chapter 1) and then directional peer interactions (Chapter 2). We devote Part II to principles that permit the preparation of students to cooperate (Chapter 3) and the structuring of academic group work (Chapter 4).

Chapter 1

Mutual peer interactions

This chapter defines what represents mutual peer interactions for learning and explains the social and educational relevance of peer interactions, as well as the principles that promote it. We will present the main characteristics of cooperative and collaborative learning. We propose to take 'cooperative learning' as an umbrella term useful for teachers willing to structure mutual peer interactions in their formal learning in the classroom at primary and secondary schools as well as in higher education. Further, in order to help teachers use cooperative learning in their classrooms, examples of methods are synthesised as pedagogical designs to deliberately promote cooperation. Finally, this chapter presents a brief summary of the evidence supporting cooperative learning through results of meta-analyses and reviews of research.

1.1. Collaborative and cooperative learning

1.1.1. Perspectives and definitions

We have seen that both *cooperative learning* and *collaborative learning* involve high equality between learners. Nevertheless, these two approaches include a variety of practices, and there is no consensual scientific position. Some authors use the two terms synonymously (Jacobs, 2015). (The Latin roots of both 'cooperative' and 'collaborative' refer to working together.) So in teaching, both approaches can be understood as the use of small groups of students working together to achieve common goals of learning. Both involve active engagement, small-group learning and development of thinking capabilities (Davidson & Major, 2014). This proximity is illustrated by the fact that some authors espouse cooperative learning under the collaborative banner (cf. Gillies, 2015b).

However, some differences between the two approaches are proposed, which we will discuss briefly. Cooperative learning is rooted in American tradition and anchored in social interdependence, cognitive-developmental and behavioural theories. Collaboration is rooted in British tradition and the linguistic and social nature of knowledge (Brody & Davidson, 1998). For Brody (2009), the difference lies more in the philosophical traditions than in clear differences in practices. For others, differences are more pronounced. For some, 'collaboration' would be a more general term that reflects a philosophy or lifestyle or a way of understanding interactions, in which cooperative learning would be a subcategory (Cuseo, 1992). For others, collaborative learning is a personal general philosophy of interaction, while cooperative learning is a structure of interaction that helps to achieve a specific goal. In this conception, collaborative learning involves shared responsibilities among students in a student-centred approach in which teachers share the authority with students (Panitz, 1999);

groups of students work together with the teacher in order to develop knowledge (Davidson & Major, 2014).

In line with Bruffee (1995), collaborative learning would be relevant for open-ended, nonfoundational knowledge, in which students challenge the teacher's input and the whole community participates in evaluation; whereas cooperative learning would be more appropriate for foundational knowledge, for which the teacher proposes a specific goal or the development of an end product (the teacher proposes what to learn with the material and organises how to learn in structuring interactions, group composition, timing and evaluation). Cooperative learning aims to help students learn academic content (Davidson & Major, 2014). Others see cooperative learning as a more artificial or induced group working form, in comparison with the spontaneous and flexible nature of collaboration (Kneser & Ploetzner, 2001). Panitz (1999) proposed that collaborative learning is more student-centred whereas cooperative learning is more teacher-centred.

What seems consensual for distinguishing cooperative from collaborative learning is the degree of structuring of the interactions between the members of the group (McWhaw, Schnackenberg, Sclater & Abrami, 2003; Millis & Cottell, 1998). Cooperative learning constitutes a generally more structured setting (the teacher acting as an organiser and facilitator and designing the specific goal to achieve the end product), while more freedom is usually given to students who can use open strategies in collaborative learning. The degree of structuring is part of cooperative learning definition illustrated by Davidson and Major's quote, "The group work is carefully organized and structured so as to promote the participation and learning of all group members. The teacher takes an active role, circulating from group to group, providing assistance and encouragement, and asking thought-provoking questions as needed" (Davidson & Major, 2014, pp. 13–14).

1.1.2. Cooperative learning: Structured mutual peer interactions

We propose to use cooperative learning as a generic term for structured mutual peer interactions in foundational knowledge, while recognising that some cooperative learning is more student-centred than others, as we will see in presenting cooperative methods. But who structures, and with what purpose, the interactions between group members? In the formal education contexts on which we focus, the group interaction is defined by the teacher, who designs the specific goal or the end product to develop, and makes decisions about groups, roles, tasks and forms of work that ensure the participation of every one of the group members. As does a coach in the sports field, the teacher organises the group life, so that it becomes a team, where, as we will see later, the participation of all and each one of its members is required for the success of the team.

Why do we propose teachers to structure interaction? Teachers know that if they do not organise the interaction of the group to convert it into a team, to bring out the cooperation, it is most probable that some students will not participate and others will be loaded with all the work. It is not sufficient to put students together and ask them to work together for it to actually happen and students learn. Dysfunctions in group work are not uncommon.

Simple group work is characterised by the dissipation of responsibilities and the fact that some students work to offset – or sometimes impede – the work of others. This fact has been widely shown in research, leading to frustration in teachers and students (Lindauer & Petrie, 1997). This is what used to happen in simple group work, without structuring interaction. Some teachers have mistaken group work for collaborative/cooperative learning. Structuring interaction in the teams is thus a valuable pedagogical aid. Thanks to this, students have the opportunity to learn to work with others and to succeed in cooperation. It is not surprising that the comparison of results between students working in structured groups (teams) and unstructured groups offers clearly better outcomes for the first option, both at primary school (Buchs, Wiederkehr, Filippou, Sommet & Darnon, 2015), high school (Gillies, 2008) or university (Buchs, Gilles, Antonietti & Butera, 2016). Some of these structured interventions will be developed in Chapter 5.

1.1.3. Favoured approaches in specific contexts

However, so far as pedagogy is concerned, structuring among the group members should be gradually removed as students learn to cooperate. Learning to cooperate is a core competence for all educational levels, including higher education. In this sense, we would not agree with assuming cooperative learning operates only in schools or basic education, and collaboration by contrast in university (Bruffe, 1995). Doing this, not offering this aid that involves structuring, could lead us often to say that university students do not know how to cooperate.

In our opinion, on the one hand, cooperative learning with a higher degree of structuring interactions fits the needs of formal education (from primary school to higher education), in contexts with the following characteristics:

- When the context does not favour cooperation. For example, when teams remain artificial, based on external constraints, with members who may not previously have worked together, or when educational systems promote individualistic values or focus on selection, so that grading and ranking is likely to promote competitive goals (Harackiewicz, Barron & Elliot, 1998), structuring interaction may help in promoting constructive peer interactions.
- When students lack social skills and they are neither used to nor socialised for cooperative learning and students need to develop social skills aimed at working in groups, teachers can help them to get into cooperation by structuring interactions. The structure may be gradually transferred to the students themselves, leaving them to decide their forms of organisation, closer to more collaborative formats.
- When the teacher identifies predetermined knowledge she/he wants students to understand and master. Using resources among teams – through previous knowledge or new knowledge built after activities proposed by the teacher – groups solve the task. The structure offered by the teacher is necessary to achieve the goal.

On the other hand, collaborative learning, in which the teacher does not structure the group interaction, is more suitable for informal learning and professional settings.

- When ad hoc teams are initiated by members themselves in order to solve a task or a real problem, which could not be solved individually, in contexts that value teamwork, the degree of structuring is not so important.
- When the members of the team have enough motivation or skills to manage the team by themselves, the team is able to work with success with fewer constraints.
- When the task is open-ended, real problems and not a mere learning task, with no determined result expected or any pre-built knowledge to rebuild, it is necessary to build joint knowledge from the participation of all members. This authentic participation, organised by the members of the group, is what makes the structure emerge.

Having made this clarification, focused as we are in formal education, we will now discuss cooperative learning as an inclusive concept for structured mutual peer interactions. In that broad sense, cooperative learning can be defined as "the instructional use of small groups in which students work together to maximise their own and each other's learning" (Johnson & Johnson, 1999, p. 73). Educational practice is of such richness that it has generated a wide variety of methods, models and instructional practices, under the umbrella of cooperative learning. "In this sense, in the classroom, cooperative learning could be understood as a diversified body of methods of instruction which organise students to work in groups toward a common goal or outcome, or share a common problem or task, in such a way that they can only succeed in completing the work through behaviour that demonstrates interdependence, while holding individual contributions and efforts accountable" (Brody & Davidson, 1998, p. 8).

1.2. Educational relevance of cooperation

Although traditionally classrooms and education centres have been organised around individual and competitive learning, today we know that offering opportunities for students to cooperate or work together is absolutely necessary, for several reasons (Duran, 2009).

Cooperation is a core competence for the knowledge society. So it is recognised by UNESCO (1996) itself; and by the OECD (Deseco, 2002), who define three key competences: use of tools, autonomy and cooperation. Therefore, it makes sense that cooperation or teamwork appears in listings of competences of all educational stages; and is one of the main competences of brain workers. Business values it more each day and conceives it not only as a necessary employee competence, but also as a mechanism of inter-business development. In these fields, the combination of cooperation and competition is called *coopetition* (Brandenburguer & Nalebuff, 1998).

Cooperation develops skills and attitudes needed for a democratic society. Teamwork allows playing with skills and attitudes in real-life situations, and favours interpersonal and cognitive skills useful to the argumentation of ideas, attentive listening to others' points of views, resolution of conflicts through negotiation and assumption of shared agreements (Slavin, 1996). For example, cooperative learning is seen as an effective resource for intercultural education (Y. Sharan, 2010a, 2015) and a necessary competence for the creation of social transformation collectives (Perrenoud, 2001).

Cooperation is a significant learning engine. Interactions with others allow creating optimal conditions for the emergence of the socio-cognitive conflict (supported by the theories of Piaget) and are necessary for mediation (in terms of the theory of Vygotsky and sociocultural perspectives). Learning is not an individual achievement. It can emerge from the confrontation of different points of view (Buchs, Butera, Mugny & Darnon, 2004; Darnon, Buchs & Butera, 2002) or from social activity with other more experienced members, offering assistance that allows the apprentice to become an increasingly competent and autonomous participant (Wells, 1999). Cooperation means to learn from each other and with the other, a necessary competence to learn throughout our lives.

Cooperative learning is an instructional strategy for quality education for all. It allows using knowledge differences among students pedagogically, seeing diversity not as a problem but as an opportunity for learning (Stainback & Stainback, 1999). Diversity within the team, heterogeneity, is a requirement for the establishment of relations of mutual aid. In addition, we can use those differences to give opportunities to students to act as mediators in the construction of the knowledge of their peers. This is what happens in the cooperative learning techniques and methods this chapter presents.

Following Johnson and Johnson (2014), cooperative learning is essential to meet the four crucial challenges in the twenty-first century:

1. Global interdependence. Future citizens must understand the nature of interdependent systems, how cooperation works, the benefits of diversity and effective decision making.
2. An increasing number of democracies. Cooperative learning is a microcosm of democracy, giving opportunities to understand how to engage in political discourse, to make effective decisions, face-to-face and virtually.
3. The need for creative entrepreneurs. Structuring learning situations cooperatively, giving assignments that require higher-level reasoning and problem solving as well as using constructive controversies are steps to promote creative entrepreneurs.
4. Interpersonal relationships. Cooperation will play a vital role in building positive relationships in face-to-face interactions and online.

Having identified the relevance of the use of cooperative learning, we will see below the principles that teachers must take into account to promote it; and the benefits for students, which is undoubtedly the main reason that makes cooperative learning valuable.

1.3. Principles for cooperative learning

Processes that explain the effectiveness of peer learning (Topping, 2005a) place dialogue and interaction as responsible for the negotiation of meanings, which allows shared self-regulation and processes of scaffolding to aid in a framework of intersubjectivity. This co-construction of knowledge, however, does not occur spontaneously, but it requires careful planning. As has been said many times, for cooperation it is not enough to just put students together. It is necessary that the teacher structures the interaction within the group to stimulate the emergence of cooperation. In order to overcome simple working in groups, with the disadvantages mentioned before, and to turn it into a true team or cooperative group, the teacher must arrange interactions between team members. This chapter proposes to summarise principles widely accepted by the scientific community to guide the teachers' actions to promote cooperative learning. We choose to focus here on the principles common to all cooperative methods proposed by Davidson and Major (2014).

1. A task or learning activity suitable for group work. It is essential for the task to be a real group task that students are not able to do alone (B. Cohen & Cohen, 1991).
2. Student-to-student interaction in small groups. Working in teams is the core of cooperative learning. The teams have to be small so all students can have face-to-face simultaneous interactions with other members.
3. Positive interdependence. Students must perceive they share a common goal, and the success of each member is connected to the rest of the team and vice versa. This is established through team goals (learn and make sure that the other group members also learn), group recognition (rewards are not individual, but for the team and depend on members' contributions), division of resources (distribution of information and limitation of materials) and complementary roles. Positive interdependence shows that one's contribution has a direct effect on the achievement of the team.

4 Individual accountability and personal responsibility. This principle tries to avoid the main drawback of teamwork: the diffusion of responsibilities, which is reflected in the student that contributes little or nothing ("social loafing") or in the student who capitalises on the work of others ("free rider"). To ensure this, teachers can rely on individual assessment, or a random choice of spokesperson or personal work reports. The contribution of each student should be possible and necessary, and each student's learning has to be visible.

5 Promotive interactions. This refers to cooperative, mutually helpful behaviour among students. Maximising interaction opportunities among the team members allows interpersonal dynamics of aid, assistance, support, animation and reinforcement. This involves confidence, resource sharing, motivation, feedback and decision-making.

These principles useful for structuring peer interactions in academic tasks will be developed in Chapter 4. We will also rely on some other principles that are recognised to be useful for working cooperatively, e.g. Johnson and Johnson's propositions (Johnson & Johnson, 2009b; Johnson, Johnson & Holubec, 2008) in order to point out the importance of preparing students for constructive interactions. Students cooperate to learn, but at the same time learn to cooperate.

6 Preparing students for the appropriate use of social skills. The skills necessary for cooperation (proper communication, acceptance and support of each other to resolve conflicts constructively) must be taught deliberately and precisely as academic skills.

7 Making students reflect on group processing. The members of the team spend some time to reflect together on the workflow, the achievement of objectives and working relationships, and to make decisions of readjustment and improvement.

In addition to these two principles, Chapter 3 develops the importance of a positive framework for learning. We propose that it is crucial to create a climate in the classroom that encourages social support and cooperative attitudes, focused on learning.

Understanding these principles, teachers can use them as valuable guides to design interactions that promote cooperation. Kagan (S. Kagan & Kagan, 2009) poses a slight variation to the conditions of the Johnson brothers. Coinciding with interdependence and individual accountability, surely the core elements, he adds equal participation (active involvement of all team members) and simultaneous interaction (high degree of participation of the members). In a similar way, Villa, Thousand and Nevin (2013) prefer to use monitoring as a concept instead of talking about group processing.

In order to help organise the interaction within the groups, turning them into teams, cooperative structures have arisen. These are didactic designs, some more complex than others, that, following the above conditions, promote cooperation through organisational proposals. Willingness to implement cooperative learning has resulted in the creation and development of many of these structures which constitute a rich universe, but one which is complex and even difficult to classify (Duran & Monereo, 2012).

In general, we can divide these cooperative structures into methods and techniques, equivalents to formal and informal cooperative learning (Johnson, Johnson & Holubec, 2013). The methods rely on common principles for structuring peer interactions in academic tasks. Some are more sophisticated, complex structures and often require more extension in time and initial training of students, making it advisable to use them regularly. On the other hand, some of the techniques are simple structures that can be applied with easy steps, without initial training, creating what could be called a few minutes of cooperative learning in the classroom. They are useful for scripts and scaffolds for peer interactions in order to create simultaneous interaction with equal participation.

The differences between these structures are so great that some authors are beginning to point out that we cannot refer to cooperative learning as a single entity, but rather should talk of various methods and specific techniques, each of which has an objective and different effect from the others (Y. Sharan, 2010b). Given the multiplicity and the difference between them, the goal is not to know all of them (which is impossible), or implement "as such" (this would be valid only for techniques, not for methods). It is rather important to know some structures, and especially the conceptual principles on which they rest, and to be able to choose which best suits our reality, adjusting, recreating, combining or reinventing it.

The methods and techniques we present are mere examples that serve as support for teachers to introduce cooperative learning in their classrooms. With all the needed adjustments, no one better than actual teachers knows the conditions and necessities of their classrooms. This chapter proposes to sum up the main cooperative methods, and Chapter 4 will develop cooperative techniques as a means to structure peer interactions.

1.4. Cooperative learning methods

Cooperative learning methods are educational designs, some more complex than others, which aim to transform the group into a team, promoting relations of cooperation, through facilitating the conditions explained above. All of these methods propose that students work together on group tasks in small teams and structure positive interdependence and individual responsibility in order to favour promotive interactions.

Due to the large number of existing modalities, it is hard to list them or even classify them. Because of this wealth, many efforts in this regard have not been very fruitful (Davidson, 1994; Brody & Davidson, 1998; Slavin, 1995 or 2000; or S. Sharan, 1999, 2002). From this rich array of methods, we will then synthesise the most known and supported by the research, in order to illustrate the multiple ways to practice cooperative learning.

a) Learning Together. This is a "conceptual" approach to cooperative learning (Johnson & Johnson, 1991), based on the assumption that teachers apply the key principles of structuring effective cooperative learning to suit the needs of their own students. Learning Together offers an array of group structures (laboratory groups, peer editing, note-taking pairs, etc.) where students work in small groups on a task designed to promote positive interdependence, individual accountability and personal responsibility. Learning Together proposes to structure interdependence in various ways (Johnson & Johnson, 1989; Johnson, Johnson, & Holubec, 2008). Positive goal interdependence is necessary (a joint product like a team presentation/report or the mastery/learning of all members of the team) and can be reinforced by other dimensions (Johnson et al., 2013) such as reward (the reward each member receives depends on the contribution of all members), or resource, task or roles (each member proposes complementary contributions). In order to boost promotive interactions, these methods propose to explicitly teach social skills and to make students reflect on group processing.

b) Constructive Controversy. Designed by Johnson and Johnson (1991), each team, usually of four members, receives an issue, on which to write a report and pass a test. Each team is divided in two and receives instructional materials to prepare one position (either the con or the pro position). After presenting their position, teams have to discuss, argue and refute counterarguments, reverse perspectives, agree on a synthesis or integration of the best reasoning and reflect on the process (Johnson & Johnson, 2007). An example will be developed in Chapter 5.

c) Jigsaw. Conceived by Aronson (1978) and developed by Slavin (1980) as Jigsaw II. Each member has to become an expert for one part of the material, so the whole can be combined within the base team. Jigsaw combines two types of grouping; first students are in heterogeneous teams and then in a group of experts. The educational objective is divided into as many parts as there are members of the heterogeneous teams (three, four, five, ...). Or the opposite, teams are created with as many members as there are parts in the objective. Then, each student meets with peers from the other teams to specialise – become an expert – in a thematic part that corresponds to a part of the assignment (piece of the puzzle). Finally, the base heterogeneous team, with their respective experts, meets again, and each student shares their built expertise with the rest of the team members, in order to achieve the whole objective. Interdependence is created, and individual responsibility is reinforced since part of the essential knowledge to achieve the goal is distributed to each team member. By its simplicity and versatility, Jigsaw is one of the most well-known types of cooperative learning. Nevertheless, caution is needed regarding the quality of learning of the whole material as will be developed in Chapter 4. Jigsaw II structures positive reward interdependence (Slavin, 1995).

d) Teams-Games-Tournaments. Devised by DeVries and Edwards (1973) and developed by DeVries and Slavin (1978), students are assigned to heterogeneous teams with the aim of learning specific content which will be evaluated in a tournament. In this phase the team members must cooperate, because then each of them will compete as a representative of the team and, depending on the score, will be grouped with same level students in a tournament where they will compete again. Each member earns points depending on her/his ranking. Finally, each member returns to the first team and brings the points earned, which gives sense to the initial cooperative work. It is, therefore, a sequence which combines cooperation within the team with competition between teams, a very common combination in the fields of sports and business. Reward interdependence highlights individual responsibility. The tournament is organised in such a way that each member has the same opportunity to contribute to the success of the team.

e) Student Teams–Achievement Division. Designed by Slavin (1978), students distributed in teams help each other in order to master and understand the content delivered by the teacher. Then, an individual assessment is performed. The individual progress obtained by each student is the contribution to their respective team, which receives recognition. Individual assessment stresses individual accountability and the calculation of points for reward interdependence permit the same opportunity to contribute to the success of the team.

f) Team Assisted Individualisation. Designed by Slavin, Leavey and Madden (1984), originally for mathematical subjects, students in heterogeneous teams contribute to the team with their individual progress, through activities that have been adjusted and respond to each individual level. In this way, the students will work individually, but supported by the team and by the teacher, in homogeneous groupings, so that they may attain the shared objective, master the unit and move to the next. Reward interdependence based on progress on individualised content guarantees individual accountability and offers the same opportunity to contribute to the success of the team.

g) Cooperative Integrated Reading and Composition. Designed by Madden, Slavin and Stevens (1986), the students take part in groups according to their level of literacy, to develop activities tailored to their abilities. The assessment for each group is the result of individual advances of each of its members. So equality of opportunity for its members is preserved and cooperation promoted.

h) Group Investigation. Designed by S. Sharan and Sharan (1992), Group Investigation considers the class group as a social community conducting research on a topic. In a similar way to how knowledge is constructed by the scientific community, organised in research groups, the teacher proposes an objective about a topic, through a problem, question or challenge. Students choose between subtopics or different content to achieve the goal. Located in teams working on sub-themes, the students organise a work plan that the teacher monitors to ensure interdependence and individual responsibility. Once the teams have carried out their investigations, the groups plan their presentations to share their findings in many engaging ways with the rest of the class, which evaluates their projects together with the teacher.

i) Reciprocal Teaching. This was developed by Palincsar and Brown (1984), for reading comprehension. The cognitive functions that a skilled reader does simultaneously and unconsciously are distributed among the team members. Thus, the cognitive load is distributed among their minds, which cooperate to understand the text. Cognitive functions for reading comprehension are converted into roles. Thus, for each piece of text, a student will read and summarise, another will ask questions, another will respond and, finally, one will anticipate what is to come or will formulate the conclusion at the end of the text. This interesting way to transform mental operations into roles can also be transported into another kind of task, such as problem solving, for example (an example in fractions learning will be developed in Chapter 5). In Reciprocal Teaching, the teacher models and plays an active role during the process.

j) Complex Instruction. Originally designed by E. Cohen (1994), problem-solving activities are open ended and built around a central concept or idea. Each group of up to five students has a different task that relates to the central concept, organised in learning stations. Groups rotate tasks and stations to understand the concept from different perspectives, media and modes. Students assume authority and perform procedural roles such as facilitator or materials manager in their groups. These roles rotate too. E. Cohen underlines that the status of students influences their participation and learning in the group. In order to address status, she introduces complex tasks requiring multiple abilities, so all students' abilities become necessary to solve the task. In order to empower students with low status, the teacher tries to recognise their abilities publically, so students gain in competence recognition which generalises and permits them to participate fully in their team.

As we can see, each method has its particularities and different ways of structuring and cooperative learning conditions arise more intensely in one or the other. Therefore, implementation in the classroom depends on features that belong to the method itself, but also features of educational reality.

1.5. Is cooperative learning effective?

Cooperative learning is one of the most researched topics in educational psychology and has hundreds of research studies, from kindergarten through college and across all subjects, supporting its success (Johnson & Johnson, 2009b). But, despite having proven to be a good methodology, its use in the classroom and schools has many difficulties (Y. Sharan, 2010b), which we will address in Part IV. Now we will synthesise the research that provides knowledge on the effectiveness of cooperative learning.

Research on cooperative learning has passed through different stages. Various authors (Melero & Fernandez, 1995; Dillenbourg et al., 1996; Rodríguez, Fernández, Escudero & Subirón, 2000) distinguish at least three generations of research. The first generation compared the effectiveness of cooperation with other forms of learning. In the second, research focused on the effects of cooperative methods and the conditions under which it was effective. And in the third generation were studies of interaction analysis, to identify the causes and mechanisms of learning. Referring to single studies would be too detailed for this book, so we will take into account only meta-analyses (a statistical procedure for combining data from multiple studies) and reviews of groups of research. And we will focus exclusively on the first two generations, since the third has not yet generated meta-analyses.

1.5.1. Cooperative learning versus competitive and individualistic learning

Within the first generation, meta-analyses focused on the comparison of the effectiveness of cooperation versus competitive and individualistic learning. Reviewing studies in all educational levels (elementary to adult education), cooperation both with and without intergroup competition is more effective than interpersonal competition and individual efforts (Johnson, Maruyama, Johnson, Nelson & Skon, 1981). The same results in favour of cooperation are obtained in problem solving (Qin, Johnson & Johnson, 1995) and in college (Johnson, Johnson & Smith, 1998).

The results of a follow-up meta-analysis (Johnson & Johnson, 2002) indicated that cooperative learning, in comparison to competitive and individualistic learning, has very powerful effects on achievement, motivation, socialisation and personal and self-development and more positive peer relationships (Roseth, Johnson & Johnson, 2008). There is only one meta-analysis which does not find differences in favour of cooperation (Thanh, Gillies & Renshaw, 2008), which highlights the possible difficulties for the use of cooperative learning in the cultures of Asian students.

Based on two major syntheses (Johnson & Johnson, 1989, with 470 studies; Slavin, 1983, with 46 studies) we can conclude that cooperation is a powerful tool for learning but that the benefits are not automatic. As pointed out by Buchs, Lehraus and Crahay (2012), on average these reviews indicate that more than half of the comparisons (57.89 per cent) showed superiority of cooperative learning compared to competitive or individual work for academic achievement. Results show that the benefits of cooperative learning can be described as moderate to strong and are found for verbal, mathematical and procedural tasks.

1.5.2. Effects of cooperative methods

Within the second generation, Slavin (1980) reviews research on the use of cooperative learning methods in primary and secondary schools. Results show increasing achievement, more positive race relations, mutual concern and higher self-esteem. Comparing cooperative learning methods in secondary education, Newmann and Thompson (1987) obtained similar results, stressing that group reward and individual accountability are necessary. The effect of group reward is also stated in Slavin (1996). Nastasi and Clements (1991) reported the importance of higher-order thinking, motivation and social skills to explain the benefits of cooperative learning for cognitive development, academic achievement and social–emotional growth.

Another meta-analysis (Lou, Abrami, Spence, Poulson, Chambers & d'Apollonia, 1996) showed that learning in small groups has positive effects in achievement and attitudes in primary and secondary education. Good results of cooperative learning methods are also consistent in all educational levels: for early childhood, from four to eight years old (Vermette, Harper & DiMillo, 2004) and in science achievement for secondary and post-secondary students (Romero, 2010). Finally, in higher education, the meta-analysis of Springer, Stanne and Donovan (1999) found better results for students working in cooperative groups in science, mathematics, engineering and technology. Bowen (2000) found similar results in chemical education. A recent meta-analysis of the effects of face-to-face cooperative learning (Kyndt, Raes, Lismont, Timmers, Cascallar & Dochy, 2013) conclude that, in general, students in cooperative learning environments outperform students in traditional learning environments in achievement (particularly in non-linguistic courses, like mathematics or sciences) and attitudes.

Finally, there are some research reviews focusing on students with difficulties. The first one (Tateyama-Sniezek, 1990) could not draw a definitive conclusion. Marr (1997), reviewing research published from 1965 to 1995, reported that research evidence supported the use of cooperative learning activities to promote academic achievement and pro-social development. Reviewing research published from 1990 to 2000, McMaster & Fuchs (2002) conclude that cooperative learning strategies that incorporate individual accountability and group rewards are more likely to improve the achievement of students with disabilities.

The great potential of cooperative learning for students with learning disabilities depends on the characteristics of the students themselves and on the way teachers implement cooperative learning (Jenkins & O'Connor, 2003). Researchers suggest that the assistance provided by peers during cooperative learning may not be sufficient for students with learning disabilities. In this sense, it could be a mistake to withdraw or replace inclusion supports for peer support. Material or personal special support has to remain available.

The review of research about the effectiveness of cooperative learning among other students with unique characteristics, like students with emotional and behavioural disorders (Sutherland, Wehby & Günter, 2000) or gifted and high-achievement students (Neber, Finsterwald & Urban, 2001) remains inconclusive; more research is needed in order for us to know how to take full advantage of the cooperative learning potential.

At this moment, there are many studies corresponding to the third generation of research on cooperative learning trying to identify the interactive causes that explain the potential of cooperation. The first meta-analysis about the effects of positive interdependency on motivation in cooperative learning (Johnson & Johnson, 2014) is just one that will help to improve understanding the effects of cooperative learning.

Chapter 2

Peer learning
Directional peer interactions

As referred to in Chapter 1, peer interactions in daily class practice can lead to learning for all the students involved. However, as argued before, simply placing students in pairs or small groups will not necessarily result in these hoped-for learning effects. Instead, teachers need to be aware of and apply specific approaches and take into account and implement important principles. This will make peer interactions in their classes constructive and consequently ensure student learning.

In this respect, Chapter 1 focused on the organisation of symmetrical peer interactions, such as collaborative and cooperative learning. Complementary to this, Chapter 2 will focus on more directional relations, such as peer tutoring. Importantly, this and later chapters will focus on purposefully organised types of peer tutoring – planned, prepared and implemented by the teacher for specific subjects, curriculum areas and concrete learning objectives. Obviously, in many schools, incidental peer tutoring of a sort often takes place as well – whenever a child helps, supports or guides others during playtime or in class. However, such helping is usually quite unstructured and often the "tutor" gains little, so these cases of more informal and incidental support (which are also found in Chapter 1) are beyond the scope of this book.

This chapter starts with conceptualising peer tutoring and illustrating various formats this instructional strategy can adopt. Then, the effectiveness of peer tutoring is described, not only in terms of diverse outcomes, but also in terms of the diverse student target groups that can benefit. To finish, Chapter 2 offers critical guidelines to take into consideration when developing and implementing peer tutoring programmes in order to ensure their success.

2.1. Describing and portraying peer tutoring

The most common form of peer tutoring is to have one tutor working with one or a few tutees. This is a positive characteristic, allowing for active engagement and individualised feedback.

2.1.1. Role disparity in the relationship between the peers

Chapter 1 distinguished between mutual and directional peer learning based on the framework of Damon and Phelps (1989), who define peer tutoring as "an approach in which one child instructs another child in material on which the first is an expert and the second is a novice" (p. 11). This definition emphasises disparity in the roles and abilities of the peers involved as an essential characteristic of peer tutoring.

At any time, one of the peers adopts the role of *peer tutor*, by creating or proposing learning opportunities (especially when the tutor is provided with guidelines or material that the teacher proposes) through questioning, explaining and active scaffolding (Duran & Monereo, 2005; Roscoe & Chi, 2008). Their partner (the *peer tutee*) is intellectually or cognitively challenged by the peer tutor (Topping, 1996). The peer tutor is more experienced or has more knowledge or skills (is to some extent an "expert") and is expected to take on a supportive role in the interaction (Falchikov, 2001; McLuckie & Topping, 2004). The tutee, on the other hand, is the novice receiving academic help and support from the tutor (Falchikov, 2001; Topping, 1996). Consequently, peer tutoring aims at "the development of knowledge and skills through explicit active helping and supporting among status equals or matched companions, with the deliberate intent to help others with their learning goals" (Topping & Ehly, 2001, p. 114).

2.1.1.1. Levels of equality and mutuality and type of interaction in peer tutoring

In line with the work of Damon and Phelps (1989), Chapter 1 introduced 'equality' or 'directionality' and 'mutuality' as dimensions to determine the quality of peer interactions and to distinguish between different sorts of peer learning. In this respect, peer tutoring is mainly characterised by directional peer interactions or rather low equality, given the difference in competency between the peers involved and the unequal role of the tutor and tutee. The more competent or knowledgeable peer tutor manages the interaction and guides the learning for the less competent novice peer tutee (Damon & Phelps, 1989).

Since this type of interaction is somewhat similar to traditional teacher–student interaction, the mutuality in peer tutoring can be considered low as well. However, obviously the peer tutor does not possess the same degree of experience, knowledge or expertise regarding the learning content and instructional skills as professional adult teachers. Consequently, there is still an important discrepancy with the traditional teacher–student model. The position of a peer tutor is undeniably closer to the tutee's position, which optimises and strengthens mutuality from low to moderate. After all, since the students are of similar ages (even in cross-age tutoring), as well as emotionally and cognitively closer to each other, they will have their own ways of communicating in the vernacular. They will also intersperse their discussions with examples and everyday experiences, and adapt to the individual needs of their tutee, their level and pace of thinking and information processing, their learning style, and so on. Consequently, tutees can understand their peer tutors' explanations more easily, leading to more personalised and effective learning (Good & Brophy, 1997). This can be considered as a significant advantage compared to more traditional teacher-led learning environments.

In this respect, Damon and Phelps (1989) more particularly argue,

> Unlike adult-child instruction, [in] peer tutoring the expert party is not very far removed from the novice party in authority or knowledge; nor has the expert party any special claims to instructional competence. Such differences affect the nature of discourse between tutor and tutee, because they place the tutee in a less passive role than does the adult-child instructional relation. Being closer in knowledge and status, the tutee in a peer relation feels freer to express opinions, ask questions, and risk untested solutions. The interaction between instructor and pupil is more balanced and more lively. (p. 138)

Another dimension used to distinguish between different approaches of peer learning is the type of ongoing interaction supporting learning. Given the rather low to moderate equality and mutuality in peer tutoring, the focus here seems to be principally on the linear transmission of content and/or skills from the expert to the novice student. In this respect, information essentially flows from tutor to tutee. However, this idea of unidirectional transmission from tutor to tutee does not do justice to the inherent value of peer tutoring for the more competent tutor. The deliberate support of peer tutors directly helps tutees to achieve learning objectives, but likewise challenges and fosters peer tutors' understanding of their own learning, and can optimise the latter (De Backer, Van Keer & Valcke, 2015c).

Consequently, successful peer tutoring is advantageous for both peer tutors and tutees, as we will elaborate in the following section. In this respect, a contemporary definition of peer tutoring is needed to adequately acknowledge that peer-to-peer interaction is fruitful for both parties involved. Topping (1996) therefore defines peer tutoring as follows: "people from similar social groupings who are not professional teachers helping each other to learn, and learning themselves by teaching" (p. 322).

2.1.1.2. Same-age and cross-age peer tutoring

Both the level of equality and mutuality as well as the particular type of peer interaction depends on the constitution of the peer tutoring groups. The peer relationship can be between students of the same age or of the same grade or class group – this is *same-age peer tutoring*. Or it can be a relationship between an older tutor academically supporting a younger tutee, which is called *cross-age peer tutoring*. However, it is important to be conscious of the fact that differences in skills or proficiencies in a particular subject are often considered more important than age differences (Duran & Monereo, 2005; Graesser, Person & Magliano, 1995).

As to the peer grouping of children in same-age tutoring, the level of equality and mutuality is typically higher than in the cross-age peer tutoring variant. The same-age tutor is more easily perceived as a "true" peer, given the comparable levels of expertise and development of both tutor and tutee (Falchikov, 2001; Topping, 1996). However, to guarantee the role disparity between the children involved in peer tutoring, same-age peer tutors need additional information or resources or expertise in order to successfully take up their supportive role in cognitively challenging their tutee's understanding (Falchikov, 2001; Topping, 2005a). Chapter 6 will illustrate how this is realised in some examples of same-age peer tutoring interventions.

2.1.1.3. Reciprocal peer tutoring

With the intention of providing all students in a class with the opportunity to reap benefits from both providing and receiving academic support, respectively in the tutor and in the tutee role, teachers often opt for *reciprocal same-age tutoring*. In this specific application of same-age tutoring, students alternate on a regular basis between the tutor and tutee role (Cheng & Ku, 2009; Fantuzzo, King & Heller, 1992; Ginsburg-Block & Fantuzzo, 1997; Griffin & Griffin, 1998). This aims to prevent social divisiveness according to the perceived ability and status of students (Topping, 2005a).

Let us take a look at some brief examples from different schools and educational levels to demonstrate the idea of same-age peer tutoring more concretely:

> A second-grade teacher integrates reciprocal peer tutoring in his class as an instructional technique for multiple content areas. Children are paired daily with same-level class

mates during short exercises. Both students in the pair mutually exchange the tutor and tutee role during the practice times. Pairs can have a different composition according to the subject the students are working on (e.g., multiplication tables; spelling using flash cards; reading and comprehension monitoring by partner reading, discussing text predictions and making paragraph summaries).

A high school aims at improving the performance of at-risk students. Therefore, high-achieving classmates are selected as tutors and teamed up one-to-one with at-risk students to assist the tutees during class for the specific subject areas in which the tutee is underachieving. In this programme, the tutor and tutee roles are fixed and not alternated.

In a university Faculty of Psychology and Educational Sciences, first year undergraduate students are teamed in stable reciprocal peer tutoring groups of six, meeting once a week. The groups work face-to-face on assignments related to content-specific themes of core courses of their curriculum. The aim of the program is to deepen students' understanding of the learning content previously addressed in theoretical lectures for the entire student group. The tutor role is interchanged at each meeting within each group. Each week, the tutor receives a "tutor guide" offering additional information to use when solving the assignments in the group meeting.

Aside from the various same-age peer tutoring programmes, some programmes engage older, cross-age peer tutors to academically support younger students (Duran & Monereo, 2005; Falchikov, 2001). In this respect, the peer tutor pairings encompass a variety of combinations: secondary school students paired with primary school children, upper secondary school students grouped with younger secondary school youngsters, primary school students with disabilities meeting with younger students with disabilities, and so on (e.g., Miller & Miller, 1995).

Cross-age peer tutoring is generally *fixed peer tutoring* with students operating as either tutor or tutee (without alternating roles) for the complete duration of the programme. Role reciprocity in cross-age contexts is understandably less relevant and applicable, given the different roles and positions of the students involved. The inherent difference in cross-age tutors' and tutees' general and content-specific knowledge, skills and experiences facilitates appropriate support and scaffolding – and consequently also successful tutoring and effective learning (Roscoe & Chi, 2008; Topping, 1996). However, as referred to above, the level of equality and mutuality is naturally lower than in the same-age alternative. Cross-age peer tutors are often attributed a higher social status by their tutees (Colvin, 2007; Robinson, Schofield & Steers-Wentzell, 2005), establishing an asymmetrical relationship which might possibly undermine tutees' initiative-taking (Webb, Ing, Kersting & Nemer, 2006).

We also present some examples to illustrate the diversity of cross-age peer tutoring programmes:

At a primary school, complete classes are engaged in cross-age peer tutoring in various subject areas. All students, regardless of their academic ability, act as tutors for younger students in a lower year. For example, sixth graders are matched one-to-one with third graders to solve math word-problems. First and second graders read out loud to small groups of kindergartners. Over time, the younger tutees become tutors themselves, after their transition to the higher grades.

At a secondary school, final year students specialising in sciences tutor third-year students' physics groups during their lab practicum. Further, final-year students specialising in behavioural sciences tutor first-year students struggling with planning and organising their homework.

In an attempt to prevent drop-out and with a view to optimising the performance and study motivation of low-achieving students who are at risk due to their social and/or ethnic background, a secondary school enrols these at-risk students as cross-age tutors for primary school students with a comparable profile or background. The tutors are trained to support subject learning and to act as positive role models for their younger tutees.

At the Faculty of Medicine of a university, more advanced third-year bachelor students tutor first year students face-to-face during their clinical skills training. More particularly, throughout the semester tutors are responsible for small groups of students practising diverse technical skills (e.g., wound care, stitching, giving injections).

As part of their internship, first-year masters degree students from a university faculty of psychology and educational sciences tutor undergraduate first-year students from the same faculty in an online learning context. The tutees collaborate in stable asynchronous discussion groups. They exchange ideas and construct knowledge by debating the theoretical concepts dealt with in the face-to-face classes of the lecturer and in the course manual. The peer tutors are assigned to one of these groups to support and facilitate the online learning and interaction.

2.1.1.4. Different constellations of peer tutoring

As is already evident, "peer tutoring" is to be regarded as an umbrella term. As such, peer tutoring programmes can take many forms. They can focus on one, two, or multiple content areas. They differ as to the learning objectives targeted or the intensity and frequency of implementation. They can be face-to-face, online, or blended learning. Overall, a wide range of configurations are imaginable and can be developed and implemented in practice.

In this respect, Topping (2005a) lists no less than 13 organisational dimensions to consider in the design and implementation of a peer tutoring programme:

1. *curriculum content* (i.e., the knowledge and/or skills aimed at in the programme),
2. *contact constellation* (i.e., tutoring in a one-on-one setting or one tutor working with a group of tutees),
3. *within or between institutions* (i.e., tutors and tutees from the same or different schools or educational levels),
4. *year of study* (i.e., tutors and tutees from the same or different years of study or age),
5. *ability* (i.e., same-ability or cross-ability tutoring),
6. *role continuity* (i.e., the tutor/tutee role is permanent or exchanged throughout the programme),
7. *time* (i.e., tutoring sessions in and/or outside regular class contact time),
8. *place* (i.e., location of operation of the tutoring sessions),
9. *tutee characteristics* (i.e., all students or only a targeted subgroup of students involved),
10. *tutor characteristics* (i.e., all students or only a targeted subgroup of students involved),
11. *objectives* (i.e., academic and/or non-academic aims of the programme),

12 *voluntary or compulsory* participation of the students involved,
13 *reinforcement* (i.e., presence or absence of extrinsic reinforcement, such as certification, course credits.

2.2. Is peer tutoring effective?

There is strong and extensive empirical evidence that peer tutoring is a valuable instructional technique when organised and implemented thoughtfully. This comes from individual studies and from systematic meta-analyses. As Chapter 1 discusses, meta-analyses are simultaneous analyses of a large number of carefully selected, high-quality individual studies using strict methodological criteria in order to combine data from multiple studies and to formulate overall statements regarding effectiveness. More particularly, the literature frequently cites clear and multiple benefits for the use of both same-age and cross-age peer tutoring in various instructional settings and subject areas and for diverse student populations.

Most commonly, research refers to benefits in the realms of the academic, cognitive and metacognitive (i.e., students' thinking and reflection about their own thinking and learning). The advantages of peer tutoring, however, go beyond gains in students' achievement and improved learning. Although receiving somewhat less attention in the research literature, a host of social, affective, and motivational outcomes are recorded as well (Falchikov, 2001; Topping, 2005a).

2.2.1. Effectiveness regarding diverse outcomes

2.2.1.1. Cognitive benefits

As to the cognitive benefits, peer tutoring commonly brings about better student performance and achievement in all kinds of subjects: language arts (including spelling, reading, and writing); mathematics; science; social studies; and subject-specific courses in higher education (e.g., health education, statistics, educational sciences) (e.g., Bowman-Perrott, Davis, Vannest, Williams, Greenwood & Parker, 2013; P. Cohen, Kulik & Kulik, 1982; Miller, Topping & Thurston, 2010; Oddo, Barnett, Hawkins & Musti-Rao, 2010; Rohrbeck, Ginsburg-Block, Fantuzzo & Miller, 2003; Topping, Campbell, Douglas & Smith, 2003; Van Keer, 2004; Van Keer & Vanderlinde, 2010).

Two relatively recently published meta-analyses on the impact of peer tutoring on student achievement (Bowman-Perrott et al., 2013; Leung, 2015) refer to the performance effects not only for primary and secondary school students but also for children and students from kindergarten to higher education. The meta-analysis of Bowman-Perrott et al. (2013) on peer tutoring in reading specifically demonstrates the academic benefits regardless of the students' grade level. Leung's (2015) study confirms the overall effectiveness for different age groups on achievement, but points to larger effects for peer tutoring at secondary education level in particular.

Both meta-analyses, combining the results of 98 individual studies, accentuate the widespread added value of peer tutoring for student performance in various age groups. Additionally, research also refers to improved understanding of the learning content (Griffin & Griffin, 1998; Ritschoff & Griffin, 2001), more deep-level learning (Ashwin, 2003; King, Staffieri & Adelgais, 1998; Loke & Chow, 2007; Topping et al., 2003), and more frequent higher-order thinking (Roscoe & Chi, 2008; Topping & Bryce, 2004).

2.2.1.2. Metacognitive benefits

De Backer, Van Keer & Valcke (2012) summarise the empirical research showing that dialogue between peer tutors' and tutees' frequently triggers metacognitive processes (King et al., 1998; Roscoe, 2014; Topping, 2001). This results in increased metacognitive knowledge about when and how to use learning and problem-solving strategies (Shamir, Zion & Spector-Levi, 2008). It also results in enhanced self-regulated learning (i.e., the conscious planning, monitoring, control, and regulation of one's learning in order to optimise it) (King, 1998; Shamir & Tzuriel, 2004), and higher levels of self-control (Fantuzzo et al., 1992).

2.2.1.3. Social, affective, and motivational benefits

A wide range of other benefits can stem from tutors and tutees improving their knowledge and skills by helping others or by receiving help, consequently building self-confidence and self-esteem. Moreover, peer tutoring settings are perceived as safe learning environments, lowering distress (Cheng & Ku, 2009; Fantuzzo, Riggio, Connelly & Dimeff, 1989). Additionally, both peer tutors and tutees report improved attitudes towards school and towards the subject matter, as well as increased academic satisfaction as a result of their participation (P. Cohen et al., 1982; Fantuzzo et al., 1989; Robinson et al., 2005).

Peer tutoring further fosters the development of improved social and communication competence (Ashwin, 2003; Topping et al., 2003) and the enhancement of peer relations (Greenwood, Carta & Hall, 1988). Research is also clear on students' appreciation for peer tutoring, both in the tutor and tutee role (Ginsburg-Block & Fantuzzo, 1997; Griffin & Griffin, 1998; Topping & Bryce, 2004). The meta-analysis of Ginsburg-Block, Rohrbeck, and Fantuzzo (2006) of 36 relevant studies corroborates these results for primary school children by revealing significant social, self-concept, and behavioural effects. Importantly, this meta-analysis suggests that peer tutoring programmes focusing on academic outcomes can simultaneously improve social and self-concept outcomes as well. Topping (2005a) states: "Although these [gains in transferable social and communication skills and in affective functioning] are more elusive to measure and are not found as reliably as academic gains, they represent considerable added value for no more input" (p. 635).

2.2.2. Effectiveness for diverse students

2.2.2.1. Tutors and tutees

As mentioned above, it is important to note that research demonstrates that the benefits of peer tutoring accrue to students in both the tutor and the tutee role. This implies that either providing or receiving help leads to positive effects. In fact, the impact on the tutor is often found to be larger than that on the tutee (Fitz-Gibbon, 1988; Greenwood et al., 1988). This supports the important notion in Topping's (1996) definition – of tutors learning through teaching or being helped by providing help. This finding leads to an important recommendation for educational practice – provide all students with the opportunity to be in the role of tutor, giving guidance and support to peers who might be younger, as well as in the role of tutee, receiving help from older students or classmates (Robinson et al., 2005).

2.2.2.2. High-need and at-risk students

The meta-analysis of Bowman-Perrott et al. (2013) shows that the benefits of peer tutoring are accessible regardless of the disability status of students. In line with this, an older review of studies of both regular and special education students across a variety of subject areas (Greenwood, Carta & Kamps, 1990) concluded that cross-age and same-age peer tutoring were as effective or even more effective with both groups than the traditional teacher-mediated practices to which they were compared. In this respect, Bowman-Perrott et al. (2013) argue that the fact that students with or at risk for disabilities demonstrate greater academic gains may be due to the additional support students obtain via peer tutoring.

Regarding the academic ability of the tutees, the meta-analysis of Leung (2015) indicates that studies with high-ability tutees display larger effects than studies with tutees of other academic ability levels, followed by low-, average-, and mixed-ability levels. As to specific groups of students with disabilities, the meta-analysis of Bowman-Perrott et al. (2013) indicates that children with emotional and behavioural disorders benefit most. The positive effects of peer tutoring for high-needs children are revealed in other studies and meta-analyses as well, reporting positive results for students with learning or behavioural difficulties and for students vulnerable due to their minority or socially disadvantaged background (Bentz & Fuchs, 1996; Cook, Scruggs, Mastriopieri & Casto, 1985; Fuchs, Fuchs & Burish, 2000; Klingner & Vaughn, 1996; Mastropieri, Scruggs, Mohler, Beranek, Spencer, Boon & Talbott, 2001; Mathes & Fuchs, 1994; Okilwa & Shelby, 2010; Spencer & Balboni, 2003; Rohrbeck et al., 2003). Notwithstanding the positive effects generally found for minority students, the meta-analysis of Leung (2015) revealed larger effects for studies with 50 per cent or fewer minority participants than for studies with more than 50 per cent minority participants.

Importantly, the benefits of peer tutoring for diverse learners also hold for social and emotional effects. As to these areas, the meta-analysis of Ginsburg-Block et al. (2006) revealed that peer tutoring interventions were more effective for low-income versus higher income groups, more effective for urban versus suburban–rural groups, and more effective for minority versus nonminority students.

In educational practice, we see that teachers too often or almost exclusively select high performers as peer tutors. Research, however, shows that high-needs children, (for example with learning disabilities, emotional and behavioural difficulties, or lower achievement) can benefit substantially in both the academic and affective fields from being assigned the tutor role as well. In this respect, research refers to significant benefits in the areas of academic achievement, self-esteem, social skills, attitudes toward school and so on. As noted above, Leung (2015) showed that studies with tutors of low ability displayed even larger positive effects than studies with tutors of other academic ability levels, followed by high-, average- and mixed-ability levels. This implies that all children – at-risk or not, learning-disabled or not, high-needs or not – should be engaged in peer tutoring programmes. Even more, they all should be encouraged to take up the tutor role, which is another critical recommendation for educational practice.

In conclusion, the opportunities for students from different age groups to benefit from peer tutoring are amply described in the research literature. Both parties involved (tutors and tutees) appear to take advantage of this instructional strategy. The same goes for children from different ability groups or high-needs and at-risk students in both the tutor and tutee role. These positive results might persuade and encourage teachers to implement peer tutoring as a useful strategy in their class practice. However, it is important to remember to inform parents (or if relevant the broader community around the school) on the benefits and the objectives of your intended programme as well. Broad support in this respect – especially at the onset of the implementation – can be the difference between failure and success of the programme. Chapter 3 will further develop this assertion.

2.3. Prerequisites for effective peer tutoring

As we will discuss in Part II, peer interactions may explain a great part of the effectiveness of peer tutoring. Consequently, the quality of the interaction needs to be addressed in order to design and implement successful peer tutoring programmes. We will discuss constructive interactions, as well as principles for fostering positive peer interactions in peer learning, in Part II.

Moreover, before starting the peer tutoring programme, training is required to maximise the benefits (Falchikov, 2001; Roscoe & Chi, 2007; Topping, 1996). Primarily, both peer tutors and their tutees should be informed about the programme and the related aims and they need to be encouraged to put constructive social and communication skills into practice (Topping, 2005a). In addition, taking into account the research on questioning and explaining which we will develop in the introduction to Part II, peer tutors should be trained to challenge tutees' understanding with elaborative explanations and reflective questions, aimed at stimulating tutees' deep reasoning (Graesser & Person, 1994; King et al., 1998; Roscoe & Chi, 2008; Webb et al., 2006), as well as scaffolding tutees' learning (Azevedo & Hadwin, 2005; Chi, Siler, Jeong, Yamauchi & Hausmann, 2001). The importance of preparing students will be developed in Chapter 3.

Second, in addition to the preliminary training, ongoing supervision and support to optimise role taking and future tutoring activities is required – especially for peer tutors but also their tutees (Falchikov, 2001; Schraw, Crippen & Hartley, 2006; Topping, 1996). This intermediary support for tutoring (whether conducted by coaching individual pairs or holding group meetings) is very important. Group meetings for tutors and tutees are also important as an outlet for sharing students' experiences, both positive and negative, and consequently lead to mutual learning. Tutors and tutees respectively learn from each other and from teacher feedback and reinforcement.

Third, the meta-analysis of Leung (2015) revealed that structured tutoring produces larger effect sizes relative to unstructured tutoring. Consequently, the benefits of peer tutoring can be enlarged by providing students with scripts, structured materials or clear procedures for interaction, encouraging and supporting the interaction or specifying a sequence of interactive behaviour (e.g., Falchikov, 2001; King et al., 1998; Fantuzzo et al., 1992; Miller et al., 2010; Topping, 1996, 2005a). Chapter 4 will deal in more detail with principles that can be used to organise and structure peer interactions effectively.

2.4. Conclusion

In conclusion, decades of research have revealed that peer tutoring optimises inclusive educational practices. Peer tutoring takes the differences between students and turns them into an opportunity. Peer tutoring provides teachers with the possibility to accommodate diverse learners in their classroom, realising social and emotional enhancement, and improving academic achievement in various content areas across students' ability levels.

Moreover, as illustrated above, a wide variety of programmes exists or can be developed. This enables interested teachers or schools to find or design a format that suits their needs and objectives. To support teachers in selecting or developing relevant approaches for peer learning in their own context, Part II will more extensively discuss principles for preparing learners for constructive interactions and for structuring peer interactions in academic assignments. In connection with that and as a source of inspiration for teachers and schools, Part III will illustrate authentic peer learning programmes at different educational levels. It will also elaborate on what we can learn from these to ensure fruitful implementation in classrooms and success for all students.

Part II

General principles for peer learning

Peer learning can be considered primarily as a social process, in which peer interactions and discussions are the core elements (Chi et al., 2001; Gillies, 2015b; King et al., 1998; Roscoe, 2014; Topping, 1996). We have already said that simply bringing students together cannot guarantee the positive effects referred to above. It is not just working in groups that is essential, but rather the possibility that certain kinds of learning processes can be activated in groups (E. Cohen, 1994).

In this respect, we will summarise peer interactions that have been found to promote learning. While coming to understand the relationship between peer interactions and learning, teachers can think about what kind of peer interactions they would like to stimulate in their classrooms. In a second step, we will present general principles for organising *effective* peer learning – that is likely to foster positive interactions. We propose to differentiate these principles in two sections, which will be developed in the following chapters: preparing learners for constructive interactions (Chapter 3), and organising peer interactions in academic tasks (Chapter 4).

II.1. Constructive peer interactions for promoting learning

Numerous authors emphasise positive or promotive interactions (Gillies, 2007; Johnson, Johnson & Holubec, 1998) or simultaneous interaction (S. Kagan, 2013) as an underlying principle for effective peer learning. One important feature of peer learning is that it offers opportunities for face-to-face interaction. It proposes that a small number of students work together, so each learner benefits from individualised attention and has the opportunity to receive frequent and immediate feedback and correction. When discussing, peers can make clear what was not understood and point out misunderstandings or mistakes. This immediate and individualised feedback is not so evident in a whole class process with only one teacher for all the students.

Peer learning involves a general pattern: active participation (M. Kagan & Kagan, 2000), sharing resources and help, offering academic and personal support, encouragement and praise to each for the effort to learn (Johnson, Johnson & Holubec, 1998, 2002), providing information and assistance, and accessing resources and materials needed (Gillies, 2007). The success of peer learning is actually conditional upon the quality of the ongoing interaction between the students. More specific student interactions supporting learning have been identified: summarising, questioning, explaining, argumentation and disagreement. We will give an overview of these interactions and some practical directions, as well as research results supporting what we recommend.

II.1.1. Summarising

Many peer-learning methods require students to summarise information. Research on cognitive psychology shows the benefit of summarising (e.g., O'Donnell & King, 1999). The research underlines that the mere expectation of making an oral summary facilitates the acquisition of information, by promoting awareness of the objectives – and the strategies by which these objectives can be achieved. In addition, the actual oral presentation allows rehearsing and reviewing the material, which consolidates and reinforces it. Effective oral presentation also enhances awareness of the degree of mastery and understanding of the information.

The results of Ross and DiVesta (1976) underline that summarising a text (or having another student listen to a summary after reading it) is beneficial for understanding, retention and future recognition. Students who actively summarised the text performed better on the recall tests than those who were merely listening. In addition, the length of the summary was positively correlated with the performance of the student who made the summary, but not with the performance of the one who listened. The preparation of the summary is thus important. It makes a difference to know that you may have to summarise the text while you are reading.

Bargh and Schul (1980) found that students who individually studied a text while anticipating teaching another student about it memorised more information than students who worked on the text while anticipating answering questions. The effect of knowing that the listener would respond to questions about the text made a difference. Similarly, Annis (1983) found that students who read the material for themselves were less successful after one week than those who had read the materials anticipating having to teach a peer. Moreover, those who had read the material while anticipating having to teach a peer *and who actually taught it* were even more successful. This indicates a better understanding of the content as a result of interaction. These results underline that each time teachers suggest that their students summarise main ideas for another student, they offer opportunities for deeper processing of the material.

II.1.2. Questioning

Peer learning is likely to enhance the number of questions occurring in the interaction. The questions will be both for requesting clarification for something that has been not understood or misunderstood – and also for making sure that the partner has understood. It is easier to ask a question in presence of a few persons than in a whole class, and it may be less anxiety-inducing to ask a peer than an adult.

Both questioning and explaining are found to be important interactional qualities, leading to academic advantages for both tutor and tutee (De Backer, Van Keer & Valcke, 2015a; Graesser & Person, 1994; King, 1998; Roscoe & Chi, 2007; Webb et al., 2006). Tutor or peer explanations often result from or lead to questioning (Chi et al., 2001; Webb et al., 2006). Given that questioning prompts learners to optimise their thinking (King et al., 1998; Roscoe, 2014) and that peers generally engage more frequently in questioning than teachers during whole class instruction (Graesser & Person, 1994), peer learning thus fosters students' learning. Requests for clarification favour the development of common co-construction (Foot & Howe, 1998) – the generation of common understandings which go beyond where both students originally were. Thought-provoking questions and knowledge-building explanations as opposed to factual questions and knowledge-reviewing explanations appear especially effective in stimulating meaningful learning in peer learning (Graesser & Person, 1994; King, 1998; Roscoe & Chi, 2007). It seems especially positive to prompt students to ask comprehension questions and thinking questions for integration and connexion, as proposed by King (2007, p. 272):

Examples of comprehension questions include the following:

- Describe … in your own words
- What does … mean?
- Why is … important?
- What caused …?

Examples of thinking questions include the following:

- Explain why …
- Explain how …
- How are … and … similar?
- What is the difference between … and …?
- How does … affect …?
- What are the strengths and the weaknesses of …?
- How could … be used … to …?
- What would happen if …?
- Give another example of …

As far as cooperative groups are concerned, Webb underlined that not getting an answer to a question is negatively related to achievement (Webb, 1985, 1991). Terminal answers (giving solely the answer, without explanation) are not always positive for the giver and seem to be negative for the recipient (Topping, Dehkinet, Blanch, Corcelles & Duran, 2013). These terminal answers, unlike explanations, do not allow students to develop learning. The kinds of questions proposed by King reduce the likelihood of obtaining a terminal answer. Developing norms about the duty for peers to ask elaborated questions may support students in developing elaborated answers. Research regarding the effect of training on questioning will be summarised in Chapter 3.

II.1.3. Explaining and co-construction

Questioning and explaining are both important interactional qualities, leading to academic advantages for both tutor and tutee in peer tutoring (De Backer et al., 2015a; Graesser & Person, 1994; King, 1998; Roscoe & Chi, 2007; Webb et al., 2006) and for students working in cooperative groups (Gillies, 2015a; Webb, Franke, Ing, Turrou & Johnson, 2015).

A research study coded student interactions when working in cooperative groups and analysed the relations between the frequency of interactions and student learning (Johnson, Johnson, Roy & Zaidman, 1985). Observations while students discussed information from texts showed that intervening in the discussion, repeating studied information, adding new information and disagreeing with partners were positively related to subsequent factual recall of the studied material. Other researchers in mathematical tasks (see for example Webb,

1985; Webb, 1991) consistently underlined that those who provided more explanations were the students who performed better, even when the mathematical level was controlled. Providing explanations was positively related to performance, while giving a terminal response (directly giving the correct answer or pointing out an error without explanation) was unrelated to achievement. Furthermore, receiving elaborated help contributed to learning in mathematics on the condition that the received explanations were used subsequently in a constructive problem activity (Webb, Troper & Fall, 1995).

Students detect more easily what is not understood by their peers (as compared to the teacher) and give more easily understandable explanations (Gillies & Ashman, 1998). The gain in understanding thanks to peer learning is related to the extent students give propositions and explain their ideas (Howe et al., 2007). Research demonstrates that the peer tutoring interaction is mainly characterised by the tutor providing explanations in order to make information comprehensible for the tutee, correcting the tutee's misconceptions, and asking questions to elicit tutee thought processes (Graesser & Person, 1994; Roscoe & Chi, 2008).

With regard to the tutors on the other hand, since peer tutors are not truly either content or instructional experts, the task of providing relevant and coherent explanations requires them to permanently monitor their own understanding and to consider the learning content in depth and from different perspectives (Falchikov, 2001; King et al., 1998; Roscoe, 2014; Roscoe & Chi, 2007, 2008). This facilitates long-term retention, more comprehensive understanding, and results in academic benefits for students in the tutor role.

Interestingly, explaining (making some elaborative and metacognitive comments) for a partner who is active is a good way to interpret main ideas from a text (Spurlin, Dansereau, Larson & Brooks, 1984). In cooperative learning, shared mutual responsibility encourages both partners to be active in the discussion and promotes co-construction (Howe, 2015) – each partner adds something and they construct step by step on what the other proposes. This co-construction supporting common knowledge is also termed "cumulative" (Mercer, 1996), with partners building positively by accumulation.

II.2. Argumentation and reasoning

Argumentation plays an important role in learning (Muller Mirza & Perret-Clermont, 2009). Argumentation forces learners to make explicit and public their positions while justifying them for another person. Learners are encouraged to view the issue from different positions and to test the validity of all ideas and positions and justify their own position. This process makes them understand the rules of reasoning by making their joint reasoning explicit, in what has been labelled exploratory talk.

As suggested by Mercer, Wegerif and Dawes (1999), "In exploratory talk, knowledge is made publicly accountable and reasoning is visible in the talk" (p. 97). In exploratory talk, students are encouraged to engage critically but constructively with each other's ideas. They

- jointly consider suggestions,
- challenge the other's proposition while justifying,
- offer alternative propositions and
- justify their propositions.

As this kind of talk is not likely to appear spontaneously, we will summarise some ground rules which various authors suggest to promote it in Chapter 3.

II.3. Confrontation and socio-cognitive conflicts

In his early work, Piaget (1932) emphasised the role of cognitive conflict in cognitive development. More precisely, he pointed out the conflict between what a child anticipates as a result of her/his actions and the outcomes of her/his actually engaging in the activity. In a learning situation, hopefully information that contradicts students' beliefs may prompt them to abandon their misconception and favour a switch toward a more acceptable conception.

Nevertheless, this conceptual change remains a challenge, because it implies a radical shift in information processing. Confrontation with contradictory information does not always support conceptual change (Chan, Burtis & Bereiter, 1997). Indeed, contradictory information may lead to any of three types of processing strategy:

- assimilative activity (connecting information with surface features, ignoring it or modifying it to make it compatible, justifying the difference with surface rationalisation)
- surface-constructive (understanding information without taking it into account, juxtaposing positions, discarding information as an exception)
- knowledge building (perceiving different information as something problematic needed to be explained, constructing explanations to reconcile information, seeking connections, proposing conflicting hypotheses).

Results indicate that confrontation with contradictory information supports conceptual change only when students take the opportunity to engage in knowledge-building activity (Chan et al., 1997). Interestingly for peer learning, this research also showed that when students were confronted with contradictory information and they had to agree with a peer before answering, they scored higher on belief change. Likewise, Ames and Murray (1982) used Piagetian tasks and introduced different confrontation conditions in order to investigate which form of confrontation permitted more progress (changes for each child from pre-test to post-test). In a socio-cognitive conflict condition, they asked two children whose answers were confrontational during the pre-test to reach a common answer. This condition was compared to other situations where the children were confronted with contradictory answers without interaction: listening to a peer proposing a different answer or pretending the opposite of what they think, or being confronted with their own previously different answers. It appears from this study that the socio-cognitive conflict condition resulted in more progress at post-test than the other conditions in which children were faced with conflicting information without interaction.

Research has repeatedly pointed out the importance of conflict with others (Bell, Grossen & Perret-Clermont, 1985; Doise & Mugny, 1984; Johnson & Johnson, 2007; Levine, Resnick & Higgins, 1993; Tjosvold & Johnson, 1978). Howe (2015) proposes that the expression of difference in opinions elicited by peer learning promotes metacognitive awareness and this enhances students' receptiveness to subsequent events of relevance – thus these processes support individual learning.

Working with a peer elicits the expression of difference in opinions. Nevertheless, the relationship between socio-cognitive conflict and learning depends on how these processes are regulated (Buchs, Butera, Mugny, & Darnon, 2004; Johnson & Johnson, 2009a). Indeed, disagreeing with someone may cast doubt on the validity of both partners' answers and leave the students confused. Disagreeing may also put into question whether anyone is right and cast doubt on the competence of all partners. These interpretations lead to different regulation of conflict with different consequences for cognitive change (Butera, Darnon & Mugny, 2010).

We retain here the idea that conflicts between learners are positive when they are focused on the task or understanding the knowledge (Butera et al., 2010). This "epistemic regulation" stimulates the integration of different perspectives and promotes learning (Darnon, Muller, Schrager, Pannuzzo & Butera, 2006; Howe et al., 2007; Quiamzade & Mugny, 2001). Nevertheless, all confrontations are not positive, as we can easily imagine when we consider debates between politicians. When disagreement does not lead to constructive criticisms of suggestions (see "disputational talk", Mercer, 1996), or when learners try to impose their own point of view (see "debate", Johnson & Johnson, 2009a), confrontations do not support learning.

Indeed, when learners are focused on social comparison, confrontations challenge their respective competences and this reduces the benefits of confrontation of viewpoints (Sommet et al., 2014). Two such "relational regulations" have been documented. First, when students aim at avoiding conflict, a *protective* regulation pushes students to take the partner's position – they imitate the partner uncritically in order to end the conflict in a form of compliance. This compliance prevents learners from benefitting from confrontations. Second, a *competitive* regulation can take place in which learners compete to try to protect or demonstrate their own competence. This competitive regulation stimulates a struggle for competence and is negatively linked with learning (Buchs & Butera, 2015).

In one study (Darnon et al., 2002), the type of conflict regulation was manipulated in three interventions by a research confederate during pair (dyadic) work on a text at a university. The aim was to test the relationship between conflict regulation and student learning. Two different types of conflict regulation (epistemic conflict and competitive conflict) were compared with a controlled condition where the confederate just reformulated the content (non-conflict condition). Results indicated that in a cooperative context, epistemic conflict led to better learning than no conflict, which in turn was better than competitive conflict. When the context was not so cooperative (weak positive interdependence), conflict regulation did not lead to differences in learning. Thus for epistemic conflict to favour learning, it is necessary that partners engage in such regulation in a cooperative context.

Examples of epistemic and competitive conflicts are provided in Table II.1:

Table II.1 Examples of interventions for illustrating epistemic versus competitive conflicts

Epistemic conflicts: focus on search for understanding	Competitive conflicts: focus on competence issues
"I am not sure that I have understood the difference between those two conditions … Isn't it the same thing?"	"You haven't told me the difference between those two things … Presented like that, it is the same …"
"It's quite strange, I thought about it in another way, indeed [personal counterargument], what do you think about that?"	"And that doesn't question you? Because there are some theories that postulate the opposite [personal counterargument]. Have you never heard about it?"
"I think the meaning of the text is … but I'm not sure; how do you explain it?" [repeat the partner's answer] OK.	"Have you got it? It's simple but would you be able to explain it? In fact, it is rather different [personal reformulation].
"In the text, it says that … It's weird, I thought differently [personal counterargument]; what do you think?"	In the text, it says that … Didn't this surprise you? Because it can be different [personal counterargument]. Does this mean nothing to you?

This introduction proposes a brief summary intended to emphasise promotive interactions that explain how peer learning favours cognitive development and underlines the importance for the learner to develop a high level of communication. Understanding the relationship between peer interactions and learning, teachers can begin to figure out what kind of peer interaction they would like to promote. In our point of view, one role of teachers is to create conditions for these interactions to occur in their classrooms. In what follows, we will introduce general principles for teachers to consider which encourage these kinds of interactions.

II.4. Directions for organising peer learning

Observations in classrooms indicate that learners hardly ever engage spontaneously in promotive interactions. Western educational systems offer few opportunities for students to constructively interact with other learners (Baines, Rubie-Davies, 2009; Blatchford, Baines, Rubie-Davies, Bassett & Chowne, 2006; Blatchford, Kutnick, Baines & Galton, 2003; Pianta, Belsky, Houts & Morrison, 2007). This may result in some problems when teachers suggest that students work together (Buchs & Butera, 2015; E. Cohen, 1994; Webb, Farivar & Mastergeorge, 2002).

Different methods have been presented in Chapters 1 and 2 which aimed at educational solutions for effective learning. On one hand, some authors proposed methods like Constructive Controversy, Jigsaw, Teams-Games-Tournaments, Student Teams-Achievement Division, Team Assisted Individualisation, Cooperative Integrated Reading and Composition, Group Investigation, Reciprocal Teaching or Complex Instruction. Chapter 1 offers a brief description of these methods (see also S. Sharan, 1999 for a presentation of the methods by their proponents). They give guidance for teachers to organise a whole unit of teaching from the beginning to the end with an inner coherence.

On the other hand, other authors propose more specific cooperative techniques (e.g., S. Kagan, 2013), that represent instructional strategies which are content free, and can be used without a great deal of change in usual teaching. Some of these techniques will be presented in Chapter 4.

At the midpoint between these two directions, we will develop some general principles for organising peer interactions. We present these general principles in a detailed way in Chapters 3 and 4. These principles can be introduced in all classrooms from primary to higher education in a variety of contexts (E. Cohen, 1994), so teachers can easily adapt them to their own contexts, students and content teaching.

II.5. General principles

Peer interaction is proposed as an essential principle of peer learning. The way of naming peer interaction can vary, e.g., simultaneous interaction in M. Kagan and Kagan (2000) or face-to-face promotive interaction in Johnson and Johnson (1989) or Gillies (2007), but all cooperative learning methods stress the importance of student-to-student interaction in small groups (Davidson & Major, 2014). We propose to differentiate two aspects of interaction. First, we have introduced constructive interactions as the central element in the introduction to Part II along with explication of what peer interactions can promote learning. Second, we propose to move the question of the number of participants involved in the terminology *simultaneous* or *face-to-face* or *small groups* to Chapter 4 when addressing grouping learners. So we retain constructive (peer) interactions as the central principle of peer learning.

In addition, two principles are consensually proposed (Johnson, Johnson & Holubec, 1998; M. Kagan & Kagan, 2000; Rouiller & Howden, 2010; Y. Sharan, 2010b; Slavin, 1995):

- positive interdependence – which refers to the perception of learners that they are positively linked together making them think in terms of "us" instead of "me"
- individual accountability – by which each member is responsible for contributing and accountable for his/her own learning as well as his/her teammates' learning

According to the Learning Together method (see Chapter 1), two other principles are needed: cooperative skills (the teacher may teach skills required to work efficiently in groups) and group processing (the teacher proposes their students reflect on taskwork and teamwork). These two principles will be developed in Chapter 3. Therefore, despite the variation in terminology, constructive interactions, structuring positive interdependence and individual accountability, teaching cooperative skills and making students reflect on group processing are presented as essential for organised cooperative learning by different authors (Abrami et al., 1995; Bennett, Rolheiser & Stevahn, 1991; Clarke, Wideman & Eadie, 1990; Gillies, 2007; Howden & Kopiec, 2000; Johnson & Johnson, 2015).

Additional principles are mentioned regarding equal participation (M. Kagan & Kagan, 2000), making sure that all participants contribute meaningfully (Slavin, 1995), establishing a constructive climate in the class and team spirit (Abrami et al., 1995; Bennett et al., 1991; Howden & Kopiec, 2000; S. Kagan, 2013), and specifically working in the classroom on values (Rouiller & Howden, 2010) or norms (E. Cohen, 1994).

II.6. An organisation for general principles

These general principles may vary among authors. We propose to discuss these principles in three blocks. The first block concerns constructive interactions. Indeed, in our point of view, all the principles aim at stimulating the promotive interactions required to support learning. Promotive interactions are what the teacher is trying to elicit in peer learning. Both other blocks provide the teacher with ways for achieving this goal. Chapter 3 focuses on preparing students as in block 2 and discuss a positive framework for learning, with principles that suggest general ways of behaving with others in relation to learning (cooperative values, norms and attitudes as well as a focus on learning and mastery), the importance of cooperative skills (skills enhancing student interactions while they are working together on academic tasks in their teams), and group processing (reflexion on the way the team functions). Finally, the third block concerns the organisation of peer interactions in the task. Chapter 4 presents principles for organising peer interactions in academic tasks. We will discuss the way teachers group learners, structure positive interdependence, introduce individual accountability, offer scripts and scaffolds for peer interactions and assess learning.

Thus Chapters 3 and 4 propose general principles that can be used to organise peer learning in classrooms, along with results from research evaluating the effectiveness of these principles. Some practical directions will be proposed for each individual principle. Then, Chapters 5, 6 and 7 offer some examples of interventions involving the different principles that we have used and studied in our own practice.

Chapter 3

Preparing learners for constructive interactions

Empirical research demonstrates that students' spontaneous interaction during cooperative learning and peer tutoring can be unsatisfactory. Many researchers have reported that group work is not always effective (Blatchford et al., 2006; E. Cohen, 1994; Gillies & Ashman, 1996). Peer tutors' explanations and questions sometimes appear too shallow and limited both in frequency and level of cognitive demand, in turn eliciting too limited and rather superficial tutee responses (Chi et al., 2001; Graesser & Person, 1994; King, 1998; Roscoe & Chi, 2007; Topping, 2005a). Moreover, peer tutors sometimes tend to monopolise the interaction, leaving limited space for tutee contributions and truly interactive discussions (Chi et al., 2001). When designing and implementing successful peer tutoring programmes, these possible difficulties have to be taken into account if you are seeking to guarantee effective peer interactions.

We argue that it is especially necessary to prepare students for constructive interactions, as they are neither socialised nor used to cooperating. Indeed, students are socialised in a generally competitive environment (Kasser, Cohn, Kanner & Ryan, 2007) and educational system (Harackiewicz, Barron & Elliot, 1998). Moreover, group work is not so usual in the daily classroom (Baines et al., 2009; Blatchford et al., 2006; Blatchford et al., 2003; Pianta et al., 2007) and teachers tend not to have confidence in pupils' social interactions in groups (Blatchford et al., 2003). It is important to prepare students to cooperate (Blatchford et al., 2003; Johnson & Johnson, 2006; Tolmie et al., 2010; Webb, 2009) in order to promote constructive interactions. E. Cohen (1994) underlines that teachers lose less time in preparing students for group work than in reacting to disorganised behaviour from students.

Webb et al. (2002) suggest four areas in which the teacher can help in promoting productive helping in small groups. We propose to group the two of these (establish positive norms for group work and structure the task in ways that support learning and understanding) into a positive framework for learning in interactions. Their third element (model desired behaviours) will be developed as we talk about preparing and training students for appropriate use of cooperative skills. The fourth element (monitor group work) will be integrated when we talk about group processing.

3.1. Positive framework for learning in interactions

3.1.1. Cooperative values, norms and attitudes in the class

All teachers value some rules that they would like to be respected in classroom. For example, some teachers expect their students to do their work without worrying about what others are doing, to be attentive to what the teacher says, to refrain from giving or seeking advice from a friend, and to be quiet. Other teachers expect their students to question, to share their ideas, to explain their rationale and help each other for understanding and learning.

Cooperative values play an important role in effective peer learning. Values represent beliefs referring to desirable goals and serve as guiding principles in peoples' lives – they transcend specific situations (Schwartz, 1996). Teachers' values influence their daily interactions and their pedagogical choices. Regarding peer learning, Rouiller and Howden (2010) proposed a list of cooperative values which were important to discuss with students: respect, engagement, openness, helping each other, the right to differ, solidarity, trust, sharing, pleasure, autonomy, equality and empathic listening.

Following Johnson et al. (2002), the development of values goes through several channels. Teacher can directly teach values, through identification and modelling. They can also assign to students the underlying behaviours as social roles they have to display, or they can structure activities to work on values.

It is important to establish new cooperative norms for general rules and ways of behaving in the class that support cooperative values (Blatchford et al., 2003; E. Cohen, 1994). The role of the teacher is to introduce these norms and clearly state what is expected in the classroom. Encouraging student participation in the elaboration of these norms helps maximise student engagement, so the students respect the norms and invite their partners to follow them. Stressing individual and collective concerns (you need to do this in order to work together successfully) more than the normative aspect (you need to do this because I say it is the thing to do) may be useful. Specific activities for establishing norms and objectives along with cooperative structures may be useful for starting cooperative work with a class (Abrami et al., 1995; M. Kagan, Kagan & Kagan, 2012).

For example, a teacher can propose an activity to reflect on what supports learning in the class:

- Divide the class in two groups. Ask students from one group to reflect on their own for two minutes on things that can facilitate learning. Ask students from the other group to think about things that can hinder learning.
- The teacher gives one big sheet of paper to each group. Students write all their ideas without taking a look at the other group's work for five minutes.
- In each group, students read all ideas and categorise them. They develop a summary to describe each category.
- They elaborate a poster to summarise their discussion and organise themselves to present the poster to the class.
- The teacher invites students who are listening to the presentation to identify how the students who are presenting behave in a way that favours trust.
- Each group is invited to behave in a "trusty" way for presenting their subsequent work.

While students can be threatened by group work, it is important to reduce any risks perceived by students (Blatchford et al., 2003; Buchs & Butera, 2015). Trust appears to be very important for creating a positive climate in the classroom (Abrami et al., 1995; Bennett et al., 1991; Blatchford et al., 2006; Deutsch, 1962; Johnson, Johnson & Holubec, 1998; Kutnick, Ota & Berdondini, 2008; Tolmie et al., 2010; Wentzel, 1991). Trust involves openness, sharing, acceptance, support and cooperative intentions. It implies both being trusting (willingness to risk beneficial or harmful consequences) and being trustworthy (willingness to respond to another person's risk taking) (Johnson, Johnson & Holubec, 1998).

For example, Rouiller and Howden (2010) propose reflections for pointing out and transmitting the importance of trust. The first step is to explore why the value is important. The second step is to explore how to make students discover these values. Table 3.1 shows some propositions Rouiller and Howden (2010) have collected from teachers.

Teachers can suggest their students think about one person they trust, then ask them to describe what characteristics would be useful to explain this relationship. For young children, teachers can use stories or film extracts that involve examples and counterexamples of trusting and trustworthy behaviours, then ask students what they think of the situation and how they would have felt in these situations.

It is also possible to pair students and ask one of them to close their eyes, while the other student has the responsibility to help the partner to be confident enough to move from one point to one another with closed eyes. The teacher can propose two variations: the person responsible for guiding the partner

- is not allowed to talk and has to guide the partner's movements by touching only; or
- is not allowed to touch the partner and can guide only with the voice – this alternative also permits the beginning of a reflection on the importance of using a quiet voice when working together so as not to disturb other groups.

Roles can be reversed, and teachers can lead a collective reflection on how students feel in both roles: what characteristics they use to identify others' trustworthiness, and what characteristics make themselves worthy of others' trust. Teachers can ask if students need to open their eyes despite the instructions – and ask why. What can be done to make students more comfortable?

Trust has to be developed regarding student-student as well as teacher–student relationships. The climate starts to be built from the first welcome and is a determining factor for all activities (individual, whole-class or group work) in the classroom. Activities that allow students to discover and discuss their common points as well as recognise and welcome their differences can be useful to create and maintain trust (Abrami et al., 1995; M. Kagan et al., 2012).

Table 3.1 Propositions for reflecting on values

Why is trust important?	How to make students discover trust?
• Trust is the foundation for relationships and learning • Trust makes the work in team easier • Trust is bidirectional • Trust is easier to lose than to gain	• The teacher trusts the students • The students trust each other • Allowing students to make errors • Supporting autonomy by giving responsibilities to students • Giving students opportunities to express their ideas and listen to other's ideas • Learning to accept each other's ideas

Source: Rouiller & Howden, 2010.

3.1.2. Positive interpersonal relationships

Knowing other students is essential for interactions. In order to know each other, students must have opportunities to interact. Activities to create positive interpersonal relationships in the class and in a team that has to work together can be useful (Abrami et al., 1995; S. Kagan, 2013; Staquet, 2007). There are many books that propose examples of activities - we will not present here all the possibilities. What we would like to stress is the importance of positive interpersonal relationships and to underline some directions. In line with Abrami et al. (1995), we suggest three steps: icebreaker activities for getting to know each other, creating positive relationships in teams before teamwork, and introducing norms for supporting the quality of exchange in teams.

- Fun icebreaker activities (Abrami et al., 1995; Bennett et al., 1991; M. Kagan et al., 2012) can be useful to help students in getting to know each other (e.g., classmates' names and characteristics). Activities that propose students move around the class to stimulate quick interactions may make students comfortable at first. These activities should not be threatening.

"Find someone who ..." is an activity than can be adapted in different ways for different purposes (see for example, M. Kagan et al., 2012). Students receive a sheet with a list of questions starting with *Find Someone Who*.... This list can be worded in a sentence or related to pictures depending on the age. The questions can be related to personal characteristics (find someone who likes ices cream, rides a bike to come to school, plays music…), or be related to lesson content (find someone who can solve a problem, knows a specific fact, has already read something on the targeted topic). However, we do not recommend content-related questions for icebreaker activities. At the end, students share their findings with the class or with their team.

One variation consists of asking each student to confidentially write one thing regarding themselves (a hobby, a personal characteristic, something they have done…) that other classmates could not easily guess and give the paper to the teacher. The teacher uses it to make a list for proposing the "find someone who" activity for the class. Collective discussion enables other students to guess who possesses the attribute mentioned. All students are eventually discussed.

- Activities for stimulating positive interpersonal relationships in teams of students before they start to work together should aim for them to feel secure to contribute. Even if the class climate is positive, students have to be ready to work with their teammates. Activities that support trust and communication between members (as well as those that allow students to realise their common points and their team identity) are likely to support the quality of work (Bennett et al., 1991). A few minutes can be sufficient for students to get ready to work together in a good atmosphere. For teachers who do not wish to invest much time, the constitution of the teams can offer opportunities to connect with partners before starting work (see Chapter 4 below for some examples). Suggesting that students exchange thoughts on a topic in a personal manner as a starting point for the discussion may help promote good personal relationships.

For example, introducing discussion on the content in a way that allows students to connect with each other before going on to the task work may help. Ask students

- to share with their teammates their favourite story on a particular topic before starting to work on a literature task;
- to present their favourite animal before a biology lesson on animal classification; and
- to discuss what evokes the theme of the lesson for them, and what they would like to learn on this topic.

The cooperative structures in Chapter 4 can be useful for ensuring equal participation.

All the activities for developing positive interpersonal relationships should aim to support students' positive self-image and integrate all students. It is important to avoid competition for recognition or criticisms that create tensions. These activities should give opportunities to get to know the other members and appreciate this moment of discussion.

Staquet (2001) suggests introducing some rules:

- Everyone has the right to speak without being interrupted.
- Everyone has the right not to answer.
- Do not monopolise the floor.

The cooperative norms or ground rules introduced for supporting the quality of exchanging help serve to maintain and foster the positive relationships between partners in teams. Some examples can be found below in the norms proposed by E. Cohen (1994):

- You must complete each individual report and each group activity.
- Play your role in the group.
- You have the right to ask for help from any member of your group.
- You have a duty to help anyone that asks for help.
- Help others without doing the work for them.
- Everyone participates.

More general rules were proposed by Mercer et al. (1999):

- All relevant information is shared.
- The group seeks to reach agreement.
- The group takes responsibility for decisions.
- Reasons are expected.
- Challenges are accepted.
- Alternatives are discussed before a decision is taken.
- All in the group are encouraged to speak by other group members.

The Mercer et al. (1999) research indicated that the ground rules can be taught. Teachers should carefully explain, justify and 'scaffold' these rules and comment on subsequent positive effects on interactions and learning. In this programme, researchers proposed to teachers a series of nine structured lessons which aimed to strengthen students' awareness regarding the way they were talking together based on the ground rules for exploratory talk. In each class, students and teacher created their own rules from the original ones and worked through nine hours of activities devoted to cooperative skills (listening, sharing information and cooperating) and critical arguments (controversy for and against different cases). In order to assess the effect of this work on cooperation, researchers compared students who experienced this work to others who did not. Results indicated that these rules stimulated students' exploratory talk, improved the way students worked together on problem-solving tasks and enhanced children's individual reasoning skills.

In sum, establishing a positive climate helps students feel comfortable and ready to take risks in contributing, stimulates a high level of talk and positive interactions, and favours learning.

3.2. Focus on learning

When students work together, they should take this opportunity to go deeper in their learning processes. A focus on understanding and efforts to improve learning is particularly important to create a positive orientation for mastering the content, rather than merely highlighting the correct answers and achieving a quick consensus (Meece, Anderman & Anderman, 2006). The relationship with the teacher and the class structure are important (Stipek & Mac Iver, 1989) to orient students towards a mastery goal instead of a performance goal (Urdan, 1997). Research on motivational climate summarises essential elements in the acronym TARGET, meaning Task, Authority, Recognition, Grouping, Evaluation and Time (Ames, 1992; Maehr & Midgley, 1991; see Table 3.2.).

Mastery orientation is enhanced thanks to work on the climate and organisation of the classroom. This climate allows learners to feel secure enough to be able to learn through cooperation.

Not only are mastery goals positively related to adaptive behaviour at school, but such goals also frame the meaning of social relationships (Poortvliet & Darnon, 2010) and enhance the likelihood of help giving and help seeking (Poortvliet & Darnon, 2014). Indeed, students with mastery goals search for improvement – they are likely to recognise positive interdependence. They perceive other students as relevant sources of information, and they support cooperation and help-seeking.

In contrast, because students focused on performance goals need to outperform others to affirm their own competence, they are likely to perceive other students as potential competitors and may be more reluctant to cooperate. The relationship between performance goals and help-seeking is negative. Finally, performance goals may decrease the benefit of social interactions for learning outcomes, as they eliminate positive outcomes from socio-cognitive conflicts.

Two studies investigated the effects of achievement goals during a situation where university students worked on text. In the first study, students worked with a fictitious

Table 3.2 Elements from TARGET to enhance mastery orientation

Task	Teacher structures the task to reduce social comparison
Authority	Teacher delegates a part of their authority by involving learners in some decisions
Recognition	Teacher promotes recognition of all students and values their efforts
Grouping	Teacher groups students in order to support help
Evaluation	Teacher regulates errors and uses them to adapt their lesson
Time	Teacher manages time while limiting stress

partner via computers (Darnon, Butera & Harackiewicz, 2007). In reality the partner's answer was manipulated by the researcher in order to agree or disagree with student's proposition. In the mastery goals condition, students were informed that their task was to acquire new knowledge that could be useful later, to understand the experiences, examples and ideas of the text, and to discover new concepts. In the performance goal condition, they were informed that their task was to be efficient, to be good, and to have a good individual score at the end. Results showed that conflict fostered uncertainty and fear of failure. Nevertheless, the effects of conflict depended on the goals of the conditions. In the mastery condition, disagreements resulted in better learning than agreements. The opposite occurred in the performance goal condition, where disagreements led to deterioration in learning. Mastery goals favoured performance only with conflict. When the students agreed, the instruction regarding achievement goals did not matter. These results underline that the way instructions are given is likely to orient students in the way they should interact and learn together.

In addition, when students interact spontaneously (Darnon, Doll & Butera, 2007), the nature of the achievement goals predict the regulation of confrontation. Indeed, the degree of confrontation students report predicts epistemic regulation of conflict in the mastery condition, whereas the degree of confrontation predicted competitive regulation in the performance condition. It is thus important to keep in mind the way teachers frame their activity can affect not only the kind of social interactions that take place but also the relation between interactions and learning.

3.3. Preparing family

In order to prepare the context of peer learning, in primary and secondary education it is important to remember to inform parents (or if relevant the broader community around the school) on the benefits and the objectives of your intended programme. Broad support in this respect – especially at the onset of the implementation – can make the difference between failure and success. Sharing information (Clarke et al., 1990) and partnering (Bennett et al., 1991) with parents can be an important ingredient to success in peer learning.

Moreover it is important to keep in mind that families can share a traditional conception about learning and teaching, and be not only reluctant for their children to use group working but perceive collaboration and helping other students as a waste of time. Or on the other hand feeling embarrassed, thinking that other children waste time and opportunities while helping their son or daughter.

For this reason, it is necessary to explain to parents that learning is a social product, that cooperation is a key competence in today's society and that peer learning will offer to their son or daughter opportunities not only to develop complex social skills (like communication, empathy or praising), but a deeper knowledge about what they teach others. A good way to provide this information could be to highlight some of the main ideas explained in Part I and tailor them to particular parents' needs.

In some schools, teachers give parents the opportunity to visit classrooms when students are working in teams. This could be an excellent way for them to observe the engagement and the learning of the students. Finally, in some peer tutoring programmes, teachers invite parents to take part actively in it, as a system to discover the potential of peer learning. So, for instance, in Read On and in Reading in Pairs, parents have the opportunity to act as a reading tutor for their son or daughter at home (Topping, Duran & Van Keer, 2016).

3.4. Preparing and training students for appropriate use of cooperative skills

Cooperative skills are important for the quality of the interactive work. Nevertheless, they may not be really mastered by the learners (including adults). Therefore, when proposing a learning situation in which peer interactions are a main component, it is important to create a context in which cooperative skills can be worked upon (Howden & Kopiec, 1999). Preparing and training students before and during peer learning is important both for peer tutoring programmes (Falchikov, 2001; Roscoe & Chi, 2007; Topping, 1996) and for cooperative learning (Gillies, 2007; Johnson, Johnson & Holubec, 1998; M. Kagan et al., 2012). In peer tutoring, both peer tutors and their tutees should be informed about the programme and the related aims. They need to be encouraged to put constructive social and communication skills into practice (Topping, 2005a). In cooperative learning, explicit instructions on the required skills for working appropriately all together are key elements.

3.4.1. Type of skills

Different authors propose different labels and target different skills. We list some here in order to illustrate this variety:

- Helping each other (giving and receiving help, perceiving the needs of others and responding appropriately), communication (the ability to express oneself, to explain, to listen, to understand, to ask questions), conflict resolution (arguing, agreeing to change one's idea), encouragement and contributing to the group goal (Gaudet et al., 1998)
- Effective communication (listening, explaining and sharing) and skills on how to plan and organise for active engagement (Blatchford et al., 2003)
- Social skills like listening, paraphrasing, taking the role of other and managing group processes (S. Kagan & Kagan, 1999)
- Social skills, communication skills and advanced group work skills (Blatchford et al., 2006)
- Interpersonal skills (actively listening, stating ideas freely, accepting responsibility for one's behaviours, providing constructive criticism) and small group skills (taking turns, sharing tasks, making decisions democratically, trying to understand the other person's perspective, clarifying differences) (Gillies, 2007; Johnson, Johnson & Holubec, 1998)
- Cognitive skills (intellectual competences related to the task, like processing information, making links, drawing conclusions or making reasoned decisions) and social skills (skills for communicating, pro-social skills like listening, encouraging, dialoguing) (Abrami et al., 1995)
- Skills for ensuring communication – sending and receiving skills (Johnson, Johnson & Holubec, 1998)
- Skills related to the task work (asking questions, clarifications, summarising etc.) and skills related the teamwork (looking for consensus, encouraging others, answering others etc.) (Clarke et al., 1990)
- Teamwork and discussion skills (Y. Sharan & Sharan, 1999)
- Social skills or small group and interpersonal skills required to function in a team (Johnson et al., 2002; Johnson, Johnson & Holubec, 1998); see below for examples.

Because the skills are introduced in order to allow students to work appropriately and cooperatively with teammates on the learning task, we propose to name them *cooperative skills*. It is important to work step-by-step through cooperative skills, respecting the degree of complexity.

Johnson et al. (2002) identify four steps that can give some ideas for developing cooperative skills:

Forming skills are basic skills needed for forming the group:

- Move into groups quietly.
- Stay with the group.
- Use quiet voices.
- Take turns.
- Keep hands and feet to yourself.
- Use names.

Functioning skills are required to complete and maintain effective working relationships among members:

- Share ideas and opinions.
- Ask for facts and reasoning.
- Give direction to the group's work.
- Encourage everyone to participate.
- Ask for help or clarification.
- Express support and acceptance.
- Offer to explain or clarify.
- Paraphrase.
- Energise the group.
- Describe feelings.

Formulating skills support a deeper level of understanding and quality of reasoning strategies:

- Summarise out loud.
- Seek accuracy.
- Seek elaboration.
- Develop memory aids.
- Check for understanding.
- Ask for others to plan out loud.

Fermenting skills are needed for challenging the conclusions and reasoning of others:

- Criticise ideas without criticising people.
- Differentiate ideas and reasoning of group members.
- Integrate ideas into single positions.
- Ask for justification.
- Extend answers.
- Probe by asking in-depth questions.
- Generate further answers.

Teachers can introduce explicit work on cooperative skills while respecting an increasing order of complexity. Once basic cooperative skills are mastered, new ones can be introduced.

3.4.2. Which cooperative skills to develop?

In line with Abrami et al. (1995) and Johnson, Johnson & Holubec (1998), we propose to monitor teams, diagnose specific skills the students need to improve and analyse the cooperative skills required for completing the assignment. Moreover, these authors suggest asking students to identify skills they would want to improve.

As we propose to put cooperation into the service of learning, we recommend to design the group's scholarly task first, and then to target the appropriate cooperative skills. We underline the necessity for analysing the academic activity and bringing out the cooperative skills that students will need for working effectively together on that specific task. By proceeding in this way, the targeted skill is likely to be relevant for teamwork and helpful for learning (Abrami, et al., 1995). We suggest saving the notes from past tasks – the observations as well as the modes of interaction that arose – while taking care not to overload learners. By proceeding in this way, one skill at a time is established and consolidates those already introduced (Jacobs, Power & Wan Innm, 2002).

3.4.3 How to develop the required cooperative skills

Different authors recommend the explicit teaching of cooperative skills (Abrami et al., 1995; Bennett et al., 1991; Clarke et al., 1990; E. Cohen, 1994; Gaudet et al., 1998; Johnson et al., 2002; Rouiller & Howden, 2010) and suggest important steps to move from conceptual (knowing which and why cooperative skills are important) to procedural knowledge (knowing how to perform these cooperative skills):

3.4.3.1. Make sure that students perceive the usefulness of the targeted cooperative skills

Explaining when and why these cooperative skills will help is important. It is easier if students can participate in the choice of the skills. Teacher can use role playing, simulation, examples and counterexamples. For example, after working on a Sudoku puzzle completed in pairs, the teacher asked five-year-old students who first started playing and why. Some children said that their partner had started, but they would have preferred to have started themselves. Others indicated they started because their partner was not looking at the puzzle. From the discussion the importance emerged of "Agreeing who is starting" and "Playing turns" (activity proposed by teacher Christelle Darbre).

3.4.3.2. Define the cooperative skill

The teacher explains what is expected, and can demonstrate and model the skill. It seems important that students understand procedures and can themselves demonstrate the skills (from declarative knowledge to associative knowledge to procedural knowledge, Rouiller & Howden, 2010). For example, teachers can introduce a collective discussion regarding the way the cooperative skills can be demonstrated, inviting students to participate. The discussion can be summarised in a poster to be made available during cooperative work.

Johnson et al. (2002) refer to a T-chart (because of the shape of the chart, see Table 3.3) that describes the procedural knowledge for the cooperative skills.

Whatever the form, it is important to collectively elaborate a reference tool promoting the introduction of the targeted cooperative skills with concrete examples on how to behave in a way that make sense for students. Taking their own suggestions stimulates recognition and motivation for using the cooperative skills.

Table 3.3 The T-chart as a reference tool for cooperative skills

Targeted cooperative skills

As a member of the team: What can I say? As an observer: What can I hear?	As a member of the team: What can I do? As an observer: What can I see?

Table 3.4 An example of a reference tool for taking one's turn

Taking one's turn

(I see)	(I hear)
• A student helping another student • Students taking turns for speaking • Other students listening • All students participating • One or more student(s) providing encouragement (nodding, smiling, inviting)	• "Go ahead, I know you can do it!" • Each student speaking at least once • Students not talking too long • Students speaking kindly • "You did not tell your idea, please, tell us what you think" • "I'm sure you can explain something to us" • "Come closer"

For example, in a heterogeneous grade 4 class, the teacher wanted to introduce the skill "Take one's turn" (Table 3.4). She asked students: "If I was watching your groups without being able to hear what you say, what actions would indicate to me that you use this skill?" and "If I could hear what you say without seeing what you do, what words or phrases would indicate to me that you use this skill?" The teacher recorded the student's answers (activity proposed by teacher Fanny Olivier).

In another example with second graders, a teacher wanted to work on "Deciding Together". She recorded each student's answer and invited them to pay attention to this skill during subsequent activities (activity proposed by teacher Sonia Fratianni):

- We talk together and discuss.
- We help each other.
- We explain with patience.
- We carefully listen.
- We make sure that we truly agree.
- We express disagreement: "I did not understand", "I don't agree because…".

3.4.3.3. Practice and observation

Once a cooperative skill is introduced, it is important that students engage in this skill during subsequent group work involving activities requiring the targeted cooperative skills. Cooperative skills can become social objectives for all students or can be introduced as specific roles that certain students have to try to follow (Johnson et al., 2002). At that stage, students will be aware of the skills they have to demonstrate and why this skill is useful. Group work gives the teacher the opportunity for observing the way students express the skills, for intervening and for clarification. The observation can be unstructured or structured, with a specific grid designed to record the skills (qualitatively and/or quantitatively) (see Table 3.5). The teacher can observe the different groups for different moments and/or ask one student in each group to observe other members. While the cooperative skills are introduced as a social objective, it is important that students get some feedback on the way they use them.

3.4.3.4. Feedback and reflection

Information gathered during observation allows giving specific feedback to students on the way they demonstrated the cooperative skills. They could also engage in self-evaluation. It is important that students can reflect on the way they used the cooperative skills and propose some objectives for improvement. This reflection permits upgrading the chart to adapt it for subsequent activities (see Table 3.6).

For young students, you can use pictograms for answering or suggest students visually indicate their answer. Some examples can be found in Sabourin, Bernard, Duchesneau, Fugère & Ladouceur, 2002.

Propose that teammates give positive feedback regarding the way their partners express the cooperative skills – this may be used for reinforcing cooperative skills. For the same reason, make sure that all students receive positive feedback; teachers can propose some typical formulations and invite students to use and complete it:

"I appreciate it when you ... (ask me if I wanted to add something)".
"I feel good when you ... (welcome my proposition)".

3.4.3.5. Consolidation

The last step concerns the consolidation of the cooperative skill by putting it into practice in different contexts. Together with reflection, this allows students to become aware of their

Table 3.5 Example of an observation grid

Observation	Name	Name	Name	Name
Number of propositions				
Number of invitations for partner's participation				
Ways for inviting partners for participation				

Table 3.6 An example of self-evaluation

I paid attention that everyone participated	Rarely	Sometimes	Several times
I directly invited one partner to talk	Rarely	Sometimes	Several times

progression (Clarke et al., 1990), and may increase their motivation in using cooperative skills appropriately.

When using these different steps, learning can be very mechanical at the beginning, with students using the cooperative skills when they see teachers coming. However, when repeated, these exercises allow students to integrate cooperative skills more automatically and use them more spontaneously. Johnson, Johnson & Holubec (1998) emphasise over-learning for cooperative skills to become automatic and usual.

3.5. What about research on cooperative skills teaching?

3.5.1. General approach

Some studies propose long-term intervention in which teachers introduce the relational approach in their daily classroom activities. These studies showed that students who benefitted from this relational approach not only behaved in a more constructive way during group work, but also performed better on academic tasks than students from control groups.

Kutnick et al. (2008) proposed a developmental sequence over a school year that implied framing trust and support, with specific work on communication skills and sequences involving joint problem solving for five- to seven-year-olds. Teachers introduced this relational approach in their classroom, and progressively enhanced the number of peer learning situations. The positive perception of children regarding group work outcomes increased at the same time that their reading and mathematics attainments improved. Results also indicated that students in a class with a relational approach programme participated more during group work, communicated more efficiently with each other during lessons and were more engaged in task-related behaviours compared with students in classes without the relational approach.

At the same time, Tolmie, Topping, Christie, Donaldson, Howe, Jessiman, Livingston and Thurston (2010) proposed a developmental programme for an upper-elementary teacher with nine 12-year-old students. First the teacher had one day's training on generic relational and communication skills, with plans for a sequence of group activities for helping students to develop trust and effective communication. The teachers had to introduce in the classrooms one hour of instruction regarding group work skills training and one hour of group work on an academic task over 12 weeks. Then, teachers were trained and experimented with prepared materials on two science topics. They received further comprehensive resources and had to introduce these topics in their class during at least one hour of structured group work per week. The tasks were designed to prompt propositions and explanations during group work. Students had to discuss their ideas, reach a consensus and agree on written explanation. A last training day invited teachers to reflect on their experiences and gave the opportunity to evaluate the intervention programme. It appeared that the quality of teacher implementation was generally good and students improved their group-work skills and play relationships after the intervention. Moreover, students developed constructive interactions like giving suggestions and explanations.

The above examples underline the positive impact of a broad relational approach. Positive results regarding learning outcomes are found, with strategies for providing students with a generic set of skills (such as in communication or planning) (Prichard, Bizo & Stratford, 2006; Prichard, Bizo & Stratford, 2011; Prichard, Stratford & Bizo, 2006). Other research more specifically tested the impact of teaching students targeted cooperative skills.

3.5.2. Interpersonal and small group skills

A research programme investigated the effects of training relatively general cooperative skills, involving interpersonal skills and collaborative skills for group work. Results underlined that a relatively short training for skills led to positive results regarding both the way students interacted and their learning outcomes.

Gillies and her colleagues have tested the effect of training relatively general cooperative skills. Teachers from grades 1 and 3 (Gillies & Ashman, 1998) as well as grade 6 (Ashman & Gillies, 1997; Gillies & Ashman, 1996) initiated cooperative learning through a cooperative skills training (two 45-minute sessions). The training worked on how to demonstrate interpersonal skills (e.g., active listening, taking into account the other's perspective, the expression of ideas, constructive criticism of ideas) and collaborative skills to work in small groups (e.g., taking turns, sharing the tasks equally, resolving differences of opinion and conflicts). Ways to demonstrate cooperative skills in behaviour and speech were recorded using a cooperative learning reference tool. Younger learners were invited to play roles while older students developed their own ways through collective and small group discussions. All learners worked in teams several times a week for a couple of weeks.

Compared to learners who worked in cooperative groups during the same time but without benefiting from this cooperative skills training, the participants interacted more constructively. Benefits were observed in the quality of cooperation, helping behaviours, the quality of explanations and learning. These effects were maintained throughout the study and the differences between trained and untrained learners persisted beyond the school year (Gillies, 1999, 2000, 2002).

3.5.3. Questioning

Other strategies focus on more specific interactions. Taking into account the research on questioning and explaining, peer tutors should be trained to challenge tutees' understanding with elaborative explanations and reflective questions, aimed at stimulating tutees' deep reasoning (Graesser & Person, 1994; King et al., 1998; Roscoe & Chi, 2008; Webb et al., 2006), as well as scaffolding tutees' learning (Azevedo & Hadwin, 2005; Chi et al., 2001). Training in questioning and explaining are also recognised in cooperative learning.

The introduction to Part II offered some examples of guided peer questioning, with examples of comprehension and thinking questions (King, 2007). Students had to select some generic questions and transform them into specific questions related to the lesson topic, so they could pose their questions to their teammates during team discussion while their partners answered the questions. The fact that learners could choose the questions they wanted to ask and build them in their own way enabled them to flexibly reuse the questions in other contexts.

These questions facilitate important cognitive activities like review and consolidation of student understanding, checking comprehension, constructing new knowledge, and monitoring how well the students are thinking and learning (King, 2002). Students are cognitively engaged in order to transform generic questions to specific questions, and they prompt their partners to engage in explanation and elaboration. Moreover, this question-oriented discussion favours socio-cognitive conflict. As we pointed out in the introduction to Part II, all these interactions support effective peer learning. Using guided peer questioning also stimulates metacognition – with thinking about thinking questions.

A research programme investigated the effect of guided peer questioning both in peer tutoring and cooperative learning (King, 1989, 1999, 2007; King & Rosenshine, 1993). The training was tested with fourth-grade students. Results indicated that students who were invited to use the elaborated generic questions (thinking questions) made more inferences and elaborated in a deeper way than those who were invited to use less elaborated questions (comprehension questions) or those who had to generate questions by themselves (King & Rosenshine, 1993).

Comprehension questions facilitate paraphrasing, while thinking questions stimulate elaborated answers relying on the integration of already known and new knowledge. Another study (King, 1994) underlined the additional benefit when students were invited to use not only questions regarding the content of the text (internal questions), but also questions relating to personal experiences (external questions such as "How could ... be used to ...?" or "How this is related to what we have previously learnt"?). Students using both types of questions made more elaborated inferences and remembered better.

King (2007) has investigated the additional value of elements and proposes a whole procedure in order to promote the level of discourse while students are working on texts. Here are the suggestions from her training for asking questions with the ASK TO THINK procedure:

Review questions refer to knowledge review and involve:

- activating prior knowledge,
- paraphrasing studied knowledge (definition, concepts, formula, principles),
- summarising basic knowledge, and
- comprehension questions.

Probing questions underline the need to understand and involve probing the partner to

- expand,
- elaborate, and
- clarify.

Thinking questions require critical thinking and invite students to go beyond the text content for deeper analysis, by means of

- explanation,
- inferences,
- interpretation,
- connexion between elements,
- application, and
- comparison.

Hinting questions propose to give a hint for the partner to construct an answer without disclosing the answer:

- clues
- reminders
- partly framing the answers.

Metacognitive questions suggest thinking-about-thinking:

- self-monitoring thinking
- self-evaluation of comprehension
- strategies for remembering.

The training regarding communication skills (attentive listening, being able to provide the partner with time to think without intervening, giving adequate feedback and encouragement) involves the following:

- A training for explaining proposals with the TEL WHY procedure; see Section 3.5.4 below.
- Reciprocal roles: one partner endorse the questioner role defined by the ASK TO THINK role, while the other plays the explainer role defined by the TEL WHY procedure.

When teachers use this procedure regularly, it pushes students to give particular attention to the lesson because they anticipate they will have to manage questions on it. These questions contrast with low-level factual questions. According to King (2002), "because the questions posed are high-level ones, they promote high-level thinking and learning – going beyond the material presented to the construction of new knowledge" (p.36).

3.5.4. Explaining

In addition, students may be trained how to explain. Help-seeking is important in social interaction (Järvelä, 2011). Introducing additional training to develop cooperative skills related to elaborated help (with a focus on strategies and explanations on how to solve problems) proved positive for learning in mathematics (Fuchs et al., 1997) as well as for reading comprehension (Fuchs, Fuchs, Kazdan & Allen, 1999). The *Tell Why* programme gives tips for prompting high-level explanation (King, 1994, 2007):

> **T**ell what you know to your partner
> **E**xplain the why and how of something (don't just describe it)
> **L**ink – connect what you are explaining to something your partner already knows so they'll be sure to understand
> **W**hy – tell why
> **H**ow – tell how
> **Y**our own words.

When students are trained how to explain, they use external questions related to their own experiences which enhance deep comprehension (King, 1994). ASK TO THINK – TEL WHY©® (King, 2007) combines training for communication skills, questioning and explaining along with different roles. Researchers have investigated the additional values of these elements and conclude that when the whole programme is introduced to structure peer interaction on texts, it leads to high-level positive interactions, stimulates deep comprehension with a high level of connexion and inferences, and allows students to construct coherence in knowledge in a way that makes sense for them. This programme could also be internalised by students who could use it when they individually read texts.

In sum, all these results emphasise that training in cooperative skills (interpersonal and collaborative skills, questioning, or elaborated help) is positive for interactions and learning. These results have been found from primary school to higher education. It underlines that introducing specific training on targeted skills directly involved in the academic task is particularly beneficial for student learning. For example, adding training on conceptual mathematical explanations in addition to training for elaborated help enhances student mathematical learning (Fuchs et al., 1997).

Chapter 5 will present a very short preparation for cooperation related to targeted cooperative skills. One study was conducted in middle school (Golub & Buchs, 2014) for students working on argumentative texts. The other study was at a university, for psychology students learning statistics (Buchs et al., 2016).

3.6. Group processing

In order to improve the quality of peer learning it is important that students receive feedback and reflect on it and on the way to improve.

3.6.1. Getting feedback

Peer learning introduces two objectives, one regarding academic learning and the other regarding social objectives. Informing students what is expected during peer learning helps them to realise what aspects will be taken into account. Then it is important that learners reflect on what they did and how they did it (Johnson, Johnson, Holubec, 1998). To help them, it is important that they get some information regarding the attainment of goals. This information can be introduced though self-evaluation, peer feedback and teacher's feedback.

Self-evaluation involves introspection and can help students to realise their attainments regarding the two objectives. Teachers can create a sheet for helping students, with questions related to targeted objectives and skills. This evaluation can be done in oral or written form, depending on the age of the children (Tables 3.7 and 3.8). For example, a teacher for six-year-olds read each sentence to their students and asked them to circle the pictograms for their answer (activity proposed by teacher Sylvie Simonin).

Two types of peer feedback can be introduced in peer learning. On the one hand, one of the members can play the role of observer during teamwork. This member may use a grid provided by the teacher and record the frequency and/or the way partners display skills and

Table 3.7 An example of self-evaluation for primary school students

How do you feel in this activity?	🙂	😐	☹️
Could I participate and give my opinion?	🙂	😐	☹️
Was my opinion taken into account?	🙂	😐	☹️
Did I feel well prepared to undertake subsequent individual work?	🙂	😐	☹️

Table 3.8 An example of self-evaluation for university students

	not true for me			true for me	
I have prepared my work before the session	1	2	3	4	5
I shared my ideas with others	1	2	3	4	5
I was involved in team discussion	1	2	3	4	5
I pay attention that everybody participates	1	2	3	4	5
I listened to my partners	1	2	3	4	5
I have learned thanks to my partners	1	2	3	4	5

Table 3.9 Example of peer evaluation

1: not often 2: sometimes 3: often	Me	Member A	Member B
Encourage others to participate			
Participate in team discussion			
Answer questions with explanations			

interactive patterns. Before asking one student to observe the team, it is worth remembering that this student won't participate in the activity. Students could rotate this observer role during the activities. Proposing a very active student to observe the teamwork can be a way to invite others to be more active. On the other hand, each student can evaluate the targeted skills and behaviour that they and the partners displayed during the activities afterwards (Table 3.9).

The teacher can give some feedback based on the notes she/he takes during teamwork. Useful feedback concerns the different principles involved in teamwork, in order to give information about whether students succeed in interacting according to the structure, scripts, roles and whether they master the task content. Feedback has to be specific, immediate and positive. As students will not spontaneously use this kind of feedback it is important to guide students.

Teachers can help students to give constructive feedback (Bennett et al., 1991) when they

- ask precisely ("What have you done for this?");
- model with specific sentences (the teacher can give constructive feedback when she/he observes something and what she/he observes "I observe that in response

to a question from a partner, David started by explaining the instructions and the strategies he would use" or "It was helpful when Michael asked why he wanted to start this way");
- give some constructive criticism ("In this team, I observed several students speaking at the same time; what can we do about this next time?"); and
- train students.

It seems important that students receive personal feedback regarding the way they function in their team (Archer-Kath, Johnson & Johnson, 1994). These results point out that general feedback regarding the team as a whole is not very informative. In the Archer-Kath et al. (1994) study, eighth graders worked on learning German during a couple of weeks in cooperative groups, after being trained for praising, supporting, asking for information, giving information, asking for help and giving help. In each team, one student recorded the frequency of the targeted cooperative skills. They did it in two different ways. Either they recorded cooperative skills which occurred inside the group as a whole, or cooperative skills used by each member.

Based on this information, the teacher gave feedback for groups or individuals in the following session. The students reflected for five minutes to discuss how well the group was functioning and how they could improve. Results indicate that students who received individual feedback subsequently were more engaged in the targeted skills and spent more time on task. They performed better at homework and tended to score higher than those who received team feedback. Moreover, students who received individual feedback perceived more positive interdependence and more accepted the low-status members. They also demonstrated more intrinsic motivation.

3.7. Making students reflect on group processing

In order to improve peer learning, it is important to introduce debriefing after activities (Blatchford et al., 2006; Blatchford et al., 2003; Kutnick et al., 2008) – otherwise known as "group processing" (Gillies, 2007; Johnson, Johnson & Holubec, 1998; Johnson et al., 2002). "Group processing exists when group members discuss how well they are achieving their goals and maintaining effective working relationships. Groups need to describe what member actions are helpful and unhelpful and make decisions about what behaviors to continue or change" (Johnson, Johnson & Holubec 1998, p. 1:21). This critical reflection opens the discussion around what learners did positively and what they would like to improve during future activities (Gillies, 2007). This reflection step is often set aside because of lack of time. However, its realisation helps in discussing problematic issues which may appear during cooperation and it supports the quality of relations thanks to meta-cognitive awareness.

Three steps can be followed in order to organise the reflection in a progressive way (Clarke et al., 1990; Howden & Kopiec, 1999): introspection, individual reflection on team functioning and team reflection on team functioning.

Introspection invites each learner to position him/herself regarding her/his own functioning (what the student did, what the student learned):

- I asked questions to help my partner to explain.
- I checked whether all my teammates understood reasons.

- I played my role.
- I interrupted the other.

Individual reflection allows each member to express themselves on team processing (what the team did, how the team processed the task):

- In my team, everybody could express her/his ideas.
- In my team, we made sure that all members contribute.
- In my team, each member played her/his role.
- My partners invited me to participate.

Team reflection implicates a consensus inside the team regarding team functioning:

- Our team made sure that everyone agreed on the strategies.
- In our team it was easy to contribute.
- Three things our team did that were useful.

The way students answer the questions can be adapted to the teacher's habits. They can use: pictograms, yes/no answers, scales with numbers representing quantity or frequency, scales with discrete categories (rarely – sometimes – often), representation of traffic lights (red – orange – green), and so on.

Howden and Kopiec (1999) stress the importance of an organised critical reflection after cooperative tasks. Teachers may anticipate it and invite learners to participate in it. The reflection process can be done in many ways, such as spontaneous feedback, open discussion emerging from a series of questions, critical evaluation and reflection upon a specific dimension of the group task (a cooperative skill or role, level of participation, etc.). In any case, reflection should allow learners to verbalise their experience in order to increase their control over interactions and learning.

Howden and Kopiec (2000) propose different examples to introduce reflection. Each team member has 30 seconds to say something regarding different issues:

- What could we do to develop a positive team spirit?
- What should we do when teammates refuse to work?
- How do you explain to your teammates the importance of making effort and give them encouragement?
- What positive attitudes facilitate the realisation of teamwork?
- What should we do when a member disturbs teamwork?
- Each teammate indicates, among the behaviours adopted during the activity, those which have allowed the team to operate more efficiently and describes behaviour of the person to the left or to right which was helpful.
- Each student completes a checklist on participation in the team. The team members then pool together different lists and discuss the positive aspects of collaboration and what could be improved.
- I have carried out the prior reading.
- I let everyone state his opinion.
- I invited each member to speak during the discussion on the report.

Each student positively emphasises how teammates used certain cooperative skills and then gives written comments to others:

- I particularly liked the fact that ...
- I liked it when you ...
- The team discusses how to be effective and proposes a summary in a report for the class.

The students need a metacognitive space to process learning strategies. What was learned and what there is yet to learn becomes clearer when putting it into words. This reflection allows the teacher to become aware of learners' difficulties and their evolution, so teachers can adapt and regulate activities to the class's needs (Abrami et al., 1995).

Two studies illustrate the importance of group processing. The first study (Yager, Johnson, Johnson & Snider, 1986) with grade 5 learners showed that a regular five-minute reflection on group processing after group work improved the quality of learning. These authors compared three working conditions during 25 sessions: (1) learners working individually, (2) learners working in cooperative learning conditions without reflection and (3) learners working in cooperative learning conditions with five minutes of reflection on group processing (discussion on actions that were helpful or not, decisions on actions to modify or continue). Cognitive learning outcomes were better in the two cooperative conditions compared to individual work. In addition, cooperative learning with reflection improved daily success and long-term retention compared to cooperative learning without reflection.

Bertucci, Johnson, Johnson and Conte (2012) had students with no prior experience with cooperative learning from third to fifth grade work together during five sessions. They worked in cooperative groups either without or with group processing. When group processing was introduced, students received a list of questions to answer after completing each achievement test, with the aim of making them reflect on and discuss how well they worked together during teamwork. The questions included the following:

- "How did you help other members learn the material?"
- "How did other group members help you learn the material?"
- "List some behaviour you would like to increase in your group during the next cooperative lesson".

Students without group processing got some distracting task to do in order to prevent them from reflecting on the interactions among group members. Results indicated that students who benefitted from group processing performed better on achievement tests for the two last sessions than those who were prevented from engaging in group processing.

If teachers create conditions for reflecting on the way students work, it is important that students take an active role during group processing. Optimal conditions are when teachers give feedback and invite students to reflect on it. Another study (Johnson, Johnson, Stanne & Garibaldi, 1990) examined more specifically the importance of the active student role in the reflection process at university. College seniors engaged in problem solving. The study compared four working conditions for the first stage: students working (1) individually; (2) cooperatively without reflection; (3) cooperatively with work on three targeted cooperative skills (summarising member's actions and ideas, encouraging the participation of all and checking the agreement between group members); and (4) reflecting on group processing.

Group processing was introduced in two different forms: (1) by the teacher in a whole-class context, and (2) by the teacher but discussed with students in small groups. Results indicated that the quality of learning in the second stage was better in the three cooperative conditions compared to individual work. Regarding the cooperative learning environment, students who had taken an active part in group processing reflection had the best performance on the second academic tasks. This study emphasised that reflection on group processing, when conducted by the teacher, is not necessarily sufficient; active learners' participation is important.

After group processing inside the team, teachers may propose a collective discussion in the class based on observation and reflection (Johnson et al., 2002). Teachers have to open a discussion space for students to consider information on the way they work together based on self-evaluation and peer evaluation. They should have their students express their emotions, state what they have learned, and make explicit their strategies and their remaining difficulties. Teachers can anticipate this step with some questions, and then ask students to explain their answers. Group processing aims at helping students propose some objectives for improving subsequent team work.

For example, after a dyadic Sudoku puzzle for five-year-old students, the collective discussion introduced by the teacher noted that it was not easy to decide who starts in the dyad. Some students said they were disappointed that their partner had started without asking anything. The collective discussion gave the opportunity to express some strategies already used in other tasks for deciding who would start next time. After this discussion, the teacher and students decided a criterion for determining who would start for the next turn (pick one member randomly) and proposed to alternate for the following turn (activity proposed by teacher Christelle Darbre).

In conclusion, Chapter 3 stresses that the preparation for cooperation is part of the whole process and useful to enhance the benefits of cooperative learning. It seems important to emphasise that the time invested in this can improve not only the quality of student interactions and cooperation, but also the quality of cognitive learning. These benefits are observed both in primary and secondary school and higher education. Of course, cooperative learning must be supported by rigorous structuring of the group task, in order to strengthen the positive interdependence and individual responsibility among members in small teams. In this context, when students are well prepared to cooperate they can do better when they cooperate to learn. Chapter 4 will present principles for structuring the academic task.

Chapter 4

Organising peer interactions in academic tasks

Important conditions for effective peer learning include the need to structure the learning situation (Gillies, 2007; Gillies, Ashman & Terwel, 2008; Webb, 2009). As peer learning involves students working together, student interactions are the core of peer learning. Nevertheless it is not sufficient just to ask students to work together in order to actively and effectively engage each student in the learning activity. This chapter presents useful principles for teachers to organise interactions in academic tasks. We more particularly discuss how teachers may group the learners in small teams and structure interdependence as well as individual accountability/personal responsibility. Moreover, teachers can introduce some scripts and scaffolds for peer interactions. We will present each principle while giving practical guidelines and pointing to research results evidencing the effectiveness of these principles. We will conclude with the matter of assessment and evaluation of and in peer learning.

4.1. Grouping learners

In peer learning, students work together in groups small enough to enable and indeed require individualised face-to-face interactions. Teachers have to decide on the number of learners in a team as well as on the way to compose the teams.

4.1.1. Group size

It is sometimes suggested that larger teams yield richer interactions. But in large teams there can be "passengers" who play little part in the interactions. Consequently, a maximum of six learners is recommended and caution is proposed as the number increases beyond this (Johnson & Johnson, 2006). Larger teams present problems with the identification of learners' difficulties and require greater cooperative skills in the participants; therefore, most practitioners recommend between two and six learners in a team, and invite teachers to adapt the number of students in relation to the specific activity and learners' previous experiences with working in teams. We recommend starting with two to four learners, taking into account that a larger number of students may reduce the perception of positive interdependence and individual responsibility.

When comparing dyads with groups of four, Fuchs, Fuchs, Kazdan, Karns, Calhoon, Hamlett and Hewlitt (2000) underlined that dyads elicited more cooperation and better quality of verbalisations, whereas the small groups favoured confrontation of points of view (see the discussion of socio-cognitive conflict in the introduction to Part II). Results regarding the quality of learning after peer learning also favoured small groups (Fuchs, Fuchs, Kazdan, et al., 2000; Lou et al., 1996). One study indicated that groups of four required more practice to be effective (Bertucci, Conte, Johnson & Johnson, 2010). More specifically, the results indicated that dyads outperformed individuals after two weeks of work, while the benefits for groups of four only appeared after six weeks of work. This suggests that groups imply an initial demand on organisation that can interfere with learning.

4.1.2. Group formation

For peer tutoring, academic and social competence are the main criteria for tutor–tutee grouping. In contrast, for cooperative learning, the possibilities are numerous. Teachers have to decide between three approaches to composing the teams (Abrami et al., 1995; Clarke et al., 1990; Gaudet et al., 1998). The teacher forms the group, the students form the group, or teams are formed at random. We will consider these different grouping approaches along with some research results.

4.1.2.1. Teams formed by learners

Inviting students to select their teammates involves them in decision-making. Therefore, student-selected grouping fulfils their desire for autonomy, control and responsibility (Mitchell, Reilly, Bramwell, Solnosky & Lilly, 2004). This procedure requires little anticipation and organisation from the teacher, is generally welcomed by students and facilitates students' motivation. Students also report they are more satisfied when they can choose with whom they work (Mahenthiran & Rouse, 2000). Thus, some cooperative learning researchers underline the positive effect of letting students choose their group mates (Abrami et al., 1995; S. Kagan & Kagan, 1999; Y. Sharan & Sharan, 1999).

Research results regarding the academic outcomes of student-selected grouping are mainly positive (Mahenthiran & Rouse, 2000). Analysis of 13 studies suggested that groups of friends interact in a more productive way than groups of non-friends, especially in difficult tasks (Zajac & Hartup, 1997). In this respect, friends working together demonstrate a more positive involvement with greater cooperation and more positive relations with strong reciprocity and equity and less domination. They are more focused on the task and try their best to solve their conflicts constructively by negotiating.

However, student-selected grouping may introduce specific problem dynamics into the class. First it promotes students choosing their friends (Mitchell et al., 2004). Interviews with secondary school students revealed that after having to choose their group mates, they decreased their preference for this way of composing cooperative learning teams. Students expressed their concerns regarding the likelihood of socialising rather than working and regarding the potential conflict between being a good friend and being a good team member. Our observations underline that when students are not satisfied with the group work, working with friends can indeed create problems. It can also reduce the quality of the discussion, because students try to avoid socio-cognitive conflict and prefer to comply in order to preserve the relation with their friends (Zajac & Hartup, 1997).

Second, student-selected grouping may create tension between students and a negative class climate, because it makes isolated or unpopular students visible, as well as students with whom classmates are reluctant to work (most of the time because of learning and/or behavioural difficulties). This can create negative feelings and reactions (Abrami et al., 1995; E. Cohen, 1994).

Third, student-selected grouping can give prominence to some status hierarchies (E. Cohen, 1994) based on status characteristics often not relevant for learning, for example, criteria related to social success (Mitchell et al., 2004). Fourth, as students tend to choose partners resembling themselves (Kutnick & Kington, 2005; Slavin, 1995), it creates homogenous groups. Homogeneous grouping tends not to be effective for low-achievers (Mitchell et al., 2004). All of these reasons explain teachers' reluctance to engage with student-selected grouping.

4.1.2.2. Teams formed by teachers

Teachers who decide to form teams may use different criteria from student selection. Usually, teachers base group composition on the objectives of the learning activity and on their knowledge of the students. The fact that the grouping can be adapted to the teacher's objective is an important advantage.

Many leading figures in cooperative learning invite teachers to form heterogeneous teams (see for example, Abrami et al., 1995; Howden & Kopiec, 1999; Slavin, 1995). Some propose taking several criteria into account to optimise heterogeneity regarding students' academic competencies, gender and cultural background. Numerous advantages are underlined in the literature: heterogeneity is supposed to favour openness to others, acceptance of differences, opportunities to practice cooperative skills, enrichment with divergence of points of view, and so forth.

Further, heterogeneous teams are expected to favour the autonomy of the team because students can rely on each other strengths. When the task requires different competences and teachers know and acknowledge the strengths of their students, it can be very useful to combine these strengths in teams. In general, students appreciate heterogeneous groups more than homogenous groups (Elbaum, Schumm & Vaughn, 1997). Moreover, using homogeneous grouping is a way to enable teachers to adapt and regulate learning according to students' needs. Nevertheless, students can sometimes show resistance to the teacher's selection, especially at the beginning of a project.

Two guidelines are useful for a better understanding of the effects of team composition on learning. First, it is important to consider the level of students' academic competence, which we discuss below. Second, we take into account the type of interactions that the team composition elicits (Fuchs, Fuchs, Hamlett & Karns, 1998; Webb, 1985; Webb & Palincsar, 1996). In the introduction to Part II, we underlined the central role of explanations in learning and learning processes: students who provide more explanations are students who learn more, and receiving explanations is also positively linked with learning outcomes. In addition, confrontations focused on the task stimulate learning. Consequently, the interaction pattern that the team composition is likely to stimulate may help the teacher to decide on the actual allocation of membership.

As far as average-achievers are concerned, homogeneous teams or narrow-heterogeneity composition seems beneficial (Baer, 2003; Lou et al., 1996; Saleh, Lazonder & de Jong, 2007; Webb, 1985). Average-achievers working together have the opportunity of bringing in mutual explanations. Narrow-heterogeneity groupings permit average-achievers to bring in explanations to the interaction (in the low- and average-achievers grouping) or to receive explanations (in the average- and high-achievers grouping). In other words, they are more active and benefit more in narrow-heterogeneity grouping or in homogeneous teams than in large-heterogeneity grouping (low-, average- and high-achievers).

For low-achievers, many results underline they benefit more from heterogeneous teams (Hooper & Hannafin, 1991; Lou et al., 1996; Saleh, Lazonder & De Jong, 2005). This is both for large-heterogeneity grouping (low-, average- and high-achievers) or narrow-heterogeneity teams (low- and average-achievers) (Webb, 1985). Working with more advanced partners allows them to receive more explanations in heterogeneous than in homogenous teams (Webb, 1985), and stimulates their level of interaction (Hooper & Hannafin, 1991). Nevertheless, the superiority of heterogeneous teams for low-achievers is not found in all studies. For complex tasks, their contribution is likely to be basic and ignored when working with high-achieving partners (Fuchs et al., 1998).

Regarding high-achievers, the research results are not consistent either for the effect on learning or social interactions (Baer, 2003; Fuchs et al., 1998; Hooper & Hannafin, 1991; Lou et al., 1996; Saleh et al., 2005; Webb, 1985). A possible way to reconcile the differences in the research results may be to consider the level of task complexity (Hooper & Hannafin, 1988). High-achievers benefit from homogeneous teams when working on complex tasks (Fuchs et al., 1998), since they have more opportunities for collaboration and constructive confrontations with peers of the same level. However, for more simple tasks, heterogeneous groupings are more appropriate, providing opportunities for high-achievers to provide explanations for others. The use of heterogeneous groups should be accompanied by the implementation of strategies to help students of high and low levels to work together constructively, which can be done by explicit training on appropriate cooperative skills, as proposed in Chapter 3.

Studies on mathematical tasks suggest that considering group composition in terms of gender is also relevant. Webb (1985) tried out three compositions: (a) two boys and two girls; (b) one boy and three girls; (c) three boys and one girl. Results highlighted that girls are more active and more successful in balanced gender teams. Indeed, facing one boy, girls tended to mainly direct attention toward the boy, who was expected to act as the leader and to provide many explanations. When there was only one girl in the group, she tended to be ignored by the three boys. Research on the composition of groups therefore suggests caution with respect to gender and proposes that as far as possible it is better to create balanced teams in mathematical tasks.

In conclusion, it is important to keep in mind that research uses different methods in different subject areas, and with learners of different ages. As a result, it is quite hard to formulate a very clear vision for group composition. In addition, in heterogeneous groups different criteria for group composition apart from academic competence may be relevant to determine the degree of heterogeneity (e.g., students' cognitive style, self-efficacy, desire for and attitude towards working with others). The research synthesis of Lou et al. (1996) suggests that working in small groups is more effective when *several* criteria are taken into consideration when organising the composition of teams.

4.1.2.3. Random grouping

Taking into account that there is no one ideal grouping approach, we would like to point to some positive outcomes for random grouping. First, this procedure is welcomed by students. Second, it permits variation of the composition of the teams and gives opportunities to work with different partners each time. Third, random grouping can meet different objectives, such as when proposing quick informal groups, introducing activities for fostering a positive class climate, or introducing the content of the following lesson or learning activity. We will give some examples for each of these objectives below.

- Examples for quick informal groups:
  - Teachers can invite students to turn to their neighbour to form groups.
  - Teachers can cut pictures into different parts and distribute the pieces of these different images. All students having the pieces of the same picture form a group.
  - If teachers want to form groups of four, they can distribute cards from a card game and asks students to form groups depending on the card they received. Further, they can use the suits (clubs, diamonds, spades and hearts) to introduce different roles in the groups.
- Random groupings can be combined with teambuilding activities: teachers can use the formation of teams to introduce activities for creating a positive climate at the same time. Here are some practical suggestions:
  - Teachers can ask a question and ask their students to form a line related to their response, then their position in the line is used to form the group. The question may concern some aspect teachers would like their students to discuss. For example, a primary school teacher can ask students to form a line regarding their month and day of birth, while a secondary school teacher can ask students to form a line depending on their distance from home to school, and a teacher educator can ask students to form a line regarding their previous experience in teaching.

    The teacher can decide to compose teams of students next to each other, for example for 16 students ([S1, S2, S3, S4]; … [S13, S14, S15, S16]), or to mix them by separating in the middle with symmetry ([S1, S2, S15, S16]; … [S3, S4, S13, S14]), or by separating in the middle and slipping ([S1, S2, S9, S10]; … [S7, S8, S15, S16]), or by separating in four lines and slipping ([S1, S5, S9, S13]; … [S4, S8, S12, S16]). Teachers can propose a question or a theme to discuss quickly, while students walk through the class and discuss two by two during one minute. Afterwards, students move to the next partner until the teacher proposes stopping and forming dyads with their partner at that moment (or to group the two nearest dyads).
- Random groupings can be combined with the introduction of the lesson. Some of the abovementioned random group composition techniques already introduce some academic content to prepare the students to work on the lesson content while forming teams. Any variant can be imagined by teachers to introduce the lesson. Teachers might prepare materials to distribute, so students have to share their knowledge or answer in order to form teams.
  - For example, when introducing a geography lesson, the teacher distributes some cards with the names of towns, the corresponding countries and the flags (Table 4.1). Students move through the class, sharing their knowledge to form triads while matching the cards.
  - For introducing a math lesson or revision, the teacher can distribute cards with different problems to solve individually, and then students move around the class to share the answer and form teams with similar responses (Table 4.2).

Table 4.1 An example of random grouping in geography

Oslo	Norway	
Rome	Italy	
Athens	Greece	
Bangkok	Thailand	

Table 4.2 An example of random grouping in mathematics

4 X 3 =	3 X 4 =	4 + 4 + 4 =	3 + 3 + 3 + 3 =
6 X 1 =	2 X 3 =	3 + 3 =	2 + 2 + 2 =

- When introducing literature, teachers distribute cards with different characters or events of a series of stories, and ask students to move around and form teams regarding the same story.
- Teachers can also arrange random choice. For example, when students are sitting next to their friends and teachers want to mix them, they can distribute Post-it notes of the same colour to people seated near to each other and ask them to move to form new teams of a different colour. Students are required to move to new partners, but they still have some freedom to choose and/or avoid other partners, insofar as they respect the different colours.

Among the advantages of random group combinations is the fact that no one feels excluded and all students will easily find partners. In addition, this process is generally well accepted by the students, as they are focused on sharing and smoothly become a group member. Practiced several times, it allows students to get to know and work with many different partners. As for limitations, however, this grouping method does not control the composition of teams, so teams do not necessarily have all the resources to help each other to learn and accomplish the task. This approach is thus not suitable for complex tasks or for long-term collaborative activities. This type of grouping is, however, ideal for short activities, such as the revision of previously studied learning content or brainstorming sessions. Further, the teacher can take advantage of observing the dynamics at work in the classroom.

As it is very difficult to accommodate all the multiple characteristics of students to form "ideal" teams for all purposes, we suggest varying the approaches used to build the teams. Teachers need to carefully organise peer interactions in academic tasks to promote constructive interactions, whether via student-chosen, teacher-chosen or random groupings. Next, we will develop principles helpful to organise peer interactions.

4.2. Positive interdependence

The way interdependence in peer learning is structured determines how students interact together, which in turn affects the results from this interaction (Deutsch, 1949; Johnson & Johnson, 1989). Social interdependence reflects the relationships between team members and the way they achieve their goals. These are related in a situation in which students share a common goal, and the outcomes of each individual student are affected by the actions of others (reciprocal relations). In this respect, social interdependence differs from "dependence" of one student to another (i.e., a unidirectional relation) or from "independence" (i.e., individual work without any relation between students' goal achievement).

Social interdependence can be negative in the case of competition – with a negative relationship with students' goal achievements. Here the more one team member achieves their academic goal, the less the others can achieve theirs (i.e., only one student can be the best one). For cooperative learning, however, social interdependence has to be positive: students have to perceive a positive relationship in their goal achievement. Positive interdependence exists "when a mutual joint goal is established so that individuals perceive they can attain their goals if and only if their groupmates attain their goals. Members know that they cannot succeed unless all other members of their group succeed" (Johnson, Johnson & Holubec, 1998, pp. 2:11–2:12). In other words, the success of a student increases the likelihood of success of other students (Abrami et al., 1995; Rouiller & Howden, 2010) – the gain for one is at the same time a gain for the others (M. Kagan & S. Kagan, 2000).

Positive interdependence is at the heart of cooperation as it allows learners to identify their common goal, so they perceive that they can achieve their goal only when the other team members also reach it. It is the most basic principle (M. Kagan & Kagan, 2000) and the one constant principle serving as an anchor for the design of cooperative learning (Y. Sharan, 2010b). Different slogans may illustrate positive interdependence during peer learning, such as "Sink or swim together" or Dumas's proposition "All for one and one for all!" (Johnson et al., 2002), or "WE as well as me" (Bennett et al., 1991).

Positive goal interdependence represents both the structure of the cooperation (ensuring that students actually work together) and the spirit of the classroom (stimulating students to take care of both their own learning and the learning of their classmates) (Abrami et al., 1995). It specifies the goal structure and determines students' motivation and actions (Bennett et al., 1991; Johnson & Johnson, 1989; Johnson, Johnson & Holubec, 1998; Johnson et al., 2002; M. Kagan & Kagan, 2000).

When students perceive positive interdependence,

- they perceive members' complementarity,
- they perceive that efforts from each member are required to achieve success,
- they realise that they should try to reach a joint outcome,
- they strive for all members' success,
- they are committed to joint work in order to achieve a common goal,
- they feel responsible for all members' learning,
- they help every member to truly understand the learning content tackled in the team work,
- they search for benefits for themselves and for other team members,
- they are motivated to help each other and to support partners,
- they are willing to tutor teammates,
- they are concerned with others and
- they take care of preserving positive relationships in the team.

Different types of interdependence are documented (Abrami et al., 1995; Bennett et al., 1991; Howden & Kopiec, 2000; Johnson, Johnson & Holubec, 1998; Johnson et al., 2002). Teachers can mainly focus on outcomes that motivate students to work together (i.e., the reason why students cooperate – goals or rewards) or they can focus on the means that specify the way students work together (i.e., how students cooperate – roles, resources, or tasks). Nevertheless, it is crucial to clearly structure goal interdependence. As recommended by Johnson and colleagues (Johnson, Johnson & Holubec, 1998; Johnson et al., 2002), teachers first have to structure and ensure positive goal interdependence and then they may supplement this with other types of positive interdependence. Below, we elaborate on different ways to incorporate positive interdependence between students working together.

4.2.1. Positive goal interdependence

In order to structure positive goal interdependence, teachers should start by establishing a team goal and clearly specifying the task the team has to accomplish (Johnson et al., 2002). The group task should require an assignment that no single student can achieve and to which every student is expected to contribute (E. Cohen, 1994). As presented below, different ways to structure positive goal interdependence can be used.

4.2.1.1. One product for the group

Many teachers propose that their students elaborate and work on one product for the complete group. In order to highlight goal interdependence between students, it is important to make clear that you as a teacher are not merely interested in the quality of the product, but also in the quality of the learning process leading to that result or product. That is, all members have to contribute to, agree with, and are expected to be able to explain what was done, and how and why the team went through the work in this way. Some practical examples follow:

After reading a story, a primary school teacher can ask teams to discuss in order to reach an agreement regarding the way the story can be illustrated or to explore how the story might end. The instructions underline that all students need to be included and that every student should be able to tell the story of the team.

A secondary school teacher can ask teams to prepare a presentation on a topic for the whole class or to organise a debate on a self-selected issue, requiring that all team members participate actively.

A higher education teacher can ask for a team report presenting an analysis of a scientific book or an experimental report.

The team product can be one single sheet of answer for the whole team, after verifying that every member agrees and understands the answer. For example, primary school students can list some advantages and disadvantages to having a dog as a pet in towns, secondary school students can list pro and con arguments regarding nuclear energy, university students can generate possible hypotheses regarding an experiment, and pre-service teachers can indicate advantages and disadvantages of grades as a means for evaluation.

4.2.1.2. Responsibility toward partners' learning

Another way to structure positive goal interdependence is to introduce mutual learning responsibilities. Indeed, in cooperative learning, each student is responsible for understanding and learning the material they are studying, but also for making sure that all partners have understood and learnt as well.

These responsibilities are conveyed in the team goals specifying the criteria of success regarding individual learning of all team members.

Before handing in work for assessment, each member has to supervise the work of teammates and help and explain if necessary: "The goal of your team is to check the worksheets of other students before handing them in to the teacher" or "Your goal is to offer help and explain to other members if necessary, with the intention of everybody mastering the content".

The team has to ensure that all members understand what is done during the cooperation: "Your goal is to make sure that all of you can demonstrate that you have understood and can explain the different steps your team undertook" or "The team succeeds when all members are able to explain what was done during the team work and to demonstrate that they have participated".

After the cooperation, each member of the team has to score above a previously specified criterion on an individual learning test: "The goal of your team is to ensure that everyone will score over 80 per cent correct on the individual learning questionnaire" or "The goal of your team is to ensure that all members will be able to give and explain at least five reasons why voting is important".

Each member of the team should improve on their previous performance: "The goal of your team is to ensure that everyone tries their best to perform better than the last performance on a test".

4.2.2. Reward interdependence

Reward interdependence defines the relationship between team members regarding the consequences of the goal achievement. With positive reward interdependence, each team member receives the same reward for successfully completing the joint goal (Johnson & Johnson, 1989). Either all members are rewarded or none is (Bennett et al., 1991). The reward should encourage students to understand, master and learn the content or procedure and not merely to perform unthinkingly. Students should feel responsible for their own learning but also for the learning of their teammates. Just as for goal interdependence, rewards can be related either to one team product or to the team members' responsibility towards their partners' learning. Teachers have many choices as to the specific reward (Bennett et al., 1991) and can propose that students choose from a list (e.g., have the opportunity to select the next discussion topic in relation to the lesson, what to do during extra time, decide where to place posters summarising the discussion, and so forth).

4.2.2.1. One reward for the team

The fact that students receive one reward for their team product is a way to introduce positive reward interdependence. For example, they all receive the same evaluation for the joint product. It is relatively common that teachers evaluate one group product for the team (e.g., a team presentation, report, poster, or drawing). As the quality of the product depends on what the members of the team brought in, the contribution of team members affects the rewards all members receive as well.

4.2.2.2. Responsibility toward partners' learning

We have already underlined that the team goal can be framed in terms of the learning of each individual member in the team. Similarly, positive reward interdependence can be related to the individual learning of each member. In this case, the team work is perceived as an opportunity for all members to interact in order to ensure that all members will understand, master and learn the studied content. What each student learns during teamwork is central and is individually assessed afterwards. There are many alternatives to positive reward interdependence that are based on individual assessment:

The individual scores of all team members are grouped (mean score or sum score) and all members receive rewards on this basis.

Each member contributes to the score of their team depending on their individual performance (see for example Teams-Games-Tournament as a way to organise fair tournaments for ensuring the likelihood of equal participation for each member, Slavin, 1995).

The teacher can say that she will pick one learning test in each team and the evaluation of this test will provide the score for all team members.

Taking the above examples into account, we recommend being very careful with this procedure. In the case of different competences or abilities in the team, some students can feel upset because they think that their score potential will be lowered by the score of the other team members. We have to keep in mind that most of the students are socialised in a competitive society and students are looking for social recognition via academic evaluation. For teachers willing to use some strategies combining individual and team rewards, bonus points may be an alternative.

Each student receives their own individual score but is rewarded with bonus points when some conditions are met by all team members. These conditions are defined by the group goal (e.g., all members score above the criteria specified during individual test, or all members improve their previous performance). These group reward contingencies structure positive reward interdependence. The goal can be related to performance ("If all members of your team attain 80% correct, every member can benefit from bonus points") or to progress ("If all members of your team maintain or improve their score compared to the last evaluation, all team members receive one bonus point") (see Student Teams-Achievement Divisions, Slavin, 1995).

4.2.2.3. Cooperative behaviour

Cooperative learning introduces both academic and cooperative objectives. Accordingly, positive reward interdependence could also be related to the cooperative behaviour of students. Teachers can introduce conditional rewards if all members demonstrate some cooperative skills (Lew, Mesch, Johnson & Johnson, 1986a, 1986b). For example, students can receive bonus points if teachers observe that all members express the social skill targeted for the task at least 2 times.

4.3. Positive interdependence related to means

4.3.1. Positive role interdependence

Positive role interdependence refers to specific and complementary responsibilities among team members, and roles that students have to fulfil to complete the joint goal. Peer tutoring, with the complementary roles of tutor and tutee, is an excellent example.

A variety of roles can be used to give students the opportunity to improve their weaknesses, strengthen their skills and to learn new skills (Bennett et al., 1991). Assigning roles can be strategic and it is important to take into account that spontaneous roles are not always positive for the quality of the interaction in the team, since status characteristics (E. Cohen, 1994) may influence who is more active and more influential. Moreover, when students organise themselves spontaneously, they are likely to share responsibilities in such a way that students take the lead regarding their respective strength. This self-selection can improve team productivity and efficiency and can be a good thing for the quality of a team product, for example when students are in charge of the part they feel more comfortable and competent with.

Nevertheless, this organisation does not offer the opportunity for each student to improve their weaker competencies. Therefore, spontaneous organisation does not guarantee optimal learning opportunities. Accordingly, it is the responsibility of the teacher to invite students to practice new skills and to introduce some specific responsibilities to ensure the quality of the interaction and the learning in the team. At the beginning, however, it can be useful to let students select the roles themselves. This will help the students feel comfortable, enabling them to offer some modelling for others. Later on teachers can propose changing roles.

Roles prescribe what students have to do and what other team members can expect from their team members. Positive role interdependence introduces complementary and interconnected roles helping the team to achieve its goal and to work well together (Bennett et al., 1991; Johnson et al., 2002; Johnson, Johnson & Smith, 1998). Different types of roles can be useful to support the quality of the interactions and of learning (Abrami et al., 1995; Howden & Kopiec, 2000). More particularly, functional, social, and cognitive roles are distinguished. We will elaborate more on the different roles in the part regarding individual accountability and mutual responsibility.

4.3.2. Positive task interdependence

Task interdependence (i.e., division of labour) is related to and interconnected with resource and role interdependence. Members may or may not access the whole material, but each one is responsible for contributing to one particular aspect. It is important, however, to underline that at the end all team members are responsible for the quality of the whole product. Primary school students studying an animal can divide the task so one student will summarise information regarding alimentation, the other reproduction, the other the environment, and so on. Secondary school students can divide the study of the periods of life of an artist they have to present to the rest of the class. University students can divide the different steps of an experiment for the writing of a lab report.

4.3.3. Positive resource interdependence

Resource interdependence is related to the means that students have to combine to succeed. It strengthens the perception of complementarity, but as mentioned by Howden and Kopiec (2000), caution is needed in order to avoid introducing competition for resources or any waste of time because students have to wait. This type of interdependence can be related to common resources or complementary resources.

- Common resources:
    With common resources, students have to coordinate with others in order to achieve their goals. For example, in a team of three students a primary school teacher can give only one pen and one single sheet for inventing a story based on some pictures. Secondary school teachers can give teams only one sheet with instructions and problems to solve. A higher education teacher can ask teams to use only one computer and one set of books in order to document their answer to a question.
- Complementary resources:
    Positive resource interdependence also involves complementary resources (Johnson et al., 2002; Johnson, Johnson & Smith, 1998). We identify three different ways to introduce complementary resources. First, given students' specific abilities or skills, resources in a team are complementary in nature. Second, complementary resources can be introduced by means of instructions: each student brings a part of the resources

needed (e.g., each student has to prepare one part of the activity before the onset of a team discussion). Third, teachers can give each team member only part of the material to study or information or resources necessary for the team to accomplish its goal (each student has to explain or teach the other members regarding her/his part and has to learn from other members). In the Jigsaw method presented in Chapter 1 (Aronson, 1978; Aronson & Patnoe, 2011), complementary resources are central.

Regarding the results for resource interdependence, we consider it as promoting cooperation but it may be a pitfall for learning (Buchs, 2015). Theoretically, positive resource interdependence underlines the need to coordinate the different pieces of knowledge in order to get the whole picture. Thus, it elicits cooperation as an appropriate way of interacting and strengthens the relevance of the relationship with the partner (Gruber, 2000). It is supposed to force students to cooperate (Aronson & Patnoe, 2011; B. Cohen & Cohen, 1991). To sum up some research results, positive resource interdependence does indeed stimulate students' cooperation and engagement in the task (Buchs, Butera & Mugny, 2004; Lambiotte, Dansereau, O'Donnell et al., 1987), as further illustrated in Chapter 5. Other results point to the benefits of positive goal and resource interdependence for students' self-esteem, school- and group-mates' liking (Aronson & Patnoe, 2011; Blaney, Stephan, Rosenfield, Aronson & Sikes, 1977) and for the experience of competence, autonomy and social relatedness (Hänze & Berger, 2007).

Nevertheless, informational dependence elicited by resource interdependence makes this method challenging for learning, because students are totally dependent on the quality of the informational input from their partners. Consequently, it may be important to verify whether students learn well the part taught to them by their partners. When students have to rely on their partner to access information (as is the case in positive resource interdependence), no matter how much their partner is involved and makes an effort, if they do not succeed in understanding and/or explaining information, the other students cannot learn.

Thus, the quality of the informational input moderates the effect of resource interdependence on learning (Buchs, Butera & Mugny, 2004; Buchs, Pulfrey, Gabarrot & Butera, 2010). When the quality of the informational input is good, students benefit from the high cooperation and engagement elicited by resource interdependence and they display high learning quality. When the quality of the informational input is not guaranteed (e.g., because of the difficulty of the content or the inexperience of students to summarise or explain their part), learning can be hindered for the part not directly studied.

4.4. Other types of interdependence

In line with Johnson et al. (2002), we recommend first to structure positive goal interdependence, and then to structure additional dimensions of positive interdependence in order to reinforce it. Nevertheless, it is important to keep in mind that if multiple sources of interdependence are useful to enhance learning, multiple interdependencies create complexity as well. Students may need time to manage this complexity.

4.5. Individual accountability and mutual responsibility

Positive interdependence stresses members' complementarity, where individual accountability and mutual responsibility consists of making the contributions of all team members possible, necessary and visible. Positive interdependence and mutual responsibility are interrelated: the more students perceive they are positively linked to others, the more they feel responsible for trying their best, the more they understand their responsibilities and the more they feel that they are all related.

Individual accountability refers to the responsibility of each team member for completing his or her part of the learning task. It is an essential principle for avoiding social loafing and encouraging students to actively engage in the learning activity (E. Cohen, 1994; Johnson & Johnson, 1989; Johnson, Johnson & Holubec, 1998; M. Kagan & Kagan, 2000; Mercer, 1996; Y. Sharan, 2010b; Slavin, 1995). Mutual responsibility on the other hand makes each member responsible for contributing to the search and acquisition of knowledge to accomplish the group's learning goal (Y. Sharan, 2010b). Each member shares the responsibility for productivity of other members (mutual responsibility) and each member has to support and assist others (mutual obligation) (Johnson, Johnson & Smith, 1998).

In order to avoid unequal contribution to the task, each team member must be accountable for contributing his or her share of the work and for mastery of the content – and the team must be accountable for achieving its goals (Bennett et al., 1991; M. Kagan & Kagan, 2000). Therefore, the team has to be clear about its goals and be able to measure both the team progress in achieving the goals on the one hand and the individual efforts of each of its members on the other hand (Johnson, Johnson & Holubec, 1998). Each member is responsible for their own learning and is responsible for helping their teammates to learn (Abrami et al., 1995; Bennett et al., 1991).

For structuring this principle, teachers have to make sure that all members have the possibility to contribute, and structure the learning task so that the contributions of all members are required and discernible and that individual learning is visible.

4.5.1 Ways to structure individual accountability/responsibility

Teachers have to think about ways to make each member's contribution easy and necessary:

- In order to feel comfortable to contribute, it is important that students receive time for individual reflection/preparation before the actual teamwork.
- Ensure a positive climate for students to feel secure to contribute.
- Propose small group sizes, since small groups stress individual contribution requirements.
- Introduce ways to identify and make individual contributions public, to urge students to take their part. For example, when they have to solve problems together, students use different coloured pens so teachers can identify the different contributions.
- Observe the contributions of each member during team work.
- Inform the students that a randomly selected student may be asked to explain how team discussion contributed to reinforce accountability.
- Ask students to sign the group product to indicate that they contributed, agree, can explain team decisions and ideas, and can present the team work when asked for.

4.5.2. Individual accountability related to positive reward interdependence

When teachers propose joint goals in terms of responsibility towards all partners' learning, it reinforces individual accountability. In addition, according to Slavin (1995), it provides incentives to students for helping one another to learn. He proposes that teams are rewarded on the basis of the learning of all team members. Teachers use all members' individual scores for computing the score that each teammate receives as mean bonus points (or the sum of individual learning scores). Therefore, students need to make sure that they, as well as all their teammates, have learned.

For Slavin (1995), two strategies are useful to maintain individual responsibility in team work. First, assigning each student the responsibility for one part of the task makes each student accountable for their own performance. Second, teams need to be recognised or rewarded for their success. Individual accountability exists when the performance of each team member is assessed and the results are given back to the team. Giving feedback to individuals *and* the team permits them to compare the results to preset criteria and to identify who needs help, support, and encouragement, or to reassign responsibilities (Johnson, Johnson & Holubec, 1998).

Johnson et al. (2002) introduce both group accountability (feedback is given to all team members regarding group performance) and individual accountability (feedback is given regarding individual performance to individual and team members). Self-evaluation and peer-evaluation can be useful to make students responsible for their outcomes.

4.5.3. Mutual responsibility related to positive mean interdependence

A simple way to introduce mutual responsibility is to propose a structure for the participation. As we will present in the next section, regarding scripts and scaffolds for peer interactions, introducing structure indicating how to interact is useful for encouraging students' participation. In the same way, mutual responsibility can be introduced by task or role interdependence (E. Cohen, 1994).

The fact that each member has a specific role to play reinforces a student's self-worth in the team (Bennett et al., 1991). Roles in cooperative learning are very well known. Most teachers introduce useful roles, such as roles to facilitate behavioural engagement in the task and to work on the learning activity in good conditions. Nevertheless, we would like to underline that other types of roles also ensure social and cognitive engagement (Abrami et al., 1995; Howden & Kopiec, 2000).

We give some classical examples without being exhaustive:

- Functional roles help the team to manage functional aspects: for example, the secretary (responsible for taking notes), the resource person responsible for material (before and after the task), the chair person responsible for the agenda (ensuring that the time available will cover the different necessary steps), the reader, the timekeeper, the person responsible for the volume level of the discussion, and so on.
- Social roles give positive energy to the team and personal and academic support. For example, the person responsible for encouraging, the person responsible for reaching a consensus, the animator, the observator, the motivator, and so on.
- Cognitive roles invite students to deepen the learning process and to be cognitively active and engaged: for example, the person responsible for summarising, the person responsible for deepening ideas, the checker, and so on.

According to the literature, some roles appear to be essential. For instance, E. Cohen (1994) proposes the systematic introduction of a facilitator role, ensuring well-functioning teams (e.g., ensuring that everybody participates, preserving task orientation, avoiding team members getting lost in details, guaranteeing clear decisions within preset deadlines). Nevertheless, this facilitator may not influence the content of the decisions. Further, Johnson et al. (2002) pointed out the crucial role of the "checker for comprehension", who asks others to explain their reasoning and the underlying rationale for the team answer.

Two means of reflecting on selecting roles may be useful. Either teachers can rely on their observations of teams at work, or they can decompose the learning objectives into sub-objectives and related strategies, skills, procedures, behaviours and identify possible obstacles/introduce roles as an answer to these acknowledged challenges.

It is not useful here to give an exhaustive list of possible roles, because teachers can create all types of roles useful for their own context, taking into account the needs of the task or their students. However, we will offer some illustrative examples:

With second graders working in a grammar lesson on the construction of sentences and the identification of the different types of words (subject, verb, pronoun), the teacher provides material for the team (i.e., the different pieces of the sentences) and identifies four sub-tasks to complete:

- Propose the correct order of the different parts of the sentence.
- Underline the verb in red and circle the different types of sentence groups in different colours.
- Replace the subject with a corresponding pronoun.
- Ensure the verb corresponds to the subject.

The teacher proposes that each student in the team endorse one sub-task for the first sentence, and roles are rotated for the three other sentences. Each student practices each sub-task once (activity proposed by teacher Sylvie Simonin).

At a middle school, fraction exercises in triads involved the introduction of three roles, each involving one mathematical skill and one social responsibility (Buchs et al., 2015; see Chapter 5 for a more detailed presentation):

- One of the pupils is responsible for explaining his/her reasoning and for ensuring that everybody understands.
- Another pupil is responsible for checking mathematical writing equivalence and making sure that everyone agrees.
- The third pupil is responsible for verifying that all partners use adequate vocabulary and for reporting the common answer on the team sheet.

Teachers can assign secondary students working in foreign language classes with rotating roles for each paragraph:

- One student reads a paragraph.
- One reads the question related to the paragraph.
- The other student answers the question.

University students working on mathematical equations can alternate responsibility:

- One student reads the problem instruction.
- The second proposes the corresponding equation.
- The third explains the underlying reasoning.

However, teachers should to be careful not to overload students and to choose the appropriate roles carefully (Bennett et al., 1991). It is important that the learning task is relatively easy when introducing complex new roles.

Three guidelines should be considered when attributing roles (E. Cohen, 1994). First, the teacher has to assign the specific roles clearly and publically. In this respect, the teacher delegates a specific part of their authority to that student. Second, it has to be clear for the student in charge of the role what to do when taking up a specific role. Third, all other students have to know what the person with a specific role has to do as well.

Teachers have the responsibility to make explicit why these roles are helpful and to explain the strategies, skills, procedures, and type of interactions required by the roles. As with essential cooperative skills (see Chapter 3), roles need to be taught and the attached responsibilities clarified (Howden & Kopiec, 2000). Consequently, it is important to explain what is expected and how to put it in action (i.e., what it sounds like and what it looks like). For example, for the secretary role, does it mean to summarise what is said or to make sure that all contributions are written down? This can be done during a collective discussion involving students in the way to pursue the roles.

Displaying posters in class for remembering what the role sounds and looks like can be very useful (E. Cohen, 1994). Based on the advice of Bennett et al. (1991), we also suggest giving role cards or pictures to each student indicating both their role and what they can say and/or do in taking up this role. Because the role endorsed by each member is clearly identified and written on the card, it legitimises students' interventions and avoids tension. To introduce the role of checker, for example, Howden and Kopiec (1999) propose a two-sided card. The side directed toward other members indicated the role "Checker" and the side toward the student who had to endorse this role reminded that student what to say and what to do (see Table 4.3). Chapter 5 will present other examples.

Finally, it is important to mention that stimulating students to reflect on the way they have endorsed their roles (what was useful, what can be modified) allows improving role efficiency.

Several studies illustrate the positive effects of the introduction of roles. For examples, we present one study at university level and one at primary school level. The first (Schellens, Van Keer, De Wever & Valcke, 2007) studied the effect of introducing roles in asynchronous discussions with university students. For some students, four roles were introduced: the *moderator* stimulated the discussion actively (i.e., managed the discussion, asked critical questions, requested the opinion of others, offered tips or hints); the *theoretician* ensured that the relevant theories were discussed (i.e., introduced theoretical information, verified that all

Table 4.3 Example of a role card

Checker	**What can I do (non-verbal)** • Attend to others • Invite others to ask questions by using inviting body language **What can I say (verbal)** • Does everybody understand? • Can you repeat that please? • Can you say more about that? • Do we all have the same answer? • Are we satisfied with this?

concepts were used); the *source seeker* encouraged going beyond texts (i.e., looked for other interesting and relevant sources); the *summariser* highlighted the different points of view (i.e., proposed an intermediate synthesis, offered a final synopsis, identified the similarities and inconsistencies). The students worked for 12 weeks on four different topics or discussion themes, each theme being worked for three weeks in groups of ten. The four roles were randomly assigned to four students for the first theme and four other students for each new theme discussed. Also, the roles were changed for each discussion topic. The introduction of these roles helped to improve the level of knowledge construction and allowed students to achieve better results in the final examination of the course. Being in charge of summarising the information proved particularly beneficial for the construction of knowledge.

Further, an analysis of longer-term development (De Wever, Van Keer, Schellens & Valcke, 2009) showed that roles were more beneficial to the construction of knowledge when introduced at the beginning of the semester (in the first six weeks) than towards the end of the semester (in the last six weeks). It is interesting to note that the groups in which the roles were introduced from the starting point maintained their superiority even when the roles were no longer assigned to students. It can therefore be hypothesised that the students had internalised the activities related to the roles.

In another study, primary students were asked to take up roles related to cooperative skills (Saleh et al., 2007) in very heterogeneous groups with low-, medium- and high-achievers. The learners were encouraged to use specific rules to give and to receive help. They took turns playing the role of facilitator on the basis of these rules. An additional rule (i.e., it was not allowed to initiate explanations more than two times) prevented all explanations coming from a single student. The results indicated that the introduction of this structuring promoted student learning and favoured the participation of average students. Average-level students contributed more and were more motivated with this structuring, while high- or low-level students were not bothered by the introduction of roles. Chapter 5 will present another intervention which introduced roles and high-structure interaction in primary school for a mathematical task (Buchs et al., 2015).

4.6. Scripts and scaffolds for peer interactions

As has been said, peer interactions have to be structured in order to guarantee peer learning. In peer tutoring and cooperative learning, teachers have to organise the interaction between the team members to promote positive interdependence and individual accountability.

In peer tutoring, the literature refers to the effectiveness of embedding support for tutors by means of scripts or structured materials. In this way, the expected roles and activities related to the desired tutor behaviour are made explicit to the students (Topping, 2005a). The meta-analysis of Leung (2015) showed that structured peer tutoring was more effective relative to unstructured tutoring. This implies that the benefits of peer tutoring can be enlarged by providing students with scripts, structured materials or clear procedures for interaction, encouraging and supporting the interaction or specifying a sequence of interactive behaviour (e.g., Falchikov, 2001; King et al., 1998; Fantuzzo et al., 1992; Miller et al., 2010; Topping, 1996, 2005a). Chapters 6 and 7 will present concrete examples of how peer tutoring includes structured relationships between tutor and tutee.

Concerning cooperative learning, the methods presented in Chapter 1 are pedagogical designs that help teachers to structure the interaction among the team members. We have selected as examples versatile and simple techniques that can be used easily in classrooms.

We will introduce three of them for each of the four sections in which we have organised them. (You can find some of these structures in Johnson, Johnson & Smith, 1998, and more than 140 in Kagan & Kagan, 2009.) In these structures, students follow the guidelines for interaction and in their team they all do the same tasks, taking turns.

4.6.1. Techniques for dialogue

The three following techniques encourage dialogue, ensuring participation of all team members with different simple procedures.

Active Knowledge Sharing (Silberman, 1996). In pairs, before starting a new topic, students try to answer initial questions with a view to activating and sharing prior knowledge.

Talking Chips (S. Kagan, 1992). In order to promote dialogue and participation of team members, each student puts a small personal object in the middle of the table (e.g., a pen). As they are speaking, the objects are removed. A new turn of conversation cannot be started until all team members have participated. It is recommended to allow time for reflection on one's own and peer contributions.

Three-Step Interview (S. Kagan, 1992). It starts with a mutual interview between members of a pair. Then, each student in turn shares with the team what he or she learned from his or her partner in the interview. In addition to interpersonal relationships, this technique stimulates active listening thanks to reformulation, respect for the opinions of others and expression of one's own ideas.

4.6.2. Techniques for processing the information

The following techniques can easily be inserted between the teacher explanations or other sources of information (texts, videos, etc.), in order to keep students' attention and assure understanding.

Think-Pair-Share (Lyman, 1992). During the explanation, the teacher asks a question and leaves enough time to answer, first individually and then in pairs. At the end, the ideas are shared with the rest of the class.

Cooperative Note-Taking Pairs (Johnson, Johnson & Smith, 1998). At a point in the explanation, the teacher gives time to students to wonder in pairs about the main ideas and doubts. One student summarises and provides corrections or additional information. In the next phase of activity, the members of the pairs reverse roles.

Scripted Cooperation (O'Donnell, 1999). In each pair, one student takes up the role of recaller, while the other is engaged in the role of listener. At one point, the teacher stops the explanation and the recaller summarises the information, while the listener complements it. They end up producing a synthesis of the working subject (see Chapter 5 for a more detailed presentation).

4.6.3. Techniques for the joint construction of knowledge

Below we present three techniques that easily structure team member interaction, with the purpose of having all students contribute to knowledge construction.

Teammates Consult (S. Kagan, 1992). The teacher distributes a folder of activities to each team of students. A team member reads the activity aloud and all members leave their pencils in the centre, indicating that they will first discuss the procedures for resolving it. When they are in agreement, each takes his pencil or pen and solves the task individually. The action is repeated, and the student who reads the solution aloud will change by activity, until the activities provided by the teacher are finished.

Numbered Heads Together (S. Kagan, 1992). Each team member has a number from 1 to 4 (for teams of four students). The teacher gives an assignment to the teams, and the team members must work together to resolve it and make sure that all teammates understand it well. Later, the teacher asks all students with a certain number to explain exactly how they solved the task.

Role Playing (Barkley, Cross & Major, 2005). The teacher creates a situation in which the students take up responsibilities or identities (roles) in each team as needed to achieve learning. Each student plays their role and has to devolve knowledge and skills to participate from a particular point of view. This intends to promote student creativity to develop the situation.

4.6.4. Techniques for problem solving

Finally, three techniques aimed at structuring team interaction to solve problem solving tasks are presented. The problems have to be complex enough to make cooperation between the team members necessary.

Pair thinking-aloud problem solving (Barkley et al., 2005). Pairs of students receive a series of problems and specific roles (e.g., troubleshooter and hearer) for each problem. The troubleshooter thinks aloud while formulating the steps to resolve the problem. The hearer follows the steps, seeks to understand them and formulates suggestions in case of mistakes. This technique is particularly suitable for activities requiring the application of procedures in a reflective way, and for activities with various correct answers or solutions, depending on the decisions taken.

Send a problem (S. Kagan, 1992). Each team of students receives an envelope with a problem, tries to resolve it, includes the written solution inside the envelope and passes the envelope to another team. In the second stage, the team – without looking at the answer of the previous team – formulates its own solution and passes the problem to yet another team. Depending on the number of teams in the classroom, the process can be extended. Finally, the initial team reviews and evaluates the different answers offered by the other teams. The technique combines group problem solving with peer group assessment, which provides opportunities to learn from students comparing one's own and other resolutions, and reflecting on one's own and other mistakes.

Team-pair-solo (Cuseo, 2002). Students are given three problems: the first is solved in teams of four; the second in pairs; and the third individually. The support is removed gradually in order to ensure that the student is becoming more individually competent. It is a sort of diminishing scaffold, withdrawing peer support progressively to develop competency in problem solving.

4.7. Monitoring and assessment

We will start with a discussion of the importance of teacher monitoring. This is a way to give formative feedback to help students improve their functioning. Then, we will discuss the question of evaluation in peer learning and discuss different ways to evaluate students' learning, taking into account both cognitive and cooperative objectives.

4.7.1. Monitoring peer learning

In the case of directional peer interactions (tutoring), either same-age or cross-age, ongoing supervision and support to optimise role taking and future tutoring activities is required – especially for peer tutors but also for their tutees (Falchikov, 2001; Schraw et al., 2006; Topping, 1996). This support for tutoring (whether by coaching individual pairs or holding group meetings) is very important. Group meetings for tutors and tutees are also important as an outlet for sharing students' experiences, both positive and negative, and lead to mutual learning. Tutors and tutees learn from each other and from teacher feedback and reinforcement.

Similarly, monitoring groups in action is an important role for teachers in cooperative learning (Bennett et al., 1991; Blatchford et al., 2006; Clarke et al., 1990; Johnson, Johnson & Holubec, 1998; Proulx, 1999; Webb et al., 2002). The teacher observes the teams and intervenes when needed. When students work together, teachers have the chance to observe while the students are constructing their knowledge. Teachers get access to useful information regarding the way students interact and the way they discuss the task content. It gives an opportunity to monitor students, to offer formative feedback to students and also to regulate teaching.

Teachers' observations while peers are learning play an important role in monitoring. Teachers may observe students, either from a general point of view (moving around in the classroom and taking informal notes) or more precisely how each student engages and uses cooperative cognitive skills. For systematic observations, teachers can use a grid or chart (e.g., Table 4.4) to record the number of targeted behaviours students display, as well as take notes on how they displayed the behaviours. The more the observation is systematic, the more teachers can use specific and concrete feedback to the students.

Taking into account their observations, teachers may intervene during peer learning in order to facilitate and model activities. These interventions aim to strengthen student motivation and engagement (Rouiller & Howden, 2010). Teachers can give directions to particular teams for helping students to engage or can record these comments for the reflection phase. It is important not to intervene immediately, so students have opportunities to find the answers to their problems themselves.

Similarly, teachers may refrain from responding to all students' questions. Teachers do not have to play substitute for one team member and should give the responsibility to the team to solve problems (Bennett et al., 1991; E. Cohen, 1994). Giving the responsibility to all members to answer partners' questions before asking the teacher is useful for teamwork.

Table 4.4 Example of a grid for systematic observation

Team _____	Student _____	Student _____	Student _____
Explain her/his strategies			
Encourage others			
Make propositions for helping the team to achieve the goal			
...			

If none of the partners can answer, teachers can give directions to explore instead of just the answer. Nevertheless, when questions show that students do not have the resources for going on, teachers can offer the support needed for students to engage in the activity. Teachers' interventions referring to teams' and individuals' responsibilities reinforce student autonomy, individual accountability and positive interdependence.

4.7.2. Evaluation in peer learning

Some teachers will wonder how to evaluate team work. First of all, we would like to underline that the evaluation needs to meet the same criteria as that for other academic activities. As suggested by Howden and Kopiec (2000), it is important to clarify the objectives of the learning activity, how the learning will be evaluated and what the criteria are to judge whether the objective is met.

Some methods propose the introduction of normative evaluations in cooperative learning by comparing teams (Slavin, 1995). Because normative evaluation is based on social comparison, it activates performance goals and students can easily turn competitive despite the cooperative instructions (Buchs & Butera, 2015). We recommend being highly attentive to the social climate when deciding to introduce competition between teams. In methods that propose this kind of team competition (see Chapter 1 and Slavin, 1995, for a more detailed description), particular attention is necessary to ensure that the competition is fair and avoid a hostile atmosphere, which could be counterproductive.

Peer learning involves two objectives: academic and cooperative goals. Therefore, teachers have to make decisions regarding the assessment of both objectives as well (Abrami et al., 1995). We have underlined the importance of getting feedback on goal achievement and making students reflect on it when discussing group processing (in Chapter 3). We mentioned that peer learning can rely on self-evaluations, peer evaluations and teacher evaluations. When students work in teams, teachers have the opportunity to observe them and to collect notes that allow continuous assessment, always difficult in the traditional classroom.

Second, because students work together, teachers have to decide how this interdependence will be reflected in the evaluation and what aspects will be included for individual and collective evaluation (Abrami et al., 1995). Decisions on the way to structure positive reward interdependence have consequences on individual's assessment. Some proponents of cooperative learning propose that positive reward interdependence is important for cooperative learning gains (Johnson, Johnson & Smith, 1998; Slavin, 1995). Teachers may want to combine individual evaluation and group evaluation depending on the nature of the team work (Bennett et al., 1991; Clarke et al., 1990; Gaudet et al., 1998; Howden & Kopiec, 2000; Johnson et al., 2002). Others suggest that it is especially important when students need to be (extrinsically) motivated to interact together (B. Cohen & Cohen, 1991).

E. Cohen (1994) draws attention to the potential problems created by a collective notation for a common group result or product. If students are stimulated to have the best common product possible, it may push them to differentiate contributions depending on their perceived level of competence. This is likely to reduce cooperation and does not guarantee individual learning for all team members. In this respect, formative group feedback (see Chapter 3) appears to be more appropriate than a mark or grade. Because status characteristics may affect participation in teams, it can be problematic to evaluate students based on their respective contributions to the group product.

We perceive peer learning as a wonderful opportunity for students to learn, because it requires them to be cognitively active. Peer learning is a great experience for "learning time". Nevertheless, we are, at the end, interested in what each individual student has learned from this experience. Therefore, we use individual learning tests to assess students' understanding and mastery of the material studied in teams. Even if students are required to produce a common product, we want to ensure that all students understood and mastered the learning content they worked on. Basically, we follow Howden and Kopiec (2000), who propose that summative (outcome) evaluations may stay individual in order to avoid pressure and negative feelings towards partners. If teachers want to integrate the team outcome in the evaluation, some propositions have been discussed previously regarding reward interdependence. In addition to testing academic objectives (relative to the curriculum and the cognitive content of the task), we may add some questions for reflection about what helps teams to work together well and what would improve them as learners. The quality of this reflection can offer an individual bonus to individual score.

In Part II we discussed principles for preparing learners for constructive interactions (Chapter 3) and for organising peer interactions in academic tasks (Chapter 4). While defining each principle, we suggested some practical guidelines and research results.

Part III aims to present different examples of authentic interventions in real schools and classes, combining several principles. We more particularly describe guidelines regarding the instructions, material, tools for scripting or scaffolding interactions and specific training used. By presenting interventions in different contexts, we try to help teachers to realise how the principles described in the chapters in Part III can be implemented concretely in daily class practice.

Part III

Practical propositions for the classroom

Part I, in particular Chapter 1, introduced the educational relevance of cooperation as a key competence for our students – in all educational stages – and as a resource for learning. Contrary to what traditional teaching presumes (which primarily gives value to teacher–student interactions), we demonstrated how peer interactions may also lead to learning. Chapter 2 highlighted the value and instructional effectiveness of mutual peer learning (cooperative and collaborative learning) as well as directional peer learning (cross and same-age peer tutoring).

However, we all know that putting cooperation into practice – in a world and in educational systems that have promoted competition and individualism – is not easy. It is not enough, as so often has been said, to simply group students and expect cooperation to arise spontaneously. On the contrary, simple group work is characterised by the dissipation of responsibility and by the fact that some students work a lot to compensate – and sometimes hinder – the work of others, who often act as passengers or stowaways.

How many times do we, as teachers, ask our students to perform a task – even a task that can be solved individually – by placing them into groups and saying "Remember: work as team!"? How many times do we bother to find out that some students did nothing and others were loaded with everything? To overcome the problems of simple group work, with its well-known limitations, and turn it into true cooperative or team work, it is necessary to structure the interaction between members of the team, according to the principles outlined in Part I and Part II. Particularly in compulsory education, where students have different degrees of motivation for learning goals and different degrees of development of cooperative skills, it is necessary that the teacher carefully organises the interaction between members of the group.

As explained in detail in Part II, the structuring of interaction not only acts as a guide to student cooperation, but also puts into practice the type of peer interactions which promote effective learning: summarising, questioning, explaining and co-construction, argumentation and reasoning, and confrontation and socio-cognitive conflicts. All this is complex and requires, as Chapter 3 explains in detail, preparation, training and help for students to reflect on what they are doing. In other words, students need to learn to cooperate.

But does this mean that students cannot cooperate until they have established all these values, cooperative skills and metacognitive resources? There are some teachers that say: "I don't use cooperative learning with my students because they can't cooperate". This is turning the argument on its head – precisely because they don't know how to work in teams, teachers have to offer them opportunities to do so. Learning to cooperate is similar to learning to cycle: you obviously need some skills, but you cannot learn to cycle without a bike. Most of the complex skills involved in cooperation (as explained in Chapter 3) can be displayed only in interacting with others. It is not possible to develop empathy alone, for instance. For this, you need to interact with others, to receive opportunities to stand in someone else's shoes, to understand their point of view and so on.

As Chapter 4 explained, teachers have to organise peer interactions in academic tasks to offer their students opportunities to cooperate. In this sense, cooperation is not only a competence in itself, but also a learning resource. Students cooperate to learn in academic contexts. Both aspects, cooperation as a competence (or learning to cooperate) (Chapter 3) and cooperation as an educational resource (or cooperating to learn) (Chapter 4), are two sides of the same coin. And each side needs the other.

In fact, in educational practices both aspects go together. When teachers use peer learning in their classes (mutual or directional) they take both into consideration. So, as a part of the cooperative principles, teachers using a cooperative learning method can give opportunities to the group members to reflect on their work and to improve their cooperative skills. Likewise, when teachers use peer tutoring, they generally invest in some sessions to train students in their respective roles of tutors and tutees.

In Part III, we present some real practices of peer learning – illustrations of how teachers can implement this methodology in their classrooms. These examples show how some of the different principles – though not necessarily all of them – work together. Fortunately, despite any difficulties, resistances or challenges, peer learning is being used at all educational stages and subjects and in a very rich variety of forms. We have selected some of them from our own practices, or from practices that have been published and documented as effective.

Trying to preserve this richness, practices have been selected with different sizes (some of them are programmes with years of operation, thousands of students and a lot of research, while some others are more exploratory in one classroom), from all educational stages (primary, secondary and university), with a varied number of subjects (reading, mathematics, statistics, physical and medical education) and from different cultural and geographical locations.

This is not an exhaustive sample of peer-learning practices. The next three chapters aim at illustrating the varied range of implementation of the principles on which peer learning is based. It is not a question of just replicating them. These examples are aimed to help teachers understand the principles so that they, knowing better than anyone their own context and the needs of their students, can effectively adjust the practices to their own realities.

Following the structure adopted in the book, Chapter 5 presents six practices of mutual peer learning (cooperative learning). Table III.1 summarises them.

Table III.1 Practices of cooperative learning presented in Chapter 5

Name	Educational stage/country	Area/subject
Scripted cooperation	University (USA)	Studying texts
Scripted cooperation with complementary information	University (France)	Social Psychology
Working with cooperative skills	University (Switzerland)	Statistics
Dyadic cooperative controversy	Primary (Switzerland)	Argumentative texts
Complementary expertise	Primary (Switzerland)	Mathematics
Structured responsibilities	Primary (France)	Mathematics

Chapter 6 gives examples of same-age peer tutoring, with students in the same or different classes – even in different schools – but with similar ages or levels of abilities. Seven practices are summarised in Table III.2.

Finally, in Chapter 7, the practices relate to cross-age peer tutoring, with pairs of students from different courses working together, with the older ones playing the role of tutor. Table III.3 summarises the seven practises presented.

Each of these practices is presented following this general structure: overview and main objectives, grouping students (in teams or pairs), preparing students and the material, procedure, and evidence from research.

To sum up, the following three chapters aim to illustrate from actual practice how teachers can rely on the principles presented in the previous section in order to prepare students for cooperation and to organise peer interaction in academic tasks. The diversity of practises shows a huge variety of ways teachers can introduce peer learning in their classrooms.

Table III.2 Practices of same-age peer tutoring presented in Chapter 6

Name	Educational stage/country	Area/subject
Paired Reading	Primary (UK and USA)	Reading
Duolog Math	Primary (UK and USA)	Mathematics
E-tutoring	Primary (Catalonia and Scotland)	Foreign languages
Reading in pairs	Primary and secondary (Spain)	Reading in English as L2
ClassWide Peer Tutoring	Primary and secondary (USA)	Different contents
Reciprocal peer tutoring in Teacher Education	University (Mexico)	Teaching studies
Reciprocal peer tutoring in Educational Sciences	University (Belgium)	Instructional sciences

Table III.3 Practices of cross-age peer tutoring presented in Chapter 7

Name	Educational stage	Area/subject
Reading Together	Primary (Israel, USA)	Fluency and reading comprehension
One Book for Two	Primary (Belgium)	Reading comprehension
The Peer Tutoring Literacy Program	Primary (Canada)	Literacy in French immersion schools
Paired Maths using games	Primary and secondary (England, Scotland)	Mathematics
Peer tutoring in physical education	Primary and secondary (USA)	Physical education
Online peer tutoring in asynchronous discussion groups	University (Belgium)	Instructional sciences
Cross-age peer tutoring in medical education	University (Belgium)	Clinical skills in medical education

Chapter 5

Structuring peer interactions in symmetrical relationships (cooperative learning)

This chapter will present some educational experiences regarding cooperative learning. Some were developed in the US, others in Europe (in France and Switzerland), in different contexts from primary schools to university. The cooperative learning concerned studying texts and mathematical learning. All these interventions rely on principles discussed in Chapter 3 (preparing students for constructive interactions) and Chapter 4 (organising peer interactions in academic tasks).

5.1. Scripted cooperation for studying texts at university

Scripted cooperation generally refers to dyadic (pair) cooperative work on texts organised by the teacher in order to foster four dimensions (the cognitive, affective, metacognitive and social dimensions) when studying, processing and acquiring information from texts (Dansereau, 1988; O'Donnell, 1999). This method is proposed for university students and was successfully implemented in the United States with university students from psychology.

5.1.1. Overview and main objectives

Scripted cooperation aims to improve students' learning from reading textbooks in pairs. It proposes strategies to facilitate the acquisition of information from texts and simultaneously introduces scripts for dyadic interaction between students alternating two roles. One student summarises the information while the other listens and facilitates with metacognitive and elaborative activities (see below and Table 5.1). More particularly, the study text is cut into different passages, and for each passage students endorse one role implying specific activities – then alternate roles for the next passage.

5.1.2. Grouping students

Scripted cooperation is designed to stimulate student learning within the class. Dyads are formed with no specific requirements for pairing students; either proximity of seats in the classrooms or students' preferences is a sufficient criterion for pairing.

5.1.3. Preparing students and the material

A typical scripted cooperation intervention requires three texts:

- One text for practicing alone the strategies for studying texts
- Material for the dyadic work consisting of an extract from a textbook, of about 2,500 words divided in passages of approximately 500 words
- Another text to measure the transfer of benefits

84 Practical propositions for the classroom

Table 5.1 Summary of the strategies proposed by scripted cooperation for studying texts

	During reading	During testing
Mood	Establishing a positive state of mind to read and study	Establishing a positive state of mind to complete the test
Understand	Capturing the main ideas and the facts during reading	Clarifying the requirements of the test and understanding the questions
Recall	Summarising aloud what was read without looking at the text	Searching the information to answer from own memory
Detect	Verifying the errors and the omissions in the summary	Looking for the errors or omissions in the reminder
Elaborate	Facilitating the memorisation	Organising the information in a coherent way
Review	Reviewing the material to remember it	Reviewing the test for improving it

The projects that have tested scripted cooperation proposed one session of one hour for students to practice alone the strategies for studying texts. The taught strategies rely on six steps. The first stage consists in establishing a positive state of mind to read and study. The second stage concerns understanding during reading and seeks to capture the main ideas and facts. Then, students are intended to recall the text from memory – they have to summarise what was read without looking at the text. The fourth and the fifth stages correspond to the implementation of metacognitive activities (i.e., activities relying on detection, namely verifying the errors and the omissions in the summary) and elaborative activities (i.e., facilitating the learning by adding mental images and by connecting with prior knowledge). The last stage consists of reviewing the material to help remember it. These steps are summarised in Table 5.1.

5.1.4. Procedure

A typical scripted cooperation programme introduces three sessions: one for training, one for working on texts (i.e., targeted text and transfer text), and one for testing.

5.1.4.1. Training session

Students benefit from a one-hour session for introducing and practicing the strategies regarding recall, metacognitive and elaborative strategies (as above).

5.1.4.2. Study of textbooks session

First, students work on the targeted learning text with the cooperative strategies – 45–50 minutes of studying a descriptive text (a 2,500-word passage). They are informed that they will be individually tested. The text is split into several passages of about 500 words. For each passage, students are instructed to participate in roles that imply specific activities: one of them is engaged as recaller (in view of the recall activities), while the other one plays the role of listener/facilitator (in view of the metacognitive and elaborative activities). They alternate these roles for each passage.

- The recaller has to summarise the passage aloud from memory:
  - The recaller summarises all important information or facts.
  - The recaller can use some rough paper while making the summary, but she/he presents the main idea without looking at the passage.
- The facilitator tries to improve both partners' comprehension of the passage while looking at the passage and helping to remember it. The recaller can help in completing the summary.
- The listener–facilitator demonstrates the following metacognitive activities:
  - Detecting main information
  - Underlining any hierarchy present
  - Detecting missing information
  - Discussing important information not included
  - Discussing incorrect information
- The listener–facilitator demonstrates the following elaborative activities:
  - Proposing ways to remember important information or facts
  - Connecting new information to already known information
  - Using images and personal means of presenting information
  - Representing information with drawings or figures

After the study of the targeted text, students work alone on a second text without mentioning the strategy, in order to assess the transfer effect.

5.1.4.3. Individual test

In the following session, students have to summarise the main information and eventually answer some questions on the content of the studied and transfer texts.

5.1.4.4. Cooperative principles

Regarding the principles presented in Chapters 3 and 4, scripted cooperation prepares students for constructive interactions by introducing a positive framework for learning and targeting some cooperative skills useful for studying texts (i.e., recall, metacognitive and elaborative activities). Regarding the way to organise peer interactions in the task, scripted cooperation stimulates both positive interdependence and individual responsibility. Positive interdependence is supported on account of the target (i.e., students have to work together to facilitate both partners' learning) and the complementary roles students endorse. The roles as well as the individual test to assess the learning of each student sustain students' individual responsibility. Further, this script has the potential to favour constructive interactions. The fact that some definite passages are allocated to students in the role of recaller pushes them to be active and favours equal participation.

5.1.5. Evidence from the research

These strategies were inspired by a cognitive approach (Dansereau, 1988) and are supposed to generate benefits regarding learning. The mere anticipation of making an oral summary of information is likely to favour learning, because it enhances awareness of objectives and strategies needed to achieve the objectives (Dansereau, 1988; Ross & DiVesta, 1976).

Also, actively presenting information is a good opportunity to rehearse the material and to consolidate the encoding of the information.

The cooperative strategies use the benefit of making an oral summary while creating multiple opportunities for it (across the different passages), in order to reduce anxiety and enhance familiarity. Moreover, metacognitive activities give opportunities for students to deepen their understanding of the way to give feedback and require students to detect and correct errors, which remains a challenge. Students are invited to share and enrich their respective elaborations, thanks to the elaborative activities.

In order to test the benefits of scripted cooperation (i.e., the combination of dyadic work and the taught strategies), research compared this procedure with other approaches (i.e., dyadic work in combination with students' own strategies versus individual work in combination with students' own strategies versus individual work in combination with taught strategies). The first series of studies (McDonald, Larson, Dansereau & Spurlin, 1985) allowed the testing of the effect of the scripted cooperation on students' initial learning and the transfer texts (initial acquisition of college-level textbook materials regarding ecology and geology). In the first experiment, dyads working according to scripted cooperation were compared to dyads who developed their own strategies and to students who worked alone using their own strategies. Results indicated that learning the targeted text was better for students who worked in dyads (with or without the scripts). Moreover, students who worked beforehand in dyadic scripted cooperation succeeded better than students in both other research conditions as to the second transfer text.

The second experiment compared students working alone and using their own strategies to students who were taught recall, metacognitive and elaborative strategies and working either alone (students had to play both recaller and listener–facilitator for themselves) or in scripted cooperation (cooperative strategies and roles). Results indicated that the performance of scripted cooperative dyads was superior to the performance of both other conditions (individual work with the taught strategies and individual work with own strategies) for both the targeted and transfer texts.

Overall, these results indicate that the use of this cooperative strategy facilitates initial learning and favours a positive transfer for later individual learning. It may be that students in scripted cooperation improve their skills and strategies, which allows them to transfer to subsequent situations. It is not only the strategies or the interactions between peers that contribute to the transfer of benefits, but also the combination of both which influences the individual's later learning.

Further, it appears that scripted cooperation is effective for strengthening students' active involvement (O'Donnell & Dansereau, 1995). Students in the scripted cooperation approach reported more synthesising and elaborative activities, while students in dyads without these strategies reported more individual activities, such as note-taking and underlining (O'Donnell, Dansereau, Hall & Rocklin, 1987). Scripted cooperation benefits have been demonstrated for processing written descriptive information, as well as technical information and performances related to concrete procedures (Lambiotte, Dansereau, Rocklin, et al., 1987; Larson et al., 1985; see O'Donnell & Dansereau, 1995, for a synthesis).

Further results (Spurlin et al., 1984) underlined that students in a fixed recaller role summarised more main ideas in their individual test for the targeted text than those in a fixed listener/facilitator role. Students who alternated both the roles throughout the passages scored in between in this respect. Moreover, students who alternated the roles reported more motivation. Consequently, proposing students to alternate roles seems important for long-term implementation. Spurlin et al. (1984) also underline that the activity of listeners is important for both listeners' and recallers' performance. This study pointed out that students who have to summarise information from memory for a partner who facilitates the summary by proposing elaborative and metacognitive activities benefit the most.

5.2 Scripted cooperation with complementary information at university

Some interventions rely on scripted cooperation principles and strengthen positive interdependence by introducing positive resource interdependence (Buchs, Butera & Mugny, 2004; Lambiotte, et al., 1988; Lambiotte, Dansereau, O'Donnell, et al., 1987). With positive resource interdependence, the distribution of the information inside the dyad makes students work on complementary information. The intervention described below was conducted in a medium-sized French university during a regular social psychology workshop where students worked on social psychology texts.

5.2.1. Overview and main objectives

In line with scripted cooperation, students worked on texts in order that both students mastered all information. At each session, they worked on two texts with two different roles (i.e., a summariser and a listener). They occupied one role for one text and switched for the second text.

The original conceptualisation of scripted cooperation as described above in Section 5.1 was adapted to make it relevant for regular workshops in social psychology in France. In the social psychological unit, all students attend the lecture in a large group (more than 200 students), and several workshops are proposed for a small number of students (about 35 students) in order to make students more active. In this context, no specific session for training is proposed; roles are introduced with the corresponding stategies, and students work with the same partner for three sessions. Students work on two texts for three sessions. Students have the possibility to take notes during reading. In order to guarantee a good quality of information transmission, summarisers are not required to propose their summary from memory. They can refer to the text and their notes during the discussion, but they are invited to discuss information and avoid mere reading.

Positive resource interdependence is introduced in the programme as the distribution of information. Positive resource interdependence is at the heart of cooperative methods, such as in the jigsaw method (Aronson & Patnoe, 2011; Blaney, et al., 1977; see also Chapter 1). Each student in a team is responsible for learning a part of the material and for teaching it to other members of the team, so every member learns the whole. Positive resource interdependence is supposed to be constructive, as underlined in Chapter 4. It may reinforce positive interdependence and individual responsibility, which, in turn, can stimulate cooperation and learners' involvement. But it also creates informational dependence. Thus, caution is needed because learning can be impaired in the event of poor quality of informational input. The programme addresses the quality of cooperation and student learning when working on complementary information.

5.2.2. Grouping students

In this experience, students were grouped in pairs, creating same-sex partners where possible. Additionally, students were invited to work with someone they were not used to. Students worked with the same partner for all three sessions. This grouping procedure was introduced in order to assess the procedure while limiting possible interference with other elements. Scripted cooperation with complementary information does not require specific arrangements for pairing students; for example, pairing based on proximity of seats in the classrooms, random pairing or students' preferences is sufficient.

5.2.3. Preparing students and the material

At the beginning of the first workshop, the teacher explains to students how they will work during the three sessions. The teacher frames a positive climate for learning by informing students that the objective of the workshops is that they work cooperatively in pairs, so that both partners master information contained in the texts. The teacher invites them to try their best to understand the material and to facilitate their partner's learning by encouraging constructive interactions, underlining that it is particularly useful to listen to their partner and to explain. Students are invited to use their partner as a resource person. In line with scripted cooperation, two roles are introduced: summarisers and listeners.

The content of textbooks are rewritten so that students can read the content easily in twenty minutes during the workshop. The content of the texts are independent from each other. Each text focuses on one new psychological principle relevant to the content of the course, but not taught in the lecture.

5.2.4. Procedure

The same teacher conducts all the workshops and introduces two situations (see Table 5.2). In some workshops pairs work on identical information, and in other workshops pairs work on complementary information (i.e., with positive resource interdependence). They work on two texts at each session. For each text, 20 minutes are devoted to individual and silent reading and ten minutes for discussion, taking into account the roles. Students are required to play one role for each text, and they switch the role for the second text.

- Summarisers have to try their best to summarise and explain the information.
  - After reading the first text, the summariser is responsible for explaining verbally all the information presented in the text.
  - The summariser explains the ideas in the text, as well as how researchers tested these ideas.

Table 5.2 Summary of the procedure for adapted scripted cooperation (identical versus complementary information)

In identical information situation, each student read the two texts:	In complementary information situation, each student read only one text and accessed the other one thanks to their partner:
• both students silently read the first text for twenty minutes, • one of the students played the summariser in discussion while the other student played the listener role, • both students silently read the second text for twenty minutes, and • roles were reversed for the discussion.	• only one of the students read the first text for 20 minutes • and played the summariser in the 10-minute discussion while the other student played the listener role; • the other student read the second text for 20 minutes • and played the role of summariser.

- The summariser can take notes on a separate sheet, not on the text itself.
- Students can use the text and their notes during the discussion, but they should avoid mere lecture and prefer discussion.
- The summariser's role is comparable to the teacher's: to facilitate the learning of the partner.
* Listeners have to facilitate their partners' summarising.
  - The listener's role requires asking questions and obtaining clarifications when information is unclear.
  - Moreover, the listener's role is to detect errors or missing or strange information in what the summariser said.

After working together, students answer a questionnaire that serves as introspection for group processing (some questions intend to make them reflect on their efforts, while other questions are designed to stimulate reflection on the quality of the cooperation and the potentially threatening social comparison when working with a partner). Individual learning is assessed during a fourth session. In this session, students complete an individual test for the six texts they studied in the three sessions.

5.2.5. Evidence from research

Student interactions were studied during discussion either by analysing videotaped interactions (Buchs & Butera, 2004; Buchs, Butera & Mugny, 2004, experience 1) or via the interactions students reported in questionnaires (Buchs, Butera & Mugny, 2004, experience 2). Results indicated that when students work on complementary information, summarisers are more involved in explaining information than when they work on identical information (i.e., they spent more time on summarising and summarised more ideas) and listeners asked more questions and received more answers. When working on complementary information, students demonstrated more positive reactions towards their partner, they recognised having made efforts for explaining information and reported fewer activities related to threatening social comparison between partners in their introspection questionnaire. In sum, working on complementary information stimulated more cooperation and more involvement in the discussion.

Results also underlined that the partner is perceived as a resource person (Buchs & Butera, 2009; Buchs, Butera & Mugny, 2004, experience 2). When working on complementary information, the partner's competence is welcomed; the more students perceived their partner as competent, the better they performed. This positive pattern was not found when students worked on identical information.

Notwithstanding the positive results above, the results regarding students' learning were more ambivalent. In one experience, the texts involved many scientific experiments and were evaluated by students as relatively complex to understand. In that experience, despite the positive interaction pattern when working on complementary information, students in the listener's role were disadvantaged in their learning. They performed worse than listeners working on identical information or than summarisers. They were in informational dependence, and no matter the efforts of their partner and the cooperation, learning was a challenge.

These results are in line with those studies that failed to demonstrate benefits of the jigsaw method (see Johnson & Johnson, 2002 for a review of different studies; Lazarowitz,

Baird, Hertz-Lararowitz & Jenkins, 1985 for secondary students in sciences; Box & Little, 2003 for third grade in social sciences; Souvignier & Kronenberger, 2007 for third grade in math, Moskowitz, Malvin, Schaeffer & Schaps, 1985 for fifth grade reading and mathematics tests; Souvignier & Kronenberger, 2007 for third grade in astronomy unit). Other studies indicated benefits only for some students (Blaney et al., 1977; Hänze & Berger, 2007).

Students are likely to learn well the part they are responsible for (Hänze & Berger, 2007; Souvignier & Kronenberger, 2007). Summarisers may benefit from playing the tutor role (Annis, 1983), giving explanations (Webb et al., 2002) for someone who relies on them (Bargh & Schul, 1980). Nevertheless, students may be disadvantaged regarding the part they learn from their partners (Buchs, Butera & Mugny, 2004, experience 1; Souvignier & Kronenberger, 2007). It can therefore be concluded that the difficulty of the text seems crucial when positive resource interdependence is introduced.

In a second research study, students worked with the same procedure, but the texts were more accessible and students perceived them as easier to understand (Buchs, Butera & Mugny, 2004, experience 2). These results indicated that listeners were no longer disadvantaged. Other experiences (Buchs & Butera, 2009; Buchs et al., 2010) confirmed that the quality of information transmission has to be good to permit positive student interactions to sustain all students' learning. It is important to keep in mind that properly summarising text in a limited time may be very challenging for students.

Further results investigate this issue at primary schools (Buchs, 2015) and underline that working on complementary information represents a nudge for cooperation but a pitfall for learning. Pupils at primary schools may experience difficulties in summarising information properly and it can prevent listeners from learning well when they work on complementary information.

5.3. Preparing students to cooperate: working with cooperative skills for improving statistics learning at university

Learning statistics is mandatory for psychology students in many university degrees. Nevertheless, statistics remains difficult for a large number of students and is associated with high anxiety and a weak feeling of competence (Tomasetto, Matteucci, Carugati & Selleri, 2009). Therefore, an educational experience was devised for using peer interactions in order to facilitate students' learning during a statistics workshop.

5.3.1. Overview and main objectives

This intervention structures statistical workshops for psychology students by organising peer interaction in pairs and preparing students to work together in order to improve their learning in statistics (Buchs et al., 2016). The experience was conducted with first-year psychology students in a medium-sized Swiss university during a regular workshop in statistics that follows an introductory statistics lecture. The regular teacher agreed that a psychology teacher trained in cooperative learning conducted the intervention for one workshop session. This teacher proposed students should work in cooperative pairs in order to keep individual responsibility high. She introduced an overall cooperative learning framework, providing students with explicit norms for cooperation (i.e., why they should cooperate) and demonstrating three cooperative skills identified by the regular teacher to be highly relevant for the specific task that they had to work on (i.e., how to cooperate).

5.3.2. Grouping students

In this experience, students worked in pairs, with same-sex partners where possible. Additionally, students were invited to work with a partner whom they did not know before the onset of the workshop. For regular implementation, no specific arrangement for pairing students is required: pairing based on proximity of seats in the classrooms, random pairing or students' preferences is sufficient.

5.3.3. Preparing students and the material

The teacher presented a short preparation for students regarding why they should cooperate in this task and how to cooperate. This preparation takes less than ten minutes.

- First, the teacher introduces positive norms to develop cooperation by making the value of cooperation apparent for individual learning and by explaining why students should cooperate. The teacher indicates that several studies in psychology and educational sciences have demonstrated that explaining to someone else how one goes through an exercise produces a better personal understanding. Accordingly, the teacher also makes clear that listening to the partner allows one to discover alternative strategies and reinforces one's own understanding. Constructive interactions were emphasised by stating that explaining, active listening and discussion about problem solving allow a better understanding of the statistics principles and facilitate the application of principles in various contexts.
- Second, the teacher explains how to cooperate by introducing three specific cooperative skills identified as highly relevant for the statistics task to be solved: (a) explain how one processes problems, (b) be sure to understand the way the partner processes problems and (c) suggest alternative ways to process problems. After the introduction of these skills, the teacher presents how to translate them into a set of operational procedures (i.e., both in words and in actions) suitable for the task under study (see Table 5.3).

Table 5.3 Cooperative skills introduced in the cooperative interactions condition for improving statistics learning

How to translate cooperative skills into action	How to translate cooperative skills into words
I explain how I process problems	
• I'm involved in the discussion. • I try my best to be as clear as possible.	• I explain the different steps ('I start by …, then I …'). • I explain my rationale ('I do it because …'). • I explain my strategies. • I explain concretely how I do something.
I check that I understand the way my partner processes problems	
• I encourage my partner to develop his/her ideas. • I let my partner explain without stopping him/her. • I listen to my partner's proposition even when I don't agree.	• I express my understanding ('All right, I understand'). • I express my difficulties ('I do not understand; could you please explain again?'). • I reformulate what my partner says in order to be sure I understand. • I ask questions to invite my partner to be more explicit. • I check for potential problems.

(Continued)

Table 5.3 Cooperative skills introduced in the cooperative interactions condition for improving statistics learning (*Continued*)

How to translate cooperative skills into action	How to translate cooperative skills into words
	I suggest alternative ways to process the problems
• I'm involved in the discussion.	• I suggest some alternatives ('and what if we started by … I would rather do …'). • I propose different alternatives.

Source: Buchs et al., 2016

5.3.4. Procedure

The statistics workshop is divided into different steps:

- First, the teacher introduces the objective of the workshop and why to cooperate.
- Then students have 20 minutes to review the content of the last statistics lecture on set theory individually.
- Pairs are formed and teacher explains how to cooperate in the statistics workshops in 10 minutes.
- Then the statistics workshop takes place for 30 minutes: students have to solve two exercises, in order to master the learning content and be able to pass a test. Students work together in pairs (to guarantee individual responsibility), in order to be sure that both students understand and master the exercise (i.e., positive goal interdependence) and will be able to answer the individual test (i.e., individual accountability). They have a coloured pen that allows identifying the contribution of each student on the common sheet (reflecting individual accountability). They are encouraged to help each other, to explain and make their reasoning clear to their partner (i.e., constructive interactions).
- Students answer a questionnaire regarding their feeling of competence, the perceived quality of the relationship, and threatening social comparison (see Table 5.4). This questionnaire can serve as a kind of group processing (see Chapter 4).
- Finally, students take an individual test in order to assess their individual learning regarding set theory.

5.3.5 Evidence from research

This intervention aims to test whether a short intervention focused on why and how to cooperate can help students to improve the quality of their learning in statistics. Students worked in three situations for the exercises phase. The procedure described above was compared with two other situations. In one situation, students work in pairs with general cooperative instructions but they do not benefit from the short preparation (why and how to cooperate). In another situation, they worked alone. The objective was to test a progressive increase in benefits as the cooperative structure was reinforced (see Table 5.5) from working individually – to working in pairs with general cooperative instructions – to working in pairs with general cooperative instructions with a nudge on cooperative interaction (why and how to cooperate).

Table 5.4 Measure of feelings of competence and introspection for two cooperative conditions for improving statistics learning at university

During the exercises we worked on in the training phase with my partner:									
I realised that I had understood some things	not at all	1	2	3	4	5	6	7	completely
I felt I was able to master the work	not at all	1	2	3	4	5	6	7	completely
I felt I was competent	not at all	1	2	3	4	5	6	7	completely
I felt committed to learning the subject	not at all	1	2	3	4	5	6	7	completely
I was motivated	not at all	1	2	3	4	5	6	7	completely
I was concentrating on the exercises	not at all	1	2	3	4	5	6	7	completely
I was involved in the work	not at all	1	2	3	4	5	6	7	completely

What about the relation with your partner?:									
To what extent did you feel comfortable in the dyad?	not at all	1	2	3	4	5	6	7	completely
What do you think of quality of the relationship inside the dyad?	very bad	1	2	3	4	5	6	7	very good
What do you think of quality of collaboration in the dyad?	very bad	1	2	3	4	5	6	7	very good
To what extent did you feel to be …	two individuals	1	2	3	4	5	6	7	a team

What was the frequency of your own behaviours?:									
I wondered how to appear competent	Very infrequent	1	2	3	4	5	6	7	Very frequent
I checked what my partner said was correct	Very infrequent	1	2	3	4	5	6	7	Very frequent
I evaluated my partner's competence	Very infrequent	1	2	3	4	5	6	7	Very frequent
I tried to appear more competent than my partner	Very infrequent	1	2	3	4	5	6	7	Very frequent

Table 5.5 Summary of progressive increase in cooperative elements in three conditions for a statistics workshop

Individual learning: 75 students	Cooperative instructions without preparation: 56 students (28 dyads)	Cooperative interactions with preparation: 56 students (28 dyads)
Explaining and making their reasoning apparent on their sheet	• positive interdependence • individual accountability • constructive interactions (explaining the procedure and reasoning to the partner, helping each other)	• positive interdependence • individual accountability • constructive interactions (explaining the procedure and reasoning to the partner, helping each other • short preparation for cooperation 　• positive norms for cooperation 　• specific work on cooperative skills

Students indicated how they felt competent regarding the exercises they practiced and said how they were cognitively engaged in the statistics task. Students who worked in the cooperative conditions also answered questions about their perception of peer interactions. All students completed an individual test after the exercise phase in order to assess the way students mastered the learning content they worked on.

Results indicated a progressive increase in individual post-test learning across the conditions as the cooperative elements increased, from individual training to cooperative instructions to cooperative interactions. A similar pattern was found both for students' feeling of competence and their cognitive involvement in the statistics task. These results are likely to reduce the fear some teachers may have that introducing an additional cooperative component could overload students or distract them from the cognitive content. Moreover, students' competence perception was found to mediate the effect of exercise conditions on learning. In order words, additional cooperative elements supported the feeling of competence and this feeling was responsible for the progressive increase in learning.

Regarding the two cooperative situations, students reported a more positive relation with the partner and less competitive activities when they benefitted from the short preparation regarding cooperative learning. Therefore, specific work on why and how to cooperate seems particularly well suited to address the challenges of a competitive atmosphere at university.

5.4. Preparing students to cooperate: dyadic cooperative controversy in school

The curriculum requires grade 6 teachers to work on argumentative texts. The use of "controversy" (Johnson & Johnson, 2007; see also Chapter 1) is particularly relevant to this issue: it proposes a script for cooperatively structuring pro and con arguments. In this intervention, the controversy was adapted for dyadic work in a school in Switzerland (Golub, 2011; Golub & Buchs, 2014).

5.4.1. Overview and main objectives

Controversy encourages working on issues from pro and con positions. Each student is assigned to one position and students are invited to follow a script to discuss both positions (see procedure). In the end, students have to elaborate a common synthesis and make sure that both students master all the information and can answer questions regarding both positions. The cooperative script is supposed to stimulate constructive elaboration of confrontation and argumentation. A short preparation for cooperation was introduced in this intervention conducted by an external teacher trained in cooperative learning in two sixth-grade classes in the French-speaking area in Switzerland.

5.4.2. Grouping students

Students work in relatively homogeneous dyads regarding their ability level in French while taking account of personal dynamics to avoid very best friends and students who do not get on well together.

5.4.3. Preparing students and the material

A short preparation for cooperation is introduced for 20 minutes by the teacher in charge of the intervention. This preparation has three ingredients:

- The teacher underlines the importance of the cooperation for one's own learning by stressing that explaining to and listening to other students deepens one's own learning.
- The teacher introduces a collective reflection on the importance of showing support and different ways to demonstrate support (a cooperative skill). Students individually write down ideas, share them in their dyad and then choose one to present to the whole group. The discussion takes 10 minutes. The poster where the propositions are reported (see Table 5.6) can stay pinned to the wall during the whole activity so students can refer to it when needed.
- The teacher proposes additional specific work on the three targeted cooperative rules inspired by the work of Johnson and Johnson (2007). The teacher presents the rules on a poster in the classroom and allocates 10 minutes for students to actively reformulate the rules and try to find relevant ways to put them explicitly into practice.

Table 5.6 Poster with propositions to express support as a cooperative nudge for dyadic controversy

Class 1	Class 2
• Helping • Encouraging • Communicating together • Not giving up • Explaining • Being present for the other • Giving examples	• Not laughing at • Encouraging • Helping • Listening • Proposing ideas • Smiling • Not criticising • Praising • Giving examples

- Rule 1: I listen to my partners' ideas, making sure I understand them even if I do not agree.
  The teacher invites students to discuss what they can do and say when they do or do not understand and to find counterexamples. For example, in the case of understanding, they can nod the head or can use the expression "Hmm hmm", "I understand" or "I got it". In contrast, when they do not understand, they may use their body language (move their hands, furrow their eyebrows) and say, "Can you give me an example please?", "Can you explain me again please?", "What?" or "I did not understand".
- Rule 2: I criticise ideas, not people
  The teacher invites students to reflect on how to criticise ideas explicitly while not judging the person. Students can use sentences such as "I don't agree with your idea because …" or "It depends, on the one hand I agree because …, but on the other I don't agree because …".
- Rule 3: Students were focused on coming to the best decision possible and not on winning.
  The teacher invites students to reformulate this rule and they reach an agreement in the discussion: "We have to try to do the best thing and not scream at each other" and "We take into account both person's propositions without always trying to be right".

Regarding the material, two texts were proposed regarding keeping dogs as a pet, one in favour of having dogs as a pet and one against, as well as multiple choice questionnaires in order to assess text comprehension. Both texts contained one introduction and four arguments. The material was constructed in collaboration with the regular teachers and the teacher in charge of the intervention to make sure that students at this age (11–12 years old) could read and understand the texts.

5.4.4. Procedure

During all the controversy the teacher stresses the importance of demonstrating social support (a cooperative skill). In addition, students were reminded of the relevance of the specific targeted cooperative rules before they underwent the step of the controversy (see Table 5.7).

The teacher proposes a role-playing situation according to the different steps for the controversy in dyads (Johnson & Johnson, 2007). The procedure is summarised in Table 5.7 in relation with the learning objectives.

- Step 1: Individual preparation for position
  Students are assigned to one of the positions (either pro or con) and they prepare arguments regarding this position. They have to read, understand and think how to present their position. They can also add new and personal arguments to the document.
- Step 2: Presenting positions in pairs
  Students present their position in a compelling and interesting way. Each student has a moment to present the position he/she is defending. While one partner is presenting, the other is only allowed to ask clarification questions if needed. The teacher reminds students of the importance of the rule 1 (I listen to my partners' ideas, making sure I understand them even if I do not agree).

Table 5.7 Procedure for dyadic controversy with cooperative nudge

Controversy steps for all students	Curriculum and learning objectives	Explicit work on cooperative rules and skills introduced for half of the students (cooperative nudge)
		Collective discussion regarding how to express support (10 min)
Experimenter explained the 5 steps (15 min)		
Importance for social support and introduction of the three targeted cooperative rules (5 min)		
		Collective discussion and explicit work on the three cooperative rules + underscore the particular relevance of each rule for each specific step (10 min)
1 Individual preparation for position (7 min)	Summarising arguments for the position	
2 Presenting positions (4 min for each student)	Summarising arguments from a text	I listen to my partners' ideas, making sure I understand them even if I do not agree (reminder)
3 Open discussion = persuasive argumentation of the positions (8 min)	Expressing disagreement. Searching for an opposing argument to the ones students have heard. Taking into account others' perspective	I criticise ideas, not people (reminder)
4 Reversing positions (4 min for each student)	Summarising arguments from a text	I listen to my partners' ideas, making sure I understand them even if I do not agree (reminder)
5 Construction of a synthesis (10 min)	Taking into account others' perspective Searching for an opposing argument identify organisational marks in a letter (e.g., it's sure that... but...)	We focus on coming to the best decision possible and not on winning

- Step 3: Open discussion with persuasive argumentation of the positions in pairs
  Students conduct an open discussion while staying in their position. They are requested to persuasively argue while refuting the other's arguments and rebutting the criticisms their position receives. The teacher reminds students of the importance of the rule 2 (I criticise ideas, not people).

- Step 4: Reversing positions in pairs
  Students have to exchange their positions. They have to use the other's arguments to defend the position they refuted until now. They can add new arguments of their own. This step is to make sure that participants listened actively to what the partner presented. Again, each participant is given a certain amount of time to present his/her new position. The one who listens can ask clarification questions if needed. The teacher reminds students of rule 1 (I listen to my partners' ideas, making sure I understand them even if I do not agree).
- Step 5: Construction of a synthesis in pairs
  Students have to propose a synthesis and integrate the best evidence and reasoning into a joint position. The teacher reminds students of the importance of rule 3 (We focus on coming to the best decision possible and not on winning). Due to the time allocated for this intervention and the age of the students, the teacher gives them an incomplete letter requiring students fill in the blanks. Students receive pieces of paper each containing sentences mentioned in the original texts and some connectors for articulating the sentences. They then have to decide together which sentences and connectors they want to use to complete their letter for their consensual position.

Regarding the principles presented in Chapters 3 and 4, this intervention introduces positive goal interdependence (i.e., making sure that both students master the content of the texts and are ready to answer questions on it and propose a consensual joint position) and positive resource interdependence (i.e., each student accesses only one part of the information). These two elements along with the roles in the dyads reinforce students' individual responsibility. The controversy favours constructive interactions because it requires summarising, explaining and questioning while demonstrating social support.

The moment students have to confront and argue is important for constructive conflict. Indeed, they confront after each one has presented her/his own position. First, students are more likely to see weaknesses of the position they did not yet defend. Therefore, the open discussion is a good opportunity to detect points to improve. Secondly, during this open discussion, students already anticipate that they will have to reverse the position; therefore they have to listen carefully to the other's propositions and arguments because they will have to rely on what the partner is saying for defending that position afterwards. The fact that a definite time is allocated for each step and position permits ensuring that both students are likely to participate on an equal basis.

5.4.5. Evidence from research

One of the objectives of this intervention was to test the effect of short preparation for cooperation (Golub, 2011; Golub & Buchs, 2014). For that purpose, two forms of dyadic controversy were compared: one only introduced rules and skills and one additionally included a short cooperative nudge. In the two situations, the teacher introduced the cooperative skill and the three cooperative rules (presented on a poster in the classroom) as part of the controversy. But in the condition with short preparation, the teacher devoted ten minutes to discussing how to demonstrate social support and ten minutes to reformulating the rules to try to find relevant ways for students to put them explicitly into practice. Thus, the difference between the two is the cooperative nudge. Half of the students from each class were in the two situations. Students were placed in the two conditions, so the level in the two conditions was as similar as possible.

After the dyadic controversy, students answered some questions regarding both texts. All dyads were videotaped from steps two to five of the controversy and two raters computed the number of clarification questions pupils asked, as well as the number of critiques of the partner (i.e., when a pupil openly criticised or accused her/his partner, e.g., "You suck", "You steal my arguments", "Stop behaving like this", and/or used abusive language). The raters also coded the occurrence of attention toward the partner (i.e., involvement in the interaction by means of visual contacts and postural openness towards the partner), social support (i.e., identified with smiling, encouraging, and positive remarks such as "Come on, you can do it" and "Do not be stressed"), active listening (i.e., when the students reacted in a way related to what was said, or when they expressed interest in verbal and/or nonverbal ways, expressing connection and alignment). At the end, both observers evaluated the degree of cooperation within the dyad.

Results underlined that students who benefited from the preparation for cooperation achieved marginally better on the question regarding both texts than those who did not benefit from this preparation. However, the difference was small. Regarding student interactions during controversy, the numbers of critiques against their partner as well as active listening were similar in both conditions. These observations may be interpreted in terms of the general cooperative framework. Nevertheless, students who were prepared to cooperate displayed more social support, asked more questions and paid more attention to their partner. The overall quality of the cooperation in the dyad was also evaluated as more positive for students who received the preparation to cooperate by the raters.

This intervention showed that when the preparation to cooperate is framed in a specific way (i.e., adapted to the situation and inviting students to participate in the construction of rules and skills), benefits for the quality of the relationship can appear even after a short intervention. It is important to note that this specific preparation for cooperation took 20 minutes, which is realistic in a usual classroom context.

5.5. Creating complementary expertise in mathematics in grade 4 for empowering low-achievers

Here we summarise what a teacher introduced in her class after an initiation to cooperative learning. She decided to change the way she proposed exercises to her students in order to create complementary exercises and she invites her students to play expert roles for the others and empowers low-achievers.

5.5.1. Overview and main objectives

The aim of the fourth-grade teacher (Olivier, 2013) was to provide low-achievers in mathematics the opportunity to participate fully in cooperative work in maths in a heterogeneous context (ten out of 20 students experienced difficulties in mathematics, while the other ten were high-achievers). In line with E. Cohen (1994), the teacher was interested in student's status (see also Chapter 3) and prepared them in order that they could actively participate in the interactions.

In this intervention, the teacher regularly introduced some cooperative principles in her teaching and was particularly involved in creating a positive climate for learning. We do not explain all she introduced in her daily practice, but we focus on one particular intervention where the teacher mixed peer tutoring and jigsaw to permit all students to gain expertise. To play expert roles for these exercises they would also benefit from the expertise of other classmates. In this organisation, all students access the whole lesson and content (to avoid informational dependence), but each student was trained to become an expert for a specific exercise. Students were required to help each other to learn and to make sure that all partners mastered all the exercises. Two steps were introduced. First students gain expertise in heterogeneous expert groups, then they benefit from reciprocal teaching in homogeneous pairs. Complementary expertise reinforces positive interdependence and individual responsibility because it creates different roles (i.e., experts and learners). More particularly, scripts for the interaction are included indicating who is acting as expert and learner – and the roles require different ways of behaving.

5.5.2. Grouping students

The teacher grouped students according their previous result on a pre-test regarding subtraction and addition problems. This information was necessary to form homogenous groups and pairs, as well as heterogeneous expert groups.

5.5.3. Preparing students and the material

Because the teacher wanted to give opportunities to low-achievers to be recognised as true experts, the teacher introduced several activities in order to make the participation of low-achievers likely.

Activities for valuing all students in the class:

- The teacher conducts a collective reflection on the conditions that favour learning and the importance of integrating all students. The discussion points out that helping each other is at stake.
- The teacher proposes that each student chooses one theme that she/he would like to teach to the class. Each student has the opportunity to teach it during the month before the intervention.

Activities for ensuring all students' engagement in the mathematical task:

- The teacher conducts a collective reflection on mathematical strategies useful for subtractive and additive problems, so students can use these during the activity.
- The teacher takes care of preparing low-achievers to be good experts:
  - Before the onset of the heterogeneous expert groups, low-achievers have some time to work together, with the help of the teacher. Therefore, they may feel comfortable when they join expert groups.
  - In each expert group, one high-achiever is assigned a role as moderator by the teacher: the moderator is required to encourage the participation of all students, to underline what is useful for managing the task, and to make sure that everyone understands why it is useful.
  - At the end of the expert groups, all students receive a summary of the answer and mathematical procedure to make sure that everyone will be able to explain in homogeneous dyads.
  - During the reciprocal teaching in homogeneous pairs, the expert can use the summary from their expert group to ensure that they are able to explain in a proper manner.

The following activities ensure that all students are likely to play their part and role:

- The teachers conduct a collective discussion for reflecting on cooperative skills "Taking one's turn" (see Table 5.8).
- The teacher and the students discuss the way they can play the listener and expert role (see Table 5.9).

The material is a mathematical task proposed in the curriculum.

5.5.4. Procedure

The teacher introduces several steps:

- The teacher proposes different activities which favour a positive climate for learning and preparing students for constructive interactions (see below).
- Students have a pre-test on subtractive and additive problems.
- The ten students identified as low-achievers benefit from 30 minutes training in groups on one exercise with the help of the teacher who regulates the activities of the groups.
  - Five low-achievers work together on exercise A.
  - Five low-achievers work together on exercise B.

Table 5.8 Illustrating cooperative skills for complementary expertise in mathematical exercises

Taking one's turn

(I see)	(I hear)
• A student helping another student • Students taking turns for speaking • Other students listening • All students participating • One or more student(s) providing encouragement (nodding, smiling, inviting)	• "Go ahead, I know you can do it!" • Each student speaking at least once • Students not talking too long • Students speaking kindly • "You did not tell your idea, please, tell us what you think". • "I'm sure you can explain something to us". • "Come closer".

Table 5.9 Explanation of roles for complementary expertise in mathematical exercises

Expert role	Listener role
• To explain the exercise clearly • To be sure the partner understood • To respect the partner • To help the partner • To encourage the partner • To let the partner try by him/her self • To let the partner speak	• To be attentive • To try his/her best • To respect the partner • To make effort
Avoid: • Giving the answer • Distracting the partner • Giving orders	Avoid: • Interrupting

- The 10 high-achievers discover one of the exercises (they have 5 minutes to look at the exercise) while low-achievers stay available if high-achievers have questions.
  - Five high-achievers discover exercise A.
  - Five high-achievers discover exercise B.
- Afterwards, students are grouped in heterogeneous groups with five low-achievers and five high-achievers, to become experts for one exercise. At the end of the expert groups, they propose a consensual answer regarding the way to solve the exercise, which is verified by the teacher. The teacher prepares a summary of what the group proposes and each student receives one copy of the summary.
  - One expert group with five low- and five high-achievers on exercise A.
  - One expert group with five low- and five high-achievers on exercise B.
- Students who become expert at one exercise are paired with students who have become expert in the other exercise in order to tutor each other. They work in homogeneous pairs with each student tutoring for the exercise she/he has become an expert in and explaining the exercise to the other student.
  - Homogeneous pairs of high-achievers with one student tutoring for exercise A and the other tutoring for exercise B.
  - Homogeneous pairs of low-achievers with one student tutoring for exercise A and the other tutoring for exercise B.

5.5.5. Evidence from observation research

After the exercise, students answer an individual post-test similar to the pre-test. The evolution from pre-test to post-test indicates that low-achievers progressed, with some spectacular progress (+ 7 points out of 20). However, it should be taken into account that low-achievers also had more room for progression than high-achievers.

The teacher videotaped students' interactions in order to analyse the way low-achievers interact. These data indicate that during expert groups, low-achievers expressed more difficulties, received more help and were invited to participate more than high-achievers. Three hundred and eighty-four interactions were analysed, revealing that 48 per cent came from low-achievers. Notably, the number of elaborated student interventions focused on synthesis or explaining the mathematical procedure was quite similar for both types of students (27 for high-achievers, with one single high-achiever bringing in ten out of the 27 interventions; and 24 for low-achievers). Consequently, this organisation seems favourable for the contribution of low-achievers.

Observations confirmed that students adequately succeeded in playing their roles: experts were more active as to managing the task, giving directions and helping their partner, while listeners expressed more difficulties. Nevertheless, sharing complementary expertise in homogeneous dyads permits quite equitable participation. Both partners participated to the same extent and both discussed the mathematical content. Accordingly, it can be concluded that the intervention allowed both students to be involved in the discussion and the expert succeeded in making the listener active.

5.6. Structured responsibilities for mathematical learning in fractions in school

In primary school, learning fractions is a central mathematical objective, but many students have difficulty in mastering the basic procedures in different contexts (Carette, Content, Rey, Coché & Gabriel, 2009; Lin, Wenli, Lin, Su & Xie, 2014; Martin & Strutchens, 2007).

The aim of this intervention (Buchs et al., 2015) was to introduce structured cooperative learning as a means to improve students' learning, particularly for average achievers.

5.6.1. Overview and main objectives

As discussed in Chapter 4, some results indicate that large-heterogeneity groups (high-, average- and low-achievers in the same team) might be deleterious for average-achievers, because they are excluded by the teacher–learner relationship that is likely to take place between low- and high-achieving students (Webb, 1985). In line with Saleh, Lazonder and de Jong (2007), highly structured cooperative learning might stimulate all students' involvement in wide range grouping and be especially positive for average-achievers. Students were invited to endorse specific responsibilities when working in heterogeneous triads in order to stimulate all students' engagement. Students from nine classes in France participated in this intervention.

5.6.2. Grouping students

Students formed triads according to their performance on the standardised baseline test. Specifically, within each class, each pupil was placed in a heterogeneous triad with one low-, one average-, and one high-achiever.

5.6.3. Preparing students and the material

Students were required to work cooperatively in triads and to try their best to master the learning content and to facilitate their partners' mastery of the content. Students were invited to help each other to make sure that both of them were prepared to answer an individual post-test after the teamwork.

Three cooperative skills or social responsibilities were also introduced, along with cards explaining the role:

- Checking whether everyone understands
- Verifying that everyone agrees on the common answer
- Reporting the common answer

The material was constructed according to the mathematical learning objectives from a standardised national evaluation on fractions. This related to the pre-test and the post-test, the exercise for teamwork and the exercise for checking individual understanding.

5.6.3.1. Pre-test

These tests consist of nine exercises to cover the whole concept with typical exercises used in the national curriculum included.

5.6.3.2. Exercise on fractions

During the exercise phase, the triads have to express the length of one segment in terms of fractions of a standard measurement. The standard measure is graduated with different subunits, respectively representing $\left(\frac{1}{4}\right)$, $\left(\frac{1}{8}\right)$ and $\left(\frac{1}{16}\right)$, called "the rulers". Students in the triads are required to use the three rulers and to respect three mathematical skills introduced during the lecture:

- Understanding specific fraction reasoning, more particularly the addition of a whole number and a fraction, the addition of fractions and fractional notation
- Figuring out the equivalence of the notations $\left(1+\frac{1}{3}\right)$, $\left(\frac{1}{3}+\frac{1}{3}+\frac{1}{3}+\frac{1}{3}\right)$, and $\left(\frac{4}{3}\right)$
- Being able to use adequate vocabulary

In sum, the preparation invites students in triads to agree, to ensure that every member understands, and to report the common answer for indicating the length of the segment using as many notations as possible with the adequate vocabulary and checking that all notations were equivalent (i.e., the three social responsibilities and the three mathematical skills).

5.6.3.3. Individual understanding

In order to assess individual learning regarding the exercise on fractions, students individually perform a similar fraction exercise as those carried out in the triads, but with a new ruler graduated in $\frac{1}{5}$.

5.6.3.4 Post-test

Post-test comprises the same type of tasks than pre-test; only the mathematical values change. The difference from pre- to post-test allows assessing individual progress in fraction learning.

5.6.4. Procedure

The regular teachers from the nine classes agreed that an ad hoc teacher conducted the intervention for two sessions (Buchs et al., 2015), in order to follow the same procedure in nine classes. In session 1, students have an individual pre-test, then the ad-hoc teacher gives a lecture on fractions and introduces the three mathematical skills, with some visual reminders displayed in the classroom during the whole intervention.

The second session is divided into three steps.

- Step 1. Students work in large-heterogeneity triads on one exercise
  The teacher starts by reminding the students of the three mathematical skills (i.e., explaining reasonings, checking the equivalence of notation, using adequate vocabulary) through visual posters, which stay visible in the classroom throughout the session and are reproduced on responsibility cards (See Table 5.10). The teacher then introduces general cooperative learning instructions and the three cooperative skills or social responsibilities (i.e., checking whether everyone understands; verifying that everyone agrees on the common answer; and reporting the common answer).
  This procedure supports positive goal interdependence because students have to take care of all partners' learning and report their consensual answer on the single group sheet. Individual responsibility is sustained by the information that students will complete an individual learning test after the group work. Students are invited to encourage

each other, explain their reasoning and use both cooperative and mathematical skills, which can help stimulate constructive interactions. The structure is intended to ensure that all students in the teams are engaged in mathematical discussions and group decisions.

- Complementary expertise
  Each member has to train with one of the rulers for ten minutes and discuss with students who get the same ruler for five minutes to become an expert with it. Then, each student shares with two other members of the team, who become expert for the other rulers for ten minutes. This permits the reinforcement of positive interdependence via the complementary task and expertise before the work in triads. Students gain complementary expertise because they train with different rulers, but the mathematical reasoning and mathematical skills are the same. Therefore, this expertise does not create informational dependence. It pushes all students to take an active role for explaining what they have worked on.

- Complementary responsibilities
  During the teamwork in triads, students endorse complementary responsibilities related to both mathematical and cooperative skills. In order to help pupils organise their responsibilities, they can rely on responsibility cards (see Table 5.10). Each card recalls one mathematical skill introduced in the lecture and reproduces the poster shown in the classroom as well as the one targeting social responsibility. Students alternate these responsibilities (see Table 5.11).

Table 5.10 Responsibility cards for mathematical learning in fractions

	Making sure that everyone understands		
Card for • Making sure that everyone understands (cooperative skills) • Explaining the three reasonings (mathematical skills)	• "Did you have some questions?" • "Is it clear enough for you?"		
	Responsible for reasoning		
	Explaining the three reasonings "I want to share equally 4 identical pizzas among 3 guests".		
	Reasoning 1: We can give each guest one pizza and then cut the last one in three and give one part to each guest.	Reasoning 2: We can cut each pizza into three parts and distribute one portion of each pizza to every guest.	Reasoning 3: We can cut all the pizza in three parts and give three parts representing a whole pizza and one part of another pizza to each guest.
	$1 + \dfrac{1}{3}$	$\dfrac{1}{3} + \dfrac{1}{3} + \dfrac{1}{3} + \dfrac{1}{3}$	$\dfrac{4}{3}$
	Addition of whole number and fractions	Addition of fractions	Fractional notation

(Continued)

Table 5.10 Responsibility cards for mathematical learning in fractions (Continued)

Making sure that everyone agrees

Card for	
• Making sure that everyone agrees (cooperative skills) • Verifying the equivalence of writing (mathematical skills)	• "Do you agree?" • "Can we write the answer on the sheet?" **Responsible for notation equivalence** Verifying the equivalence of notations "Equivalent notions are writing which represents all the same number". $1 + \dfrac{1}{3}$ $\dfrac{1}{3} + \dfrac{1}{3} + \dfrac{1}{3} + \dfrac{1}{3}$ $\dfrac{4}{3}$ Addition of whole number and fractions Addition of fractions Fractional notation

Reporting the team answer on the sheet

Card for	
• Writing the common answer (cooperative skills) • Communicating with appropriate vocabulary (mathematical skills)	**Responsible for vocabulary** Communicate with the appropriate vocabulary In a fraction, • the number above the bar represents the number of the parts we take and it is called the numerator. $\dfrac{1}{6}$ • the number below the bar indicates how much we share the unit and it is called the denominator. $\dfrac{2}{6}$ ~~Two on six~~ = two sixth $\dfrac{1}{3}$ ~~One on three~~ = a third

Source: Buchs et al., 2015

- Step 2. Students answer the individual understanding exercise
- Step 3. Students answer the individual post-test

5.6.5. Evidence from the research

This intervention (Buchs et al., 2015) is aimed at introducing structured cooperative learning as a means of improving students' learning of fractions, particularly for average-achievers. In order to assess the effect of the structure, two situations were compared. In the high-structured condition, each student gained complementary expertise and they alternated different responsibilities during the exercise. In the low-structured condition, no specific structure

Table 5.11 Structured responsibilities for mathematical learning in fractions

Math:	Explain reasoning	Adequate vocabulary	Notation equivalence
Social:	Everyone understands	Write common answer	Everyone agrees
Round 1	Ruler $\frac{1}{4}$	Ruler $\frac{1}{8}$	Ruler $\frac{1}{16}$
Round 2	Ruler $\frac{1}{8}$	Ruler $\frac{1}{16}$	Ruler $\frac{1}{4}$
Round 3	Ruler $\frac{1}{16}$	Ruler $\frac{1}{4}$	Ruler $\frac{1}{8}$

Source: Buchs et al., 2015

was provided (i.e., students had 15 minutes to train themselves with the three rulers before working in triads where they organised the cooperative work as they wished with all the responsibility and mathematical skills).

Triads were randomly assigned to the low-structured or high-structured cooperative learning condition to test whether the highly structured cooperative learning would improve average-achievers' understanding of the content targeted in the group work, as well as show progress in terms of fractions learning when compared to low-structured cooperative learning. The results indicate that highly structured cooperative learning favoured the understanding of the targeted task (i.e., expressing the length of a segment in terms of fractions of a standard measurement, using as many notations as possible while using adequate vocabulary, and checking whether all writings were equivalent). Students performed better after having worked in the high-structure condition. It is important to note that the overall benefits of structure came to average-ability students, who benefitted from the structure. In the low-structured condition, average-achievers performed the same as low-achievers, whereas, in the high-structure condition, average-achievers performed the same as high-achievers. The degree of structure, however, did not affect low- or high-achievers' learning.

Moreover, students at all levels progressed from the baseline test to the post-test. Thus, cooperative learning offered some benefits for such a challenging domain as learning fractions. Regarding the effect of the structure, the high-structure condition was only beneficial for average-achievers. Indeed, low- and high-achievers had the same progression in both conditions, whereas average-achievers progressed more in the highly structured condition.

In sum, these findings underscore that more (versus less) structure appears to be more effective for average-achievers than for low- or high-achievers. The other important point is that the degree of structure has no effect on either the understanding or the progression of low- and high-achievers, who might benefit from cooperation irrespective of its level of structure. As indicated in Chapter 4, building heterogeneous groups in a class requires special attention for average-achievers. They are often excluded from social interactions in classic heterogeneous group work (Saleh et al., 2005; Webb, 1985). In this respect, cooperative structure might be a solution to balance the interactions among group members. As such, this intervention proposes an interesting pedagogical cooperative learning method that can be used in classrooms to improve the organisation of these interactions in heterogeneous work groups.

Conclusion

These educational interventions based on cooperative principles illustrate the variety of ways teachers can introduce cooperative learning in their classrooms. In all interventions, the cooperative activities are built on regular activities where teachers reflect on the way they can structure these activities in order to foster constructive interactions with equal participation from all students. For that purpose, teachers can rely on principles for preparing students and for organising peer interaction in academic tasks. The general picture from these interventions is that the structure the teacher proposes stimulates positive social outcomes and support learning.

Of course, it may be difficult to introduce all the principles discussed in Chapters 3 and 4 in all activities. Therefore, we suggest teachers reflect on the type of interactions they wish for their students in a targeted activity, and then reflect on the most useful principles that can push students to be actively engaged in these constructive interactions. Because we present short-term activities, we do not stress the importance of group processing. Group processing is particularly useful in pointing out what students need to work on for improving the efficiency of teamwork. Thus, for improving long-term efficiency of peer learning, introducing group processing may be particularly useful (Bertucci et al., 2012; Yager et al., 1986).

Chapter 6

Structuring directional peer interactions in same-age tutoring

This chapter presents seven educational experiences applying same-age tutoring. These experiences have been selected from a diverse range of contexts at different educational levels (i.e., from primary school to university), in different countries (i.e., USA, UK, Spain, Mexico and Belgium), and addressing varying subjects (i.e., reading, maths, foreign languages, teacher education). All of these are examples of educational practices based on same-age peer tutoring, some of them in fixed and others in reciprocal roles.

6.1. Paired Reading. Evidence-based good practice for reading

Paired Reading (PR) is a peer tutoring method, with children or parents as tutors, aimed at improving reading (Topping, 1995). It is designed to complement professional teaching without interfering with it, implying that it can be implemented in combination with many other educational practices. For instance, the Read On project complements PR with Thinking, Writing and Spelling peer tutoring. You can find information and resources on Read On at www.dundee.ac.uk/esw/research/resources/readon/resourcesforteachers/.

The elements in the structure of the method are described below.

6.1.1. Overview and main objectives

Paired Reading is a technique – explained below in detail in Figure 6.1 – that offers the opportunity to improve fluency and accuracy in reading, in relation to the meaning of the text and comprehension. Students are likely to increase enthusiasm for reading, favour expression while reading, increase praise while reading and improve understanding and text meaning. They avoid failure by taking opportunities for guessing new or difficult words and obtaining examples of how to pronounce difficult words.

6.1.2. Pairing students, contact time, place and position

Pairs can be composed on a same-age or cross-age basis. Pairs commit themselves to an initial trial period of at least 15 minutes per day, at least 3 times per week, for an initial period of about 8 weeks. PR works best when there is consistently one main tutor to start. Later, other peers, siblings, parents or grandparents, or even friends and neighbours can help. However, they must all apply PR in just the same way, or the child will get mixed up.

For peer tutoring, the three sessions per week should be in regular scheduled class time, with the possibility of doing more during break (recess) if the pair wishes. This frequency of usage over the initial period enables the pair to become fluent in the method and is sufficient to begin to see some changes in the tutee's reading.

110   Practical propositions for the classroom

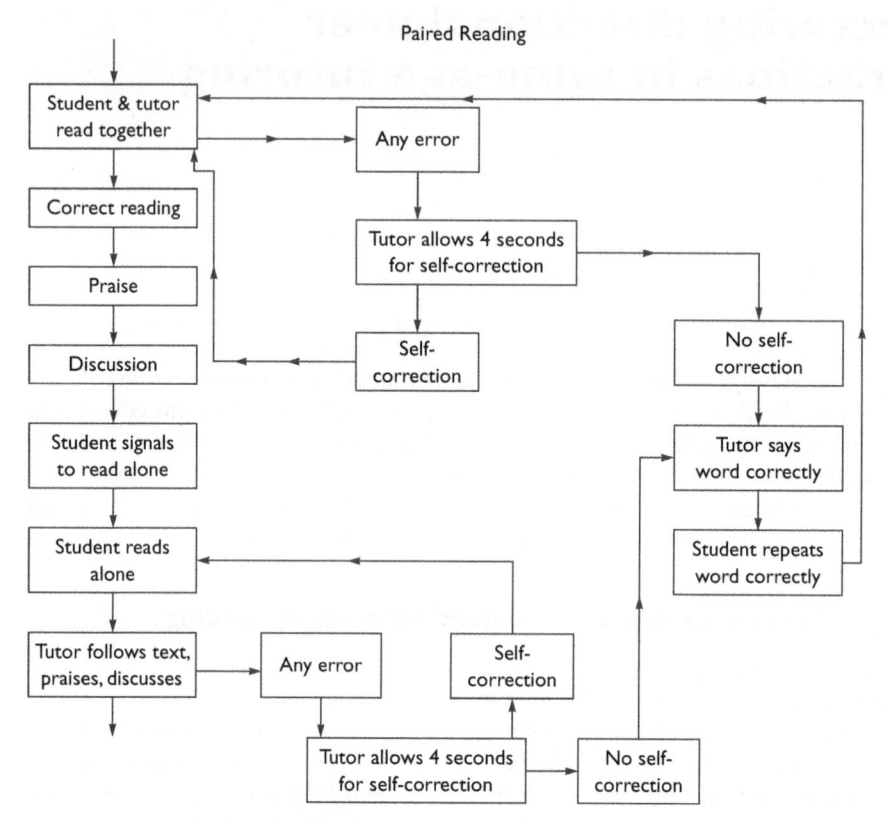

Figure 6.1 Paired Reading flowchart.

Finding a relatively quiet and comfortable place is desirable. Pairs should keep away from televisions or computers, and other distracting noise or activity. It is important that both members of the pair are sitting comfortably together side by side and can see the book equally easily. At home, PR provides an all too rare opportunity to get close to each other.

6.1.3. Initial training

Training is quick but essential and should be carried out with both tutor and tutee present. A training session should include verbal, visual and written information (bilingual if necessary). It should also include a demonstration, immediate practice with an authentic reading activity, feedback for participants about how they did and further individual coaching for those who are struggling. A video and resources are available and can be used as part of a training session to introduce PR in class (www.tes.com/article.aspx?storyCode=6339142).

6.1.4. Selecting reading material

The tutees choose reading material of high interest to them, from school, the community library or home. Newspapers and magazines are fine. However, if the tutee has a fanatical interest in one topic or type of book that is not shared by the tutor, some negotiation with the tutor will be needed, to avoid boredom for them.

Because PR is a kind of supported or assisted reading, tutees are encouraged to choose material above their independent reading level. Tutees will not benefit if they select easy books within their own independent reading level. But of course, the material must not be above the independent reading level of the tutor.

The pair can use the "five finger test" of readability, which consists of the following procedure: open a random page in the book, spread five fingers, place fingertips on the page at random, and attempt to read the five words. If after repeating it on another four pages, the tutor has struggled on more than one word in total, the book will be too hard. If the tutee struggles to read more than 10 words, the book will be too hard.

6.1.5. Paired Reading procedure

The tutoring session is organised following the PR procedure, as presented in Figure 6.1.

Reading together and alone: Two different ways of reading are proposed depending on the difficulty experienced by the tutee. For difficult sections, tutors support tutees by Reading Together – both members of the pair read all the words out loud together, with the tutor modulating their speed to match that of the tutee, while giving a good model of competent reading.

When an easy section of text is encountered, the tutee may wish to read a little without the support of Reading Together. At the start, the tutor and tutee agree on a way for the tutee to signal for the tutor to stop Reading Together. This could be a knock, a sign, a nudge, or a squeeze. When the tutee signals, the tutor stops reading out loud right away, while praising the tutee for being so confident. Sooner or later while Reading Alone the tutee will make an error which they cannot self-correct within four seconds (see below). Then the tutor applies the usual correction procedure and joins back in Reading Together.

Correct errors. A very simple and ubiquitously applicable correction procedure is prescribed. When the tutee reads a word wrong, the tutor just tells the tutee the correct way to read the word. After the tutee repeats this correctly, the pair carries on. However, tutors should not jump in and put the correct word straight away. The guideline is that tutors pause and give the tutees four seconds to see if they will correct themselves. Tutees will not learn to self-correct if they are not provided with the opportunity to practice this. Holding off for four seconds is, however, not easy for tutors. Therefore, tutors can be encouraged to count slowly to four in their heads before allowing themselves to interrupt.

Evidently, there will be some words neither tutee nor tutor will know, since tutors are not expected to know everything. In this case, tutors must not bluff. If they do not understand, they must communicate this to the tutee. Then the tutee can ask a teacher for help, or the pair can look words up themselves.

Praise. Praise for good reading is essential. Tutors should look pleased nonverbally and provide positive feedback. Praise is particularly required for good reading of hard words, getting all the words in a sentence right and correcting wrong words before the tutor does (self-correction). PR does not proscribe undesirable behaviours (since that is usually ineffective), but instead promotes effective and desirable behaviours which are incompatible with the undesirable ones.

The pair goes on like this, switching from Reading Together to Reading Alone, providing the tutee with just as much support as is needed at any moment.

If the tutee has chosen a relatively hard book, more Reading Together will be needed, and less Reading Alone. If the tutee has chosen a relatively easier book, less Reading Together will be needed and there will be more Reading Alone.

Discussion. Pairs are encouraged to talk about the book, to develop shared enthusiasm and to ensure that the tutee really understands the content (without making it seem like a test). During and after reading, pairs should talk about the pictures; talk about interesting words, ideas or events; talk at natural breaks, such as at the end of a sentence, paragraph, page or section, or when the tutee might lose track; predict what might happen next; review the main ideas or events at the end of chapters and at the end of the book.

Monitoring progress. PR emphasises self-checking. A simple form of self-recording is desirable, and both members of the pair should participate in this. Periodic checking of these records by the coordinating professional takes relatively little time, but is highly valuable in creating a culture of all working together.

If the time is available, direct observation of the pair in action, either in school or at their home, can be extremely revealing and diagnostically helpful. This can be done on an individual basis with a pair who has a particular difficulty, or in a group setting at a more general "booster" meeting. You can find samples of resources which will be helpful at www.tes.com/article.aspx?storyCode=6339142.

6.1.6. Benefits of Paired Reading

The Paired Reading method has a number of advantages. Some of these are common to other methods of working with parents or peers in order to support students with reading, but many are specific to the PR method. First, PR obviously increases the amount of reading practice, which can probably be considered as one of the most important factors in reading progress. Practice consolidates a skill, promotes fluency and minimises forgetting. Crucially, PR ensures that this practice is positive and successful. Second, PR includes both modelling and scaffolding of correct reading, and consequently also provides a bridge between listening comprehension and independent reading comprehension. Good and weak readers typically differ much less in listening comprehension than they do in independent reading comprehension. Simultaneous reading and listening, as in Reading Together, is likely to free the struggling reader from a preoccupation with laborious decoding and enables other substantive reading strategies to come into play. If the 'limited processing capacity' of the weaker reader is totally devoted to accurate word recognition or phonic analysis and synthesis, no processing capacity is left to deploy other more content-related strategies, such as using contextual clues.

However, while Reading Alone, the tutees are free to use whatever reading strategies they wish at any moment, strategically deploying a range of decoding or psycholinguistic strategies from word to word or sentence to sentence. They may use strategies they have been explicitly taught or strategies they have developed for themselves. Nevertheless, if they cannot select and successfully apply a strategy with the speed and fluency dictated by the four-second pause, the feedback and support of Reading Together switches in before the tutee becomes disconnected from the process of extracting meaning from the text.

In conclusion, PR provides modelling, successful practice focusing on the extraction of meaning, scaffolding, feedback, praise and other social reinforcement, and supported opportunities to experiment with the use and effectiveness of a wide range of reading strategies in a wide range of applications. Further, PR also enables tutees to pursue their own interests and motivation; is highly adapted to the individual learner's needs of the moment; promotes learner-managed learning and self-efficacy; eliminates the tutee's fear of failure; and reduces any anxiety and confusion in the tutor.

6.1.7. Empirical evidence on Paired Reading

Paired Reading is one of the most intensively evaluated interventions in education. There has been a great deal of research on PR, particularly in the UK, North America, Australia and New Zealand. By the early 1990s, PR had been the subject of hundreds of studies.

These were reviewed by Topping and Lindsay (1992) and Topping (1995). The general picture in published studies is that Paired Readers progress at about 4.2 times the "normal" rates in reading accuracy on tests during the initial period of commitment. Gains in reading comprehension appear to be even larger.

You can find a synthesis of recent studies in Topping, Duran and Van Keer (2016) – including not only small-scale studies and situations where teachers volunteered or self-selected to participate. For example, the Fife Peer Learning Project deployed peer tutoring in reading, encompassing 129 schools (with children aged 9 and 11 years), following children for two years (involving teachers from two consecutive classes), randomly allocating intervention types and assessing quality of implementation.

Concerning scores on all kinds of reading tests, short-term evaluations show effectiveness for same-age and cross-age tutoring. As to long-term evaluations, however, cross-age tutoring works better (Tymms, Merrell, Andor, Topping & Thurston, 2011). Although the PR implementation was somewhat variable (Topping, Thurston, McGavock & Colin, 2012), significant pre- to post-test gains in self-esteem were seen in both same-age and cross-age pairs, for both tutees and tutors, but not for students allocated to control groups which did not follow PR (Miller et al., 2010).

Not surprisingly, in a recent review discussing the effectiveness of 20 different interventions in reading, Paired Reading is ranked as one of the most effective (Brooks, 2013). In conclusion, PR has been demonstrated to be effective with thousands of children in hundreds of schools in many different countries. Additionally, implementing PR typically involves very modest additional costs in time and materials, with strong implications for relative cost-effectiveness.

6.2. Duolog Math. Peer tutoring dialogue for thinking in mathematics

Duolog Math is a structured procedure of peer tutoring designed to be applicable to any mathematics curriculum material available in the school, particularly mathematical problem solving. In contrast with other peer tutoring projects mainly prescribing mechanical drill and practice procedures based on paper materials, Duolog Math encourages dialogue on the nature of tutees' thinking in mathematics, with more emphasis on understanding and effective processes than on merely obtaining correct results (Topping, Miller, Murray, Henderson, Fortuna & Conlin, 2011).

6.2.1. Overview and main objectives

The objective for both the tutee and tutor is to highlight the different methods that can be employed when doing maths. Based on previous projects with different names (i.e., Paired Maths or Shared Maths), Duolog Math was developed in the UK, although the name was developed with teachers in Texas, hence the US spelling. You can find information and resources on Duolog Math at www.dundee.ac.uk/esw/research/resources/problemsolving/. Its goal is to help students to connect real-world situations to the abstract language of mathematics.

The interactions are structured in order for the tutor to help the tutee gain a clearer understanding of the solution and the path to the solution. Tutors employ strategies such as questioning, thinking out loud, praising, and summarising and generalising. To facilitate the discussion in the pairs, eight behaviours or strategies for interaction between tutors and tutees are proposed: Read, Listen, Check, Praise, Pause for Think-Aloud, Question, Make it Real, Summarise and Generalise. All these processes are presented in Figure 6.2.

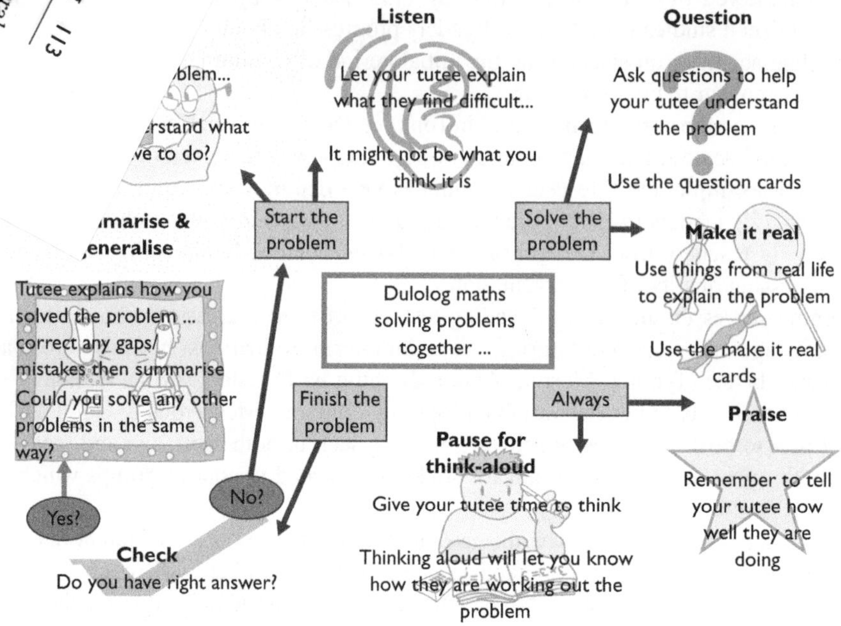

for the classroom

Figure 6.2 Process in Duolog Math.

6.2.2. Pairing students

This method relies on a dialogue between two pupils – tutor and tutee – about a mathematical question. Duolog Math can be used in a cross- or same-age tutoring project. In same-age tutoring, a class is ranked by math ability, divided into tutors above and tutees below the central line, and the most able tutor is matched with the most able tutee, and so on. This implies that in same-age classes, the weakest tutee is helped by an average-achieving tutor. Small matching adjustments can be made on grounds of social compatibility.

6.2.3. Preparing students and the material

Normally teachers train tutors and tutees in the first four relatively easy steps together (read, listen, check, praise and encourage). The second four steps (pause for think-aloud, question, make it real, summarise and generalise) are considerably harder, and teachers may wish to introduce these one week at a time, devoting a mini-lesson to exploration of each behaviour. A description of each behaviour is given below.

'Real-world' problems (also known as 'word' problems) are questions related to a concrete setting, such as, "Bill has five apples and gives Mary three. How many has he left?" or "A lorry is 7m long. A car is 2m long. There are 3 lorries and some cars in a queue. The queue is 33m long. How many cars are in the queue?"

6.2.4. Procedure in Duolog Math

The different steps involved in the Dualog Math procedure (Figure 6.2) are synthesised below. They have to be seen like steps with a relationship between them, rather than ordinated steps in a simple line.

Read. The tutee might be having trouble reading a word problem. If so, the tutor reads it and checks the tutee's understanding.

Listen. The tutor gives tutees time to explain what their difficulty is and then asks them to explain how they might solve it. In this respect, tutors do not just jump in to fix what they assume the problem is.

Check. The tutor checks whether his or her tutee eventually gets an appropriate answer. This, however, requires keeping in mind that there is probably more than one 'right' way to solve the problem. If the answer is wrong, the tutor rereads the problem and the tutee tries again. Only if the tutor support fails (through questioning and making it real), then the tutor shows how do it while thinking aloud.

Praise and Encourage. The tutor has to provide praise and encouragement to their tutee as often as possible, even for a small success with a single step in solving a problem. This is important to keep the tutee's confidence high.

Pause for Think-Aloud. The tutor has to allow their tutee with some thinking time, before expecting an answer. Further, it is important that they encourage tutees to think aloud continually. Only in this case can the tutor detect where and how tutees' thinking is going wrong. In this respect, it is also important to take into account that tutors need time to think as well. Moreover, in case the tutor is not sure how to solve the problem, (s)he has to recognise this and accept it. Tutors are not supposed to know everything.

Question. The tutor has to ask helpful and intelligent questions, which give clues, stimulate and guide tutees' thinking, and challenge their misconceptions. It is important not to say "That's wrong!", but to ask another question to provide a hint. Ask why, for instance. The tutor should try to avoid closed questions requiring only a yes or no answer; questions only relying on memory; questions containing the answer; or the simple "Did you understand that?", expecting a positive answer. Examples of effective questions include the following:

- 'What kind of problem is this?'
- 'What are we trying to find out here?'
- 'Can you state the problem in different words or in a different way?'
- 'What important information do we already have?'
- 'Can we break the problem into parts or steps?'
- 'How did you arrive at that answer?'
- 'Does that make sense?'
- 'Where was the last place you knew you were right?'
- 'Where do you think you might have gone wrong?'
- 'What kind of mistake do you think you might have made?'

Make It Real. The tutor has to try to make the problem seem real and related to the life of their tutee. A possible way to do this is to ask the tutee to imagine what the problem would look like in real life. The following are some ideas to try:

- Use previous knowledge: make tutees think of what they have learned before or problems they have solved before, relevant to the current problem.
- Simplify the problem: work through a similar but simpler problem; or make up a similar problem using the student's own name and try to use everyday language.
- Connect the problem with life: ask tutees to reflect on how the problem can be related to people, places, events and experiences in their home/community life (or those of someone they know or have seen on television).

- Use supports: encourage tutees to use fingers, counters, cubes, sticks or any other objects to show the reality of the problem; have them draw dots, a picture, a list, table, diagram, graph or map.
- Work with supports: with the tutee's permission, mark their notes with lines, arrows, colours or numbering to help them.

Summarise and Generalise. The tutor has to help their tutee to summarise the key strategies and steps in solving the problem. First, the tutor points out any errors or gaps and summarises the key strategies. Then, the tutor and tutee talk about how what is learned can be applied to another similar problem (generalising it to another maths question) or how the learning might be useful in a wider context.

6.2.5. Evidence from the research

In exploratory studies (Topping, 2005b; Topping et al., 2003) Duolog Math showed relatively good effectiveness, taking into account the difficulties in developing a math tutoring procedure not purely focused on 'drills and skills'. The results of a two-year randomised controlled trial in 86 schools (Topping, Miller, Murray & Conlin, 2011), however, showed effectiveness, but difficulties with teachers introducing the problem, suggesting ways to concretise the problem and holding plenary sessions. Crucially, it appeared that there was very little summarising or generalising, which improved in the second intervention year. The latter implies that well-thought-out teacher training is needed.

Further, it is important to mention that some studies point at the effectiveness of Duolog Math, but only for specific groups of students. Topping et al. (2011) found significant pre- to post-test gains in mathematics attainment compared with students not participating, but this was however only the case for cross-age tutoring and girls and especially for low-performing students. Improving the quality of the practice could extend these results.

6.3. E-tutoring: International online reciprocal peer tutoring for the improvement of linguistic abilities in Spanish and English

E-tutoring is an international online reciprocal peer tutoring project between teachers and researchers from the University of Dundee (Scotland) and Universitat Autònoma de Barcelona (Catalonia).

6.3.1. Overview and main objectives

The project seeks to improve Spanish and English language competence, taking advantage of the knowledge differences among students in their respective languages by means of information and communication technology.

The objectives are to improve reading comprehension in students' first language (L1) – when students act as tutors, learning by offering feedback – and to enhance writing skills in a foreign or second language (L2) – when acting as tutees, learning through the feedback received to improve their texts. In a virtual platform, students exchanged their texts with their international peers and received feedback to improve the text. More particularly, each student was required to write five texts in L2 and improve these based on the corrections received from their international peers, and in turn correct five texts from their partner, using their first language.

6.3.2. Pairing students, contact time, place and position

Students aged 9–12 from Scotland and Catalonia were paired to act as tutors in their own language and as tutees in English (in the case of the Catalan students) and in Spanish (in the case of the Scottish students). Thus the project opts for reciprocal peer tutoring. This means, for instance, that the Scottish student with the best marks in English reading comprehension is paired with the Catalan student with the best marks in Spanish reading comprehension. The schools work on the project for four hours per week during five weeks. Students interact through a virtual learning platform, each with an individual password.

6.3.3. Preparing students and the material

First, students receive information as to which kind of errors they need to detect in their tutees' texts. Tutors do not need to correct all of them, but select errors while keeping the following in mind: the fact that errors are an excellent opportunity to learn; the degree of tutees' knowledge; the nature of the error, prioritising communicative or repetitive mistakes, and remembering that tutees also have the support of their peers, text materials and their teacher.

The most important point in the tutor training is that students must avoid giving the answer or simply correcting when finding an error, because this does not allow tutees to learn by correcting their own mistakes. Instead, tutors have to point out the error and provide clues about how it can be corrected. The key is that tutors learn different levels of support and offer the least support possible in order to help their tutees to identify and correct the error by themselves. The lowest level of support is just to point out the error. More support is given when tutors mark the error and provide prompts. See, for example, Table 6.1.

Table 6.1 Levels of support for correcting errors in E-tutoring

1. Mark the error when you think that your partner will be able to correct it by himself/herself
1.1 Relating to the text (e.g., improve the cohesion between paragraphs)
1.2 Relating to the paragraph (e.g., on two occasions there is a comma between the subject and verb)
1.3 Relating to the sentence (e.g., you know how to say goodbye)
1.4 Relating to the speech (e.g., there is a typographical error)
2. Mark the error and provide a prompt. How can I give him/her prompts?
2.1 *Reminding*: refer to an error that has been corrected in the past (e.g., Do you remember how to say hello?)
2.2 *Questioning*: question your partner to give them a clue to help them identify the error and the answer… –about the error characteristics (e.g., she is not a girl?) –about the strategy to use in order to detect it (e.g., Why you don't read the phrase again? Have you reviewed this paragraph? Does it sound good?)
2.3 *Explaining*: provide some information about the use of language that helps to correct the error (e.g., You cannot put a comma between the subject and the verb)
2.4 Provide *opportunities to practice*, with examples or short texts (e.g., using an error bank).

Finally, the tutor training teaches tutors to encourage their tutees. Tutors have to be aware that they will be asking tutees to make an effort in correcting errors and in improving and rewriting texts. It is therefore important to encourage tutees to recognise the effort made. This can be done by pointing at aspects of the text that are good or have being improved (e.g., "Brilliant, you have learned to write the adjectives after the name") or by giving encouragement for the effort (e.g., "Good, every time you are putting more work into it").

6.3.4. Procedure

The project is developed through six implementation phases, described below.

Training of two teachers from each school (i.e., the English and Spanish language teachers) by researchers involved in each university – the training includes peer tutoring and technology resources.

Initial assessment of linguistic competence. All the students are evaluated in reading comprehension in L1 and in writing ability in L2.

Creation of international pairs. From the results of the initial assessment, matched pairs are created taking into account students' first-language proficiency, in which they will act as tutors.

Initial student training enables students to develop their tutor and tutee roles efficiently, making use of the virtual platform which hosts all exchanges. During this training, students learn strategies to correct the texts when acting as tutors.

Exchange of texts. The writing assignment consists of free texts chosen by the students. However, if necessary, teachers can offer guidance or thematic vocabulary. A text is exchanged every week – the text is written, sent, commented on with feedback by the tutor for correction, improved by the tutee and resent to the peer tutor. This process is repeated until each student has sent a total of five texts in L2, responded to feedback and resent an improved version; and has received five texts in their L1 and given feedback for correction. The project recommends teachers create a "bank of mistakes" in the classroom, where the students list the common errors found and construct explanations and examples. This activity helps tutors to improve their level of knowledge and promotes meta-linguistic reflection in their own language.

Final assessment of linguistic competence. To detect improvements in the learning objectives, students are evaluated again on reading comprehension in L1 and on writing in L2.

6.3.5. Evidence from the research

Preliminary studies on this project showed how Internet technology can be leveraged with reciprocal peer tutoring to enhance language learning taking advantage of intercultural differences (Dekhinet, Topping, Duran & Blanch, 2008). The use of the computer as a means to engage students in authentic situations contributed to increased motivation and engagement in learning, and improved writing (Duran, Blanch, Dekhinet & Topping, 2010). In another study, including more schools and using a comparison group, students involved in the project showed improvements in both language abilities and attitudes towards L2 (Thurston, Duran, Cunningham, Blanch & Topping, 2009).

A qualitative analysis (Duran, Blanch, Thurston & Topping, 2010) of the process of error correction found large differences between tutors in their spontaneous feedback. For this reason, subsequent research (Blanch, Corcelles, Duran, Dekhinet & Topping, 2014), studied the effects on learning with different levels of tutor support, after training tutors in scaffolding feedback as explained above. The results showed the effectiveness of the project for the improvement of linguistic abilities in both languages, but with differences in relation to the kind of feedback provided. More particularly, a paradox appeared (Topping et al., 2013): the more the tutor learned (by providing feedback with a greater level of support, including resolving the error), the less the tutee learned. At the same time, the opposite also applied: the more the tutee learned (when receiving less structured feedback, requiring tutee action), the less the tutor learned.

A possible origin of this paradox may lie in the fact that the asynchronous nature of the peer interaction in this project did not allow for real time interaction, which is possibly more effective in ensuring accurate and adjusted feedback from tutor to tutee. A possible way to resolve this paradox could be to ask tutors to prepare rich support but give it only when the tutee asks for more help. Online peer tutoring is an extremely interesting area, and projects like this will increase in the future. However, they are dependent on the development of technology and the access in schools to computers.

6.4. Reading in Pairs: peer tutoring for oral expression and reading comprehension in English as a foreign language

Reading in Pairs comprises of a set of materials shaping an educational programme that uses peer tutoring in the school between two students, and at home between a family member and a student (Duran, Flores, Oller, Thomson-Garay & Vera, 2016).

6.4.1. Overview and main objectives

The main objective of the programme is to improve the reading comprehension and oral language skills in English as a foreign language among students of primary (10–12 years old) or secondary (12–14 years old) education. These materials (more information and free resources at http://grupsderecerca.uab.cat/grai/en/node/3882) are adjustable to the school context and needs, and must allow schools to generate new interventions in order to achieve the following objectives:

- Providing teachers with inclusive methodologies. Peer tutoring provides the opportunity of seeing diversity as a positive opportunity. Knowledge of English in multilingual societies is extremely variable, depending on students' home language, their exposure to English, whether they receive extra classes or not, and so on.
- Developing new instruction techniques for English as L2. Peer tutoring and family involvement can enhance teaching and learning interventions for linguistic competence, as they provide numerous opportunities for oral interaction.
- Improving students' speaking skills and reading competence (especially reading comprehension). Well-organised work on reading comprehension strategies can ease the challenge. Moreover, increasing exposure to oral communication provides students with more opportunities to develop their oral skills.
- Encouraging cooperation among students. Beyond cooperation for learning, cooperation is a really valuable competence, because it develops social skills and basic attitudes for democratic life and for the knowledge society we live in.
- Fostering family involvement in school activities. Schools can offer more opportunities for family participation, giving parents the possibility (after initial training) to become tutors

of their children at home. In the case where parents have little knowledge of English, it is useful to interchange the roles; that is, children can act as tutors of their parents as well.

6.4.2. Pairing students, contact time, place and position

After an individual evaluation of students' reading comprehension in English as L2, teachers rank each student according to his or her marks within the class group. Next, this list is divided in two, and student 1 of the first half is paired to student 1 from the other half, and so on. If two or more groups of students from the same age are participating in the programme, all students will be ranked in one single list before pairing them.

With students of the same class, there is the possibility of opting for reciprocal peer tutoring, in which tutor and tutee alternate roles in each session or every week. In this approach, reciprocal tutoring requires matching pairs in such a way that students have a similar level of competence. Consequently, following the example of the above listing, student 1 will be paired with student 2; student 3 with student 4, and so on.

6.4.3. Preparing students and material

Students receive three training sessions before starting the tutoring sessions to learn the programme principles, the structure of the interaction (which is explained in the next section), the materials, and the features and the functions of the roles. Families receive training through a meeting with the teachers. The programme attempts to create authentic situations of reading comprehension and oral expression, on the basis of actual texts extracted from the everyday environment of the students. These texts are the basis for *Activity Sheets* that outline the activities of the session. An example of an Activity Sheet is presented in Figure 6.3.

These Activity Sheets, accompanied with an audio file (on which a native speaker reads the text aloud) and language support (i.e., structures to help the conversation and answer the questions), is presented to the tutors some days in advance of the tutoring. Tutors use these materials at home to prepare the session they will have with their tutees: reading the text; listening to the audio file, paying special attention to intonation and pronunciation; understanding the text and the questions about it, and also answering the questions; being aware of possible unexpected questions from their tutees; thinking about other questions to ask their tutees taking into account their interests, knowledge, feelings, and so on. The main idea is that students can keep the conversation going in the L2 language, avoiding transferring to L1.

The aim of the Activity Sheets is to serve as examples for the tutors in order to allow them – once they are familiar with the formats, text characteristics and the variety of activities – to develop similar materials, under the teacher's guidance and supervision. Although a resource bank for teachers is offered (i.e., sheets for different courses, self-assessment guidelines, etc.), it is recommended that teachers adapt and adjust the materials to their reality, school and students.

6.4.4. Procedure

After the initial training, the peer tutoring sessions take place. The programme includes 24 sessions at the school and 24 sessions at home with the families. Each peer tutoring session takes place in a highly structured interaction, that makes it easy for both members of the pair to know what they have to do at all times. Once the pair have learned to perform the tasks derived from their respective roles, control of the activity will be gradually transferred, encouraging a more free and creative use.

ACTIVITY SHEET (number) _____   LEVEL _____

Before reading...
Looking at the title and the author, what do you think you are going to read? Do you know anything about the text or the author? Have you ever heard it? Where? In your opinion, does it seem an optimistic or pessimistic text? Why?

DON'T WORRY, BE HAPPY!
By Bobby McFerrin

Here's a little song I wrote
You might want to sing it note for note
Don't worry be happy
In every life we have some trouble
When you worry you make it double
Don't worry, be happy
(Don't worry, be happy)

Don't worry, be happy (x3)

Ain't got no place to lay your head
Somebody came and took your bed
Don't worry, be happy

The landlord say your rent is late
He may have to litigate
Don't worry, be happy
(Look at me I am happy)

Don't worry, be happy
Here I give you my phone number
When you worry call me
I make you happy

Don't worry, be happy
Ain't got no cash, ain't got no style
Ain't got no girl to make you smile
But don't worry be happy
Cause when you worry

Your face will frown
And that will bring everybody down
So don't worry, be happy
(don't worry, be happy)

CHORUS

Don't worry
Don't worry don't do it, be happy
Put a smile on your face
Don't bring everybody down like this

Don't worry
It will soon pass whatever it is
Don't worry, be happy
I'm not worried, I'm happy

http://www.lyricsondemand.com/onehitwonders/dontworrybehappylyrics.html

---

Reading comprehension

1. Which detail gave you the clue to know what kind of text is? Did your opinion about the text (optimistic/pessimistic) change after reading it? Why? Give examples.
2. Could you sum up in two lines the main idea the text offers?
3. Do you know the meaning of "ain't"? Choose one of the options.
   a. There isn't ...
   b. You haven't got ...
   c. It isn't ...
4. Taking into account the information in the text, decide if the next sentences are True or False:
   a. To solve your problems you should be worry.
   b. If you are worry will bring everybody down.
   c. The author is happy.
   d. It's important to put a smile in our faces.
   e. If you have a trouble, it will continue for a long time.
5. Is there any word or expression in the text you don't understand? Try to understand it by the context. If you can't, look it up in the dictionary.
6. The author uses the adjective "little" two times in the text. Try to find them and explain the connection between them.
7. Make a list of the problems that appeared in the text. Which are the most relevant for you? Why?

(Continued)

(Continued)

> 8. Do you think that people, like the author, should say how to feel to others? Could he be not so happy? What is your opinion? Why?
>
> **Extra activities**
>
> 1. Look on the Internet for the song and listen to it. What do you think about the melody? Is it appropriate to the lyrics? Is it a happy melody? Do you think that music can modify your feelings? What kind of music do you feel happy with? And sad?
> 2. You can sing the song with your classmates.

Figure 6.3 Activity Sheet example of Reading in Pairs.

The first 15 minutes of every peer tutoring session deals with reading. The pair is requested to explore the characteristics of the text (i.e., format, title, structure, source etc.) to make a hypothesis or prediction about the text content and to think about what they know or do not know yet (i.e., anticipating potential problems that can be found). In short, the pairs activate their prior knowledge on the topic.

Reading tasks start with the tutors reading aloud, while acting as a model. They can do this as a result of their previous preparation of the text and the audio file. This task is really important because it is related to L2, and we need to offer a good oral model to tutees.

Afterwards, both students read the text aloud and tutors check the speed, pronunciation and intonation. Then, the tutee reads alone, while tutors apply the Pause, Prompt, Praise (PPP) technique (Wheldall & Colmar, 1990). In this technique, tutors indicate any error to tutees, they wait a few seconds in order to provide tutees with the opportunity to correct themselves and, in case tutees do not self-correct, tutors offer a prompt or several prompts. If tutees do not manage to self-correct, tutors finally offer the right answer. Reading always ends up with positive social reinforcement from tutors: an expression of support or a gesture of encouragement.

In the next 15 minutes, the activities focus on text understanding. After reflecting on whether the initial prediction of the text content has been fulfilled or not, the tutor helps the tutee to discover unknown words (often by means of contextual text information) which he or she has previously prepared (e.g., using the dictionary). Further, the main ideas in the text are identified and some activities with different difficulty levels are tackled (see the example of an Activity Sheet in the Figure 6.3). Some activities simply require retrieving information; others require some interpretation; and finally (the most interesting) some bring into play the pair's reflection, since they have to infer or assess information that does not appear in the text. The last few minutes of the session the students are engaged in expressive reading. In this case, after having achieved a thorough understanding of the meaning of the text, the tutee reads the text aloud for the last time.

6.4.5. Pair self-assessment and group processing

Every four sessions or two weeks, the pairs evaluate their progress. By means of a Pair Self-Assessment Guideline, both pair members assess different aspects of their reading and reading comprehension. This self-assessment also considers the tutor's performance: explanations, reinforcement, modelling and control. In addition, students are asked to propose objectives for the next sessions. These proposed new aims can range from reviewing complementary content to improving relational aspects and increasing attention.

The assessment of students' progress when participating in Reading
information from different sources, namely, Initial individual assessment;
Pair self-assessment guideline; Observing pairs through an Observation grid; Ac
prepared by tutors; portfolios of student learning; and final individual assessment.

6.4.6. Evidence from the research

The effectiveness of Reading in Pairs has strong evidence from practices in Catalan, Spanish and Basque. Research on these practices revealed good results in reading comprehension (Moliner, Flores & Duran, 2011; Flores & Duran, 2013) and fluency (Valdebenito & Duran, 2015) for all students, regardless of their age and role. Further, research also indicated improvement in reader self-concept for tutors (Flores & Duran, 2016) and pointed towards possibilities for families to act as reading tutors, even though it remains challenging to reach the families of the most disadvantaged children (Blanch, Duran, Valdebenito & Flores, 2013). Finally, research also refers to the effectiveness of teacher training on the Reading in Pairs programme based on school networks (Duran & Utset, 2014).

As to the effectiveness of Reading in Pairs in English as a foreign language, a study on a network of 15 primary and secondary schools shows positive evidence for improved reading comprehension and oral competence (Duran et al., 2016). Notwithstanding the fact that the study did not have a control group, the results show statistically significant reading comprehension improvements for all students, regardless of their specific role in the pair (i.e., tutor or tutee) and the type of tutoring (i.e., fixed role or reciprocal).

Teachers and students pointed out that the programme structure helped achieve these positive results. Moreover, reading several times during the session favoured the improvement of reading, in both intonation and pronunciation. Further, both teachers and students referred to the power of the development of the tutors' role, involving prior preparation of the texts (with the audio file), the vocabulary, and the correct pronunciation, as well as the responsibility of being tutor and acting as a good model for the tutee. An analysis of the interaction from a sample of pairs reveals the interdependence generated between students in the pairs, which promoted commitment. The individual effort made undoubtedly contributed to the success in the progress of the pair.

Regarding students' progress in oral expression, the research results show improvements for fixed tutoring, regardless of the role of the students. More particularly, temporal analysis of the interaction of a sample of pairs revealed that 42 per cent of the time, students were conducting the conversation in English (Duran et al., 2016). This implies that for between a third and half of the session students were speaking English in an act of real communication and with an active audience (i.e., the other student of the pair), which would be impossible to achieve in a traditional classroom.

6.5. ClassWide Peer Tutoring. Reciprocal peer tutoring and group reinforcement for basic academic skills

ClassWide Peer Tutoring (CWPT) is a specific type of reciprocal peer tutoring originally developed by researchers in the context of the Juniper Gardens Children's Project at the University of Kansas, in collaboration with regular classroom teachers, to improve the acquisition and retention of basic academic skills (Arreaga-Mayer, Terry & Greenwood, 1998). It has been successfully applied to passage reading, sight-word reading, reading comprehension,

, science and social studies instruction, from kindergar-

itoring with group reinforcement, taking advantage of
ational features. More particularly, after students are
ntire classroom is divided into two equal-ability teams
ig team by earning the most points during the tutoring

dural components of CWPT.

6.5.2. Pairing students, contact time, place and position

Depending on instructional goals, students are paired either randomly, matched by ability (same or different skill levels), or matched by language proficiency. When the subject content area relies on the tutors' unaided ability to identify errors (when, for instance, answers are not available to the tutor), ability matching of pairs is recommended. Since pairs are assigned to one of two teams for which they earn points, teachers should be careful to ensure that both teams are equally balanced with high- and low-performing students.

6.5.3. Preparing students and the material

Students are taught by their teacher to implement the tutoring procedures in four short lessons in which the procedures are described, modelled, role-played and practiced. This prior training includes sportsmanship (i.e., winning and losing teams), working with a partner and being in the role of a peer tutor or tutee.

Teachers have to define a set of materials appropriate for the class that has not been mastered yet. The content selected is based on the curriculum through reviewing grade-level scope, organising a hierarchical sequence and updating this sequence based on students' weekly pre-test and post-test performance.

The material (e.g., a social sciences text, a list of multiplication facts in math) is read aloud by the tutee to the tutor, and then they review the material using teacher-developed study guides (i.e., with questions, fill-in-the-blanks, fill-in-a-map, and so on).

6.5.4. Procedure

In the first 10 minutes of the CWPT session, each tutor presents the first item (e.g., word, equation, question) from the list to be learned by the tutee. The tutee responds both orally and in writing. At this time, the tutor monitors and assesses the correctness of the responses.

Tutees earn points based on the correctness of their answers. The tutor awards two points for every correct answer. As soon as the tutee makes an error in a response, the tutor provides the correct answer for the tutee as a model. One point is awarded for tutees correctly practicing an assisted answer three times in both the oral and written form. Each student performs their specific role for a specified amount of time (e.g., 10 minutes). At the end of that time, the students switch roles, allowing the same amount of time for the new tutee to earn points and to be more directly involved with the content in the responding role. At the end of the second round of tutoring, the points earned from all members of both teams are added together to determine the winning team of the day.

In CWPT, pre-tests and post-tests are used to monitor the academic effects of the weekly tutoring sessions and the mastery of the material. From the results, the teacher can make optimal adjustments in the difficulty level of new material and demonstrate that peer tutoring improves mastery or fluency levels compared to previous instructional formats. You can find more information at www.specialconnections.ku.edu/~kucrl/cgi-bin/drupal/?q=instruction/classwide_peer_tutoring.

6.5.5. Evidence from the research

According to the authors, the success of CWPT lies mainly in seven basic operational components:

1. Multi-modality format. The peer tutoring process incorporates each of the various learning modalities or styles by which children learn. The students "hear", "see", "say" and "write" their responses, and each individual student determines their strongest modality.
2. Reciprocal and distributed practice. Reciprocal tutoring provides active engagement and repeated practice for all students.
3. Immediate error correction and feedback. CWPT attempts to achieve "errorless" learning by stopping the tutee as soon as they say or write anything that is incorrect, providing immediate feedback and correct responses.
4. Game format with partner pairing and competing teams. CWPT provides a vehicle to cooperate with a peer and to compete in teams, which mixes both kinds of motivation and increases opportunities to respond.
5. Built-in reinforcement. Reinforcement occurs when students verbally reinforce one another for good work during tutoring, when the teacher acknowledges exceptional tutoring behaviours and offers classroom intrinsic reinforcement for the winning team each day. This feature provides an opportunity for students to feel good about themselves and to develop and be engaged in more appropriate social skills.
6. High mastery levels. Adjusting the grade-level materials to personal student characteristics, every student can achieve high mastery in their level, which provides daily awareness of individual learning progress.
7. Measured outcomes. Weekly outcomes (evidenced in the pre- and post-test assessments that are given at the very beginning of every new unit of material to be taught) and daily outcomes (evidenced in the points earned and the written documents produced during the tutoring sessions) provide a solid foundation for monitoring learning and overall academic improvement.

Classroom-based research studies since 1980 have demonstrated that students are able to learn more in less time using CWPT when compared to conventional forms of teacher-directed instruction. The tutoring process increases students' time on task and improves academic performance. Reading, spelling, vocabulary and maths have been documented extensively. Moreover, a lot of research has focused on students with special needs (Arreaga-Mayer, Terry & Greenwood, 1998).

The combination of cooperative and competitive motivation can yield good results. However, it is necessary to keep in mind that competitive reinforcement can depress intrinsic interest in an academic activity (Chun & Winter, 1999).

The good results based on the abovementioned different components of CWPT explain the widespread use of this practice and have promoted research on technology-based teacher support tools (Abbott, Greenwood, Buzhardt & Tapia, 2006). More particularly, a CWPT Learning Management System, including a web environment, e-mail communication and interactive multimedia resources has been developed to support teachers' and schools' use of CWPT.

6.6. Reciprocal peer tutoring in teacher education to learn and practise teaching

For a long time, different peer tutoring formats have been reported in North American and British universities (Goodlad & Hirst, 1989), as well as research evidence of their effectiveness (Topping, 1996). These practices have been extended to other geographical and cultural contexts, such as the Latin American context. Every day, peer tutoring practices are becoming more frequent in these contexts, especially practices related to Proctoring (academic orientation by last-year students acting as tutors of freshmen) (Duran & Flores, 2015). Same-age tutoring, however, is less common in this context.

For this reason, we present an institutionalised project at Universidad Autónoma Benito Juárez in Oaxaca (Mexico) which uses reciprocal peer tutoring, allowing students of education to act as peer tutors in a teaching unit. Through experiencing peer tutoring, the incorporation of this methodology into the resources of future teachers is expected.

6.6.1. Overview and main objectives

One of the main study areas of a bachelor's degree in foreign languages at Universidad Autónoma Benito Juárez is called *Fundamentos* (Basics), which introduces students to general aspects of education, helping them to position themselves in their job as a future teacher. This study area is composed of three subjects (i.e., school culture, educational theory and educational psychology) in the first two semesters, at the start of the degree. The subject selected to initiate students into peer tutoring practices was school culture, consisting of 5 hours per week. Of these weekly 5 hours, students spend 2 hours in a group, including 12 peer tutoring sessions, while the other 3 hours are occupied with supervision, partially used to help tutors to plan the session.

The school culture subject is followed by more than 40 students between 18 and 20 years old, most of them women, with great ethnic and cultural diversity. The peer tutoring practice has the following objectives:

1 To promote reflection in students so that they become aware of the importance of peer learning as a teaching resource
2 To offer students the opportunity to act as peer tutors, practising effective teaching performance
3 To act both as tutor and tutee, offering and receiving adjusted teaching aid, leading to both content learning and reflection on the educational practice of peer tutoring

6.6.2. Pairing students, contact time, place and position

Students are matched in pairs, self-selecting another peer they feel comfortable with. Every pair decides who will be the tutor in the first session. The aim is that peer tutoring sessions take place in a good working atmosphere, with students focusing on their teacher occasionally helping some tutors and making observations.

6.6.3. Preparing students and the material

Arousing students' awareness on their role of peer teachers – the first activity uses a questionnaire to promote reflection and help students to become aware of the educational relevance of peer support, based on their own everyday experiences. Sometimes the daily nature of acts makes difficult to reflect on them. Awareness of the importance and effectiveness of educational peer support can help future teachers to understand peer learning as a powerful instructional resource to be used in their future classes. More particularly, a guide consisting of questions promotes student reflection on the informal support given to peers and on its effects as a pedagogical help – both for who receives it (i.e., tutee) as well as for who provides it (i.e., tutor) – and on the limitations and opportunities of the practice as an instructional classroom method.

This introspection allows the emergence of case stories of informal practices of peer tutoring, as a frequent and effective way of learning. However, it is common that when students are asked about the importance of incorporating peer learning as an instructional strategy in the classroom, they report little conviction in implementation. This initial perception is intended to be changed through the peer tutoring practice.

6.6.4. Initial tutor training in conceptual basis, communication and planning

In order to guarantee in-depth peer tutoring (in terms of internalising it and applying it in their professional future) and student success in their tutor and tutee role, two sessions of two hours are devoted to reviewing the conceptual basis of peer tutoring and highlighting communication skills. Peer interaction requires effective dialogue, from which flows student learning. For this reason, pairs reflect on communication and interpersonal relationships, active listening and the basic tools for effective communication.

In addition, as tutors' main responsibility is focused on the preparation of the theme on which they should offer help, two more sessions are dedicated to the basic elements of planning a class. In these sessions, the teacher models the planning of content and activities. The training objectives of the 12 sessions of the teaching unit selected to develop the experience are presented in Table 6.2.

Table 6.2 Educational objectives of peer tutoring sessions

Session	Educational objective
1	Analysing the sources of evaluation in the classroom.
2	Analysing the sources of evaluation in the classroom: the teacher.
3	Analysing the sources of evaluation in the classroom: the students.
4	Analysing the sources of evaluation in the classroom: the self-assessment.

(Continued)

Table 6.2 Educational objectives of peer tutoring sessions (*Continued*)

Session	Educational objective
5	Learn about the forms of communication of the results of evaluation and their impact.
6	Reflect on the impact of private student evaluation.
7	Analyse how students adapt to institutional expectations and the consequences of disobeying the rules.
8	Recognise that personal qualities are object to evaluation and analyse how students themselves do it.
9	Describe and analyse the assessment of personal qualities of the students by the teacher.
10	Observe assessments of academic degree, institutional adaptation and personal qualities when they occur at the same time.
11	Reflect on the positive or negative weighting of the assessment.
12	Observe and analyse how evaluation emotionally impacts the students.

Students are informed of the fact that the control of the planning of teaching and learning activities will gradually be transferred to them, as long as the tutoring sessions go on. For the six sessions, when each pair member will act as a tutor, the transfer of control is agreed upon.

6.6.5. Procedure

After preparing students and creating the pairs, the reciprocal peer tutoring sessions begin. There is gradual transfer of control. The peer tutors progressively take charge of the planning, following this sequence:

- Sessions 1 and 2: the teacher provides teaching and learning activities that tutors should use.
- Sessions 3 and 4: the teacher offers different learning activities that tutors should select and use.
- Session 5: the tutor designs learning activities from information or resources offered by the teacher.
- Session 6: the tutor looks for information and resources to design his or her own learning activities.

Through this gradual transfer of control in planning, in the last session the tutors reach a level of control and responsibility similar to the teachers'. Obviously, tutors still receive support from the teacher. During the supervision time, specific sessions are scheduled for this purpose. Thus, during supervision, tutors are planning the sessions, while tutees – who acted as tutors during the previous session – review the comments of their peers and work on improvement actions.

Reflection on academic difficulties. At the end of each session, tutors stay somewhat longer to share their feelings and reflect on the academic difficulties raised. During these moments, a gradually increasing perception of learning is noticed. The more tutoring sessions go on and the more tutors' responsibility increases, the more they feel they are learning.

Relational and content evaluation. The continuous and formative evaluation of tutoring sessions covers two aspects: the relationship between the pair and the mastery of learning content. With a view to improving tutors' teaching performance, the assessment takes into account the critical perception of the tutee at the end of every session. When the session is finished and tutors gather with the teacher to reflect on their work, tutees individually value and evaluate the performance of their tutor (i.e., both relational and content aspects). The teacher, who also had the opportunity to observe the tutors, compares both observations and evaluations and provides feedback to the tutors.

Individual exam. Finally, an individual exam evaluates the content domain, referring to the teaching unit worked through peer tutoring sessions.

6.6.6. Evidence from the research

Evaluation of this project (Duran & Huerta, 2008) shows that the point of departure at which students doubted the effectiveness of peer learning (while recognising their spontaneous use of it) was modified at the end of the experience. Learning by teaching a peer allowed them to see the opportunities of this method. With regard to the second objective – namely, offering student teachers opportunities to act as teachers – this project shows an economical and accessible way to practice teaching and at the same time provide personalised attention for tutees. The educational reflection promoted by this peer tutoring practice offered students the chance not only to act as a teacher, but also to get feedback from their tutees and the supervising teacher. It allowed students to become aware of necessary improvements in their teacher training.

6.7. Reciprocal peer tutoring to develop student's metacognitive regulation

Recent views on learning and instruction highlight the need for self-regulated and lifelong learning as essential for active and effective participation in our knowledge society. Especially in higher education, students are required to apply metacognitive regulation due to the organisational structures at this educational level (i.e., large groups of students, large amounts of learning content, time pressure, less individual support from staff, etc.) and the depth of expectation associated with academic assignments (Nota, Soresi & Zimmerman, 2004).

Unfortunately, however, higher-education students' metacognitive regulation (i.e., planning, orientation, monitoring and evaluation) is often insufficient to adequately self-regulate their learning (Nota et al., 2004). This is a problem, since adequate metacognitive regulation enhances learning, understanding and performance (Winne, 2011; Zimmerman, 2002). Fostering students' metacognitive regulation is therefore an important educational objective.

6.7.1. Overview and main objectives

Same-age reciprocal peer tutoring in small groups was introduced in a first-year course for students in the Educational Sciences programme at Ghent University (Belgium). It concerns a formal component of the 5-credit compulsory course "Instructional Sciences". Two typical characteristics of same-age reciprocal peer tutoring apply here: (1) reciprocal peer tutoring allows for intensive metacognitive modelling by a peer tutor, and (2) its rotation of assigning the tutor role among learners prevents peer tutors from being too directive in regulating the group's learning. Within reciprocal peer tutoring, the tutor role is switched between participants, giving equal opportunities to all learners to benefit from the tutor and tutee role and leading to more or less equal social status attached to both roles (Falchikov, 2001).

6.7.2. Pairing students, contact time, place and position

During a complete semester, students tutor each other in face-to-face contexts, in small and stable groups of four to six tutees per tutor. Since the course and the associated peer tutoring sessions take place during the first semester of students' first year at the university, the groups are composed randomly. Students did not know each other at that time, nor did the university staff.

6.7.3. Preparing students and the material

Two weeks before the onset of the project, all students participate in a preliminary training. The focus is on the acquisition of (meta)cognitive and social skills to moderate group discussions. Participants are introduced to the multidimensional nature of tutoring in order to master a mix of tutoring skills. They are informed about and practice functional skills, such as establishing a safe learning environment, managing peer interactions, asking differentiated and thought-provoking questions, giving constructive feedback, and scaffolding (Falchikov, 2001; King, 1998; Roscoe & Chi, 2007; Topping, 2005b). These tutoring responsibilities are also summarised and illustrated in a short manual for the students.

Moreover, a session-specific tutor guide was offered at each session to students responsible for the tutor role. First, it offered additional information regarding the theoretical content of the specific assignment, for it was assumed that peer support and scaffolding were appropriate only when some difference in knowledge and expertise between the tutor and their tutees existed (Topping, 2005b). Second, the guide inspired students to tackle the assignments stepwise: exploring the learning objectives, developing an action plan, checking whether requirements were met, and reflecting on the outcomes and the processes of peer collaboration. In this way, the guide implicitly stressed the importance of, and elicited, metacognitive activities. This was all summarised on a 'tutor card' with a schematic overview of a stepwise problem-solving approach (see Figure 6.4).

The assignments for each session were divided into (1) a subtask aimed at familiarising students with the specific instructional sciences' terminology related to the task, and (2) a subtask in which students were asked to apply the theoretical notions to realistic instructional cases.

6.7.4. Procedure

The project more specifically contained at least eight successive sessions (each taking 90 to 120 minutes), preceded by a training session for all students. The sessions focused on the theoretical lectures of the course. During each session, the tutor was primarily responsible for managing peers' interactions and stimulating interaction, whereas tutees were expected to solve a group assignment. The tutor role was changed at each session.

The project was characterised by the following components:

Open and authentic assignments. During the sessions, tutors supported their tutees while working on authentic assignments, related to themes of the 'Instructional Sciences' course.

TUTOR CARD

- Let the tutees brainstorm (broadly).
- Keep the available time in mind.
- In advance:
- Let the group develop an action plan for task execution.
- Ask questions which suggest a purposeful approach for task execution.
- Let the tutees decide for themselves how to execute the task.
- In between:
- Check the available time and the progress made.
- Delegate the task to check time frequently to a tutee.
- Check whether all tutees are participating actively.
- Check whether the proposed solution is in line with the task demands.
- Check tutees' comprehension by giving feedback and by asking differentiated questions.

Examples of questions:

- What does ... mean?
- Summarise the characteristics of....
- Can you give an example of ...?
- In what is ... different from/comparable to ...?
- Why do you say that?
- Does everyone agree?
- Can you explain why ...?
- Can someone elaborate on that?
- What are the strengths/weaknesses of ...?
- What can you conclude about ...?

- Check whether the final task solution corresponds with the task demands.
- Check to what degree the learning objectives are met by all tutees.
- Check if tutees still have questions.
- Reflect on the peer collaboration.

Figure 6.4 Tutor card: schematic overview of problem-solving approach.

The assignments were identical for all groups and were open-ended tasks. The assignments were complex and extensive, implying that group members could not solve the task individually. The tasks demanded critical thinking, problem solving, negotiation and decision making (Puntambekar, 2006). In order to direct students' attention to specific learning content related to the course, each assignment started with an outline of the learning objectives for that week. These encouraged students to concentrate on the expectations concerning the focus of the peer discussions.

Overall tutor training. Building on research evidence that tutors who receive support and training yield better outcomes (Falchikov, 2001), all students participated in a compulsory and interactive preliminary training, organised two weeks before the onset of the project.

Session-specific tutor guide. At each session, the students responsible for the tutor role during a specific week received a session-specific tutor guide, to support and inspire their approach. The function of this tutor guide was to offer additional information regarding the assignment content students had to work at and the way they could tackle the assignments stepwise.

Interim support. In order to provide ongoing support during the project, an interim supervision session was organised. This supervision was directed by a university staff member and was set up in small groups of about 12 students. The supervision discussion focused on sharing experiences and reflecting upon one's tutoring performance. The multiple responsibilities of the tutor, as outlined during the tutor training, served as the starting point. All participants received different statements about specific tutor responsibilities, eliciting self-reflection on their own performance. By discussing these reflections with peers from their own and other groups, students shared experiences and informed each other about personal strengths and weaknesses and about pitfalls concerning managing peer interactions. Additionally, there was room for spontaneous discussion on student-initiated reflections, as well as for questions concerning organisational aspects, encountered problems, or insecurities concerning the preparation for the reciprocal peer tutoring sessions. In addition to the supervision session halfway the project, a university staff member also provided group-specific feedback every two weeks, focusing on group dynamics, peer collaboration, equal contribution of tutees as well as students' tutoring approaches.

6.7.5. Evidence from the research

As to the research evidence for the project described above, a first line of results refer to the impact of participation in reciprocal same-age peer tutoring on individual students' metacognitive regulation (De Backer et al., 2012, 2015b). More particularly, it can be concluded that the project had the potential to benefit higher education students' actual adoption of metacognitive regulation, as measured by means of an individual thinking-aloud learning task. However, participation in the project did not elicit a positive effect on all regulation skills. It especially generated an important impact on students' monitoring and their comprehension monitoring in particular, but the project was less influential regarding students' adoption of orientation and evaluation, and had no impact on their planning behaviour.

A second line of research results revealed information on the impact of the project on the peer tutoring groups' metacognitive regulation (De Backer, Van Keer, Moerkerke & Valcke, 2015; De Backer, Van Keer & Valcke, 2015c). More particularly, the project fostered the groups' adoption of particular metacognitive regulation behaviour. The project appeared especially fruitful for promoting orientation, evaluation, and deep-level monitoring in the groups. The research further demonstrated that the groups needed time to engage in certain regulation behaviour, highlighting the added value of middle- to long-term implementation of the peer tutoring project in view of fostering (socially shared) metacognitive regulation during learning in group.

In an additional study, the reciprocal same-age peer tutoring project was complemented with the introduction of metacognitive scaffolding support for the groups. More particularly, half of the peer tutoring groups received structuring scaffolds, while the other half were provided with problematising scaffolds (De Backer, Van Keer & Valcke, 2016). Structuring scaffolds aimed at reducing the complexity of open-ended problem solving by providing additional structure to the task (e.g., offering direct guidelines, exemplifying, or narrowing choices). Problematising scaffolds on the other hand were less directive and merely suggested students consider learning and regulation activities which they might easily overlook (e.g., reflection-provoking prompts, marking critical task features and highlighting essential problem solving steps) (Reiser, 2004). The differences between both types of scaffolding are illustrated in Table 6.3.

Table 6.3 Illustration of structuring and problematising scaffolds

Regulation skill addressed	Structuring scaffold	Problematising scaffold
Orientation (prior knowledge activation)	Read the following learning objectives and specify with which theoretical concepts you are (not yet) familiar with.	How could you orient yourselves on this assignment?
Planning (planning in advance)	This assignment is comprised of [xxx] parts. Develop an action plan to complete the assignment on time.	How could you ensure the assignment will be completed on time?
Monitoring (monitoring of progress)	You have completed the orientation task. Check whether you are still on schedule or whether your planning needs to be adjusted.	Are you still on schedule?
Monitoring (comprehension monitoring)	Check whether you all understand the theoretical concepts in the orientation task sufficiently to conduct the remaining of this assignment.	How could you check whether you all understand the theoretical concepts in the orientation task sufficiently?
Monitoring (monitoring of progress)	Check if your planning needs to be adjusted.	How could you ensure the assignment will be completed on time?
Monitoring (comprehension monitoring)	Check whether you can explain the theoretical concepts addressed in (the first part of) the assignment in your own words.	How could you check whether you all understand the theoretical concepts addressed in (the first part of) the assignment sufficiently?
Evaluation (evaluation of learning outcomes, learning process and collaboration)	Check whether your outcomes are an answer to the instructions given. Evaluate your collaboration and reflect on possible ways to optimise future tutoring sessions.	How could you evaluate the learning outcomes and your collaboration?

The research findings revealed that problematising scaffolds were most beneficial for eliciting deep-level regulation and tutee-initiated regulative acts. Problematising scaffolds more specifically appeared to stimulate orientation and monitoring.

These seven educational experiences based on same-age tutoring illustrate the variety of ways in which same-age tutoring can be used by teachers and schools. All educational levels, cultural contexts or kinds of subject seem to be suitable for it. In general, tutors prepare material in order to learn it and teach it to their tutees. The difference in knowledge among students is a resource to provide learning opportunities, whether students are playing the role of tutor or tutee. In this context, diversity is a real treasure, because it is thanks to diversity that students learn.

In Chapter 7, experiences of cross-age tutoring will show how students learn from each other in contexts where this diversity is even further increased, because of the difference of ages or academic courses between the members of the pair.

Chapter 7

Structuring directional peer interactions in cross-age tutoring

As in Chapter 6 (where we presented same-age peer tutoring programmes), the present chapter describes seven educational experiences in which *cross-age peer tutoring* is applied. Also as in Chapter 6, the seven selected experiences are examples from a diverse range of educational levels (i.e., from primary school to university), in different continents and countries (i.e., USA, UK, Canada, Israel, New Zealand, Belgium), and address a wide variety of subjects. They focus on both cognitive outcomes and on skill development (i.e., reading, maths, instructional sciences, clinical medical skills, and physical education skills).

7.1. Reading Together – cross-age tutoring in primary education

The Reading Together programme is developed for second-grade tutees and fifth-grade tutors in primary education (Hattie, 2006).

7.1.1. Overview and main objectives

Reading Together aims to improve the reading fluency, reading comprehension skills and the reading motivation of second-grade students. More particularly, the tutoring programme was designed originally to help English-speaking students in the United States progress from decoding words to reading with fluency and comprehension through older students tutoring younger students in a one-to-one setting.

The developers of the programme state that Reading Together is more than a peer-reading package, as it involves specifically written reading material, has a specific focus on different skills and affective aspects in learning (namely fluency, comprehension, and motivation) and includes specific training for the tutors and scripted sessions for them to follow. These diverse components are elaborated on below. In addition, we refer readers who might want some more detailed information and concrete examples of resources of the programme to the following website: www.readingtogether.net.nz/ReadingTogether.aspx.

7.1.2. Description

7.1.2.1 Initial training and preparing learners

The success of the Reading Together programme is conditional upon both the preparation and supervision of the peer tutors. Before meeting with their tutees, tutors participate in nine training sessions with the coordinator of the programme. These tutor training sessions are aimed at familiarising the tutors with the structure of a typical tutoring session (see Activities further on in this section), with planning procedures and with particular strategies that can be used to encourage younger peers with reading difficulties.

7.1.2.2. Grouping and matching pairs

Selection: As to the selection of the cross-age tutors, the programme works with volunteering students. After a brief programme presentation to fifth-grade classrooms, students who wish to engage as tutors are asked to volunteer. After the volunteer list is compiled, the programme coordinator and classroom teachers of the potential tutors meet in order to determine which of the volunteers have demonstrated sufficient academic proficiency, responsibility and interpersonal skills (considered necessary to support a younger reader in the programme). Input from both first and second-grade classroom teachers is crucial in determining which students are suitable to participate as tutees. More particularly, it is advised that students lacking proficiency in identifying sound–symbol correspondences, those who are able to identify and apply only very few predictable spelling patterns and those who have a very limited sight-word vocabulary are not suitable candidates for Reading Together. For these students it is assumed that their individual needs are best met with the assistance of a trained classroom teacher.

Matching Pairs: Second graders who have basic decoding skills, but who still need extra help with reading, are paired with fifth-grade students who are both good readers and sufficiently socially competent to support a younger student and to keep the interaction smooth and pleasant. The tutors and tutees are paired carefully, with input from their respective classroom teachers in order to ensure that any particular need of tutees that arise because of shyness, challenging personal behaviours and so on are anticipated and dealt with proactively.

7.1.2.3. Activities

The Reading Together programme is divided into three distinct phases. Phase 1 consists of 15 highly structured lessons, lasting eight to ten weeks in total. In this phase, tutors are provided with trade books to use as read-alouds in order to model fluent reading. The tutees experience a number of short, pleasant, reading-related activities (e.g., making predictions about a passage from the title and illustrations) under the supervision of the tutor. Further, the tutee engages in short reading passages with the tutor, who encourages and supports the tutee. At first, these passages are relatively easy and short, but gradually they become more challenging. At the end of each reading passage, some comprehension questions are asked. The questions from the tutor focus on building comprehension through predicting and retelling.

Phase 2 of the Reading Together programme consists of 12 lessons, lasting six to eight weeks. This phase is significantly different from the lessons in Phase 1. In Phase 2, the tutors and tutees read alternative sections of trade books, then the tutees make predictions about passages based on the titles and illustrations, read the text, answer review questions, reread the text, paraphrase it and then answer comprehension questions. The goal of this phase is to prepare the tutees to become independent readers by providing opportunities for silent reading during the tutoring session. This is followed by independent reading in class or at home. At the end, the tutors and tutees work together on a post-reading activity.

Finally, Phase 3 of the Reading Together programme is made up of three lessons and lasts two to three weeks. This phase further develops the tutee as an independent reader and focuses on working in the school's media centre. More particularly, the tutors model appropriate reading behaviour and selection of media centre books. The goal of these lessons is to teach the tutees how to select appropriate books from the media centre and read them independently.

7.1.2.4. Monitoring

Role of the coordinator: The Reading Together coordinator has the responsibility to select, train and supervise both tutors and tutees. Reading Together coordinators are further responsible for scheduling the 30 tutoring sessions for their campus. The weekly schedule includes two 1-hour sessions for tutor preparation and two 45-minute tutor sessions. Each tutoring session is also followed by a 15-minute debriefing time for the tutors with the coordinators. The preparation days and tutoring days are alternated.

Reflection periods: At the end of each session in Phase 1, 15 minutes is reserved for debriefing the tutors. During this debriefing, the coordinator and the tutors reflect on what happened during the tutorial meeting. In addition, each of the two weekly tutoring sessions is preceded by a preparation meeting between the tutors and the school coordinator, in order to ensure proper planning for the upcoming lessons.

7.1.3. Research results: Evidence about the practice

Research comparing students involved in the Reading Together programme with control group students (meeting the same rather stringent requirements for entry into the programme) reveals that Reading Together raises children's reading achievement in a significant and sustained manner and improves the relationships between children and parents, and between parents and teachers (Hattie, 2006).

As described above, the programme encompasses three phases to develop reading achievement and reading motivation.

There are, however, still questions about the effectiveness of the first phase of the programme. Although on the three testing occasions in the evaluation reading achievement and motivation increased during Phase 1 in almost every school, the increase was no different from that of similar children taught by a regular class teacher using conventional methods of instruction. One major unanswered question relates to the actual dynamics between the tutors and tutees during Phase 1. The tutors clearly followed the specified instructions closely, but the audiotape recordings used in the evaluation studies indicated that some were a little 'slavish' (i.e., adhered too closely to the instructions, exactly as written) in doing so (Hattie, 2006).

The advantages of Reading Together begin to accrue during Phases 2 and 3. The evaluation studies demonstrate that the students in these phases begin to creep ahead of their regular class peers in both reading achievement and reading motivation. Students who were in the Reading Together programme borrowed more books from the library and had greater reading gains than control group students. The teachers, tutors, tutees and parents typically also commented positively on the increases in children's reading achievement. It is hypothesised that the attention provided by the tutors to the tutees is the major motivator (Hattie, 2006).

In conclusion, Reading Together has been implemented, modified and evaluated over some years. Based on the positive evaluations, the programme expanded to other states and countries and became part of *after-school* tutoring programmes. It is in a constant state of improvement. Some variants of the programme also involve parents as facilitators.

7.2. One Book for Two, reading comprehension in primary education

The One Book for Two programme was developed in Flanders (Belgium) in order to support reading comprehension instruction in primary education (Van Keer, 2002; Van Keer & Vanderlinde, 2008). The programme is aimed at fifth- and sixth-grade tutors who work together with second- and third-grade tutees respectively.

Underneath we elaborate on the aims and different components of the programme. Additionally, Topping, Duran and Van Keer (2016) provide readers with more comprehensive information and specific examples of the diverse resources used in the One Book for Two programme.

7.2.1. Overview and main objectives

The main objective of the programme is to rethink and redesign reading comprehension instruction in primary schools, from traditional whole-class teacher-led instruction to instruction integrating recurrent cross-age peer tutoring involving practising explicitly taught reading comprehension strategies. Cross-age tutoring refers to older students tutoring younger students, that is, while second- or third-graders read, fifth- or sixth-grade tutors monitor and regulate their tutees' reading process and understanding.

One Book for Two aims more specifically to improve students' reading comprehension strategies. The reading comprehension strategies tackled in the programme cover the entire reading process, encouraging students to orientate towards the text, to plan, monitor and reflect on their reading behaviour and understanding.

The selected reading strategies of the programme are

- activating prior background knowledge,
- predictive reading,
- distinguishing main ideas from secondary ideas,
- monitoring and regulating the understanding of words and expressions,
- monitoring and regulating comprehension in general,
- classifying text genres and
- making a graphical summary or scheme of the text.

7.2.2. Description

7.2.2.1. Initial training and preparing learners

A series of lessons and materials are developed to assist the fifth- and sixth-grade students in becoming a good tutor. The tutor preparation sessions are scheduled at the beginning of the programme and require seven 50-minute lessons. During the preparatory sessions, tutors receive information on the goals and structure of the peer tutoring project and they learn to understand their specific tasks and responsibilities. More specifically, the preparatory sessions focus on how to show interest, how to start and close a peer tutoring session, how to provide constructive feedback, how and when to provide praise, and how to offer explanations and assistance. The tutor preparation also includes an acquaintance-forming activity between the class of the tutors and the class of the tutees before the first encounter between the reading pairs.

The following are preparatory sessions provided:

- Lesson 1: I get to know the project.
- Lesson 2: We meet second/third graders. Who do I know already?
- Lesson 3: With a good listening attitude I show interest.
- Lesson 4: Who exactly is my reading buddy?
- Lesson 5: How do I start the reading session with my tutee? How do I finish a reading session? How do I complete the reading assignment card?
- Lesson 6: How and when can I give compliments? How do I correct errors? Can I, as a tutor, make mistakes?
- Lesson 7: Understood! So I'm a good reading buddy! Tutor graduation.

The materials for initial training comprise instructions for role play, examples of appropriate behaviour to engage in while working with a partner, and worksheets for the students.

7.2.2.2. Grouping and matching pairs

Grouping: The peer tutoring activities in One Book for Two are cross-age by nature, involving older students tutoring younger students. One Book for Two pairs fifth and sixth graders with second and third graders, respectively. Peer tutoring activities are organised *class-wide*, so all students in a class become a tutor or tutee and all pairs are working simultaneously. Reading pairs collaborate during the complete programme (which lasts, more or less, a school year). However, it is of course important to make it possible to change pairings that are not functioning well.

Matching pairs: Children are assigned to fixed pairs by mutual agreement of both participating classroom teachers. At first, the composition of the pairs is based on the children's reading ability, so that poor and good fifth- or sixth-grade tutors are respectively paired with poor and good second- or third-grade tutees. A second guideline for composing the reading pairs is the personality of the students. For example, a socially and emotionally sensitive tutor can best be linked to a balanced, stable tutee.

7.2.3. Activities

7.2.3.1. Structure

The weekly peer tutoring sessions are organised as follows:

- Prior to each tutoring session, the teachers provide a short *briefing* to their respective students (i.e., tutors or tutees), pointing out the main ideas or focus for the upcoming peer tutoring session.
- Tutors pick up their tutees in second or third grade and accompany them to their (fixed) reading spot. Tutor and tutee sit side by side, so both students can see the book or text equally well.
- The pairs start reading and interacting. The application of the explicitly taught reading strategies is practiced independently by means of reading strategy assignment cards. The tutee reads the book or text aloud and answers spontaneous tutor questions or questions according to the provided strategy cards.
- Finally, each peer tutoring session ends with a short reflection in which students' experiences are discussed and combined with teachers' observations.

7.2.3.2. Scaffolds for peer interaction

To support the peer tutoring interaction, One Book for Two has a *strategy assignment card* for each reading strategy that is to be practised. The cards offer structure and visual support on the different steps in applying the reading strategies. They also include questions that students should ask themselves before, during and/or after reading. Importantly, these questions are text-independent. The different strategy cards are used by the teachers when first modelling and explaining the strategies, and remain later for students' reference in the tutoring pairs.

7.2.4. Resources

One Book for Two also includes a selection of attractive texts to practise the application of the strategies within the three phases of explicit reading strategy instruction. Fiction as well as non-fiction texts are included. These texts were not purposely written or adapted for One Book for Two, but were selected from children's literature.

7.2.5. Monitoring

7.2.5.1. Role of the teacher

Teachers are encouraged to focus specifically on extensive modelling of the use of the selected reading comprehension strategies through demonstrating and thinking aloud. The stepwise instruction for each reading strategy consists of the following phases:

- During a *whole-class instructional presentation and explanation phase*, the teacher explicitly explains and models by thinking aloud why, how and when a specific strategy can be beneficial during reading in order to enhance understanding.
- During a *phase of practice characterised by teacher support and coaching*, the teacher puts the reading strategies into practice together with the students.
- The last phase comprises of more *independent practice to internalise strategy use*. This takes place in the cross-age peer tutoring pairs.

7.2.6. Reflection periods

At the end of each peer tutoring session, teachers reflect with the tutors. The purpose of this reflection and discussion is to share difficulties and positive elements students' experienced during reading together. Together the tutors search for solutions or they confirm each other's views.

7.2.7. Research results: Evidence about the practice

The impact of One Book For Two has been examined – on students' reading comprehension, reading fluency, reading strategy awareness and use (Van Keer, 2004; Van Keer & Vanderlinde, 2010; Van Keer & Verhaeghe, 2005). The studies more particularly compare four different approaches to reading comprehension instruction (i.e., traditional whole-class, teacher-centred instruction with and without explicit instruction in reading comprehension strategies and explicit instruction in reading strategies in combination with respectively same-age and cross-age peer tutoring). The studies conclude that introducing explicit instruction in reading strategies in the reading comprehension curriculum is important. Both tutors and tutees benefit from the interactive relationship, but the positive effect of cross-age peer tutoring is larger for the tutor than for the tutees.

Tutees start to use reading strategies more during the reading process of One Book for Two, supported by tutors. It can be hypothesised that the significant findings for tutees can be attributed to two essential elements of the instructional approach, namely: (1) the individualised practice and assistance provided to the tutees, and (2) the fact that tutors appear to be sufficiently competent in offering this support regarding the use of reading strategies effectively. The strong presence of high-quality interaction between the cross-age peers, characterised by a wide range of different high-level questions and well-elaborated responses, underlie these findings.

Tutors' learning gains outperform other students' growth – and they have the most persistent long-term progress in reading comprehension. "To tutor is to learn twice" – so it actually seems! A possible explanation of this result may lie in the fact that the tutors are challenged to reflect on the learning content more thoroughly, in-depth and from different perspectives. Consequently, tutors develop a better understanding and take their knowledge and skills to a higher level. Moreover, it is important to mention that the One Book for Two approach works equally well for low-, average- and high-achievers.

In conclusion, the studies revealed the significance of combining explicit reading strategy instruction with regular practice in peer tutoring pairs, and cross-age peer tutoring in particular. In comparison with same-age peer tutoring, cross-age tutoring appears to be the most favourable for both tutees and tutors. Further research is, however, still necessary to evaluate the effectiveness in a larger variety of (international) contexts. It should also be acknowledged that due to the complexity of the innovative approaches, we are not able to draw conclusions about the relative contribution of the different constituent components in the approach. We hypothesise that it is the combination of different elements that contributes to the positive effects found. However, this is only an assumption and an issue for future research.

7.3. The Peer Tutoring Literacy Program – cross-age tutoring for French immersion schools

The Peer Tutoring Literacy Program was developed for primary education students. More particularly, second- and third-grade readers and fifth-, sixth-, and seventh-grade tutors are the target groups (Bournot-Trites, Lee & Séror, 2003; Chipman & Roy, 2006). The rationale behind, as well as the aims and the characteristics of the programme, are described below. Supplementary information – including texts and videos for training – can be consulted on the following website: http://cpf.ca/en/membership/cpf-member-resources/peer-tutoring-literacy-program/.

7.3.1. Overview and main objectives

The programme aims to foster literacy in French immersion schools in Canada. Notwithstanding the bilingual Canadian context, in Canadian immersion schools students face the academic challenge that their second language learning is mostly confined to the hours spent in the classroom. While primary schools students who are experiencing moderate to severe reading difficulties are given extra support by resource teachers, those with minor reading difficulties may not have any specific support outside the classroom. The Peer Tutoring Literacy Program was developed with specially trained intermediate students as tutors. The essential thrust is to promote the love of reading, to achieve reading fluency and to develop self-esteem in primary school students.

To organise the programme a *'core team'* is composed, consisting of a teacher coordinator, involved classroom teachers and parent volunteers. The principle of involving parents is key to the success and the nature of the programme. The parent volunteers help to set up the program and assist the teachers in supervising the tutoring sessions by interacting with the readers and helping the tutors.

7.3.2. Description

7.3.2.1. Role of the tutor

Tutors are involved in the programme to bring enthusiasm, empathy and a non-judgmental attitude – aiming to draw out and encourage their younger counterparts to improve their reading. Tutors commit to tutoring for one term at a time, twice a week, and are responsible for being punctual, dedicated and motivated.

7.3.2.2. Timing and place

During the school year, three tutoring terms are organised, averaging eight weeks each. Tutors and readers meet twice a week for a 30-minute guided reading session during class time. To minimise the loss of class instruction, tutoring takes place during silent reading time early in the morning. The programme explicitly takes place in the school library, which is organised as a natural and warm environment for reading.

7.3.2.3. Initial training and preparing learners

Multiple levels of tutor training are included in the programme, with an information session for prospective tutors, formal training and shadowing. All of the levels of training take place during the school day over several weeks.

- *Information Session for Prospective Tutors*: The purpose of this information session is to present the programme to prospective fifth-, sixth- and seventh-grade tutors. Once the students are briefed on the nature of tutoring, they receive a questionnaire to determine whether they are interested in becoming a tutor, a back-up tutor, or whether they would rather not participate. The information session takes approximately 30 minutes.
- *Formal Tutor Training*: The structure of the formal tutor training is similar to that of the information session. However, it goes into more depth and provides full explanations of all aspects of peer tutoring. The formal tutor training typically lasts an hour and is set up interactively, using sketches depicting the do's and don'ts of tutoring. In these sketches, the teacher coordinator takes up the role of facilitator, a parent volunteer is in the role of tutor and a veteran tutor is a reader. The sketches also cover possible problem areas which tutors may encounter, involving difficult behaviour and poor work habits of not only the readers, but of tutors as well.
- *Shadowing*: Shadowing is introduced as a specific term in training the tutors in the Peer Tutoring Literacy Program. It occurs one or two weeks after the formal tutor training and

is a two-step training process. In the first phase, the core team of the programme match experienced tutors with novice tutors. During a normal tutoring session, the new tutor observes the veteran tutoring, with the reader sitting in the middle. The second phase takes place at the next tutoring session, with the action roles of the expert and novice tutor reversed.

7.3.3. Selecting, grouping, and matching pairs

Selection: The difference in age is not the most significant factor in the tutor-reader relationship; rather it is the difference in students' literacy levels. Trained tutors have to have enough language ability to correct and instruct their readers/tutees using the programme's strategies. Readers are chosen on the basis of teachers' recommendations and the teacher coordinator's assessments of their reading skills. Classroom teachers have an intermediate role and submit a list of possible tutor candidates to the teacher coordinator.

Grouping: The programme is aimed at independent grade 2 and grade 3 readers who would benefit from some additional reading support. These students are grouped with trained tutors from grades 5, 6 and 7.

Matching pairs: Once the selection of tutees and tutors has been finalised, the core team of the programme meets to discuss the matching of the students. With respect to this, the core team considers the personalities of tutors and readers, their relative ability, relative age, maturity, gender and cultural background.

The classroom teachers may contribute some thoughts as to which tutors may suit which readers, or may offer insights as to what kind of qualities would be especially helpful for certain readers. For example, putting a lively tutor and a shy reader together can be a good match, as the tutor is likely to draw out the reader and create a relaxed atmosphere. The teacher coordinator may be well acquainted with both tutors and readers and be in a good position to consider which pairings would be suitable. When parent volunteers become familiar with the students involved, they can contribute to this discussion as well.

If there is any hesitation about a given pair, the teacher coordinator consults with the tutor for his/her input and makes appropriate changes before finalising the matching schedule. If parent volunteers and the teacher coordinator find that certain pairs lack good chemistry and are not working to their potential, they can obviously make changes once working together starts, providing it is not too disruptive to the other pairs.

7.3.4. Activities

The activities within the peer tutoring sessions consist of the following structured consecutive steps.

Step 1: Predictions. The reader is encouraged by the tutor to read the title, examine the book cover illustration, and guess and predict what the story might be about. The tutor asks the reader to look at the book's pictures and come up with a possible sequence of events. In addition, the tutor can use the pictures to introduce new vocabulary that may appear in the text as well.

Step 2: Choral/Interactive Reading. The tutor and reader both read the story out loud simultaneously, with the tutor adjusting his or her pace to make sure the younger reader is leading the reading. The tutor takes the opportunity to interact frequently with the reader by going over the predictions made earlier in step 1, and by relating the story to the reader. During choral reading, the tutor demonstrates the proper pronunciation of words misread by the reader. This makes it easier for the reader to be more accurate when reading alone, later in the tutor session. The tutor notes down the words that are new to the reader, and those he or she mispronounces. The tutor uses a number of strategies to help the reader decipher the meaning of new vocabulary (e.g., reading the text before and after the word to understand the word through its context; looking at the pictures for clues; looking for a small word within a large one).

Step 3: Retelling/Comprehension Questions. The tutor asks the reader to retell the story in sequence. To help the reader with the details, the tutor may ask questions about the plot or the main characters in the story.

Step 4: Individual Reading. The reader now reads the book out loud alone, with the tutor helping out with pronunciation and supplying any word the reader has trouble decoding. The latter is important in view of preventing tutee frustration.

Step 5: End Activities. At the end of the activities, flashcards and games are introduced.

Flashcards: Throughout the reading activities, the tutor notes down the words the reader has trouble pronouncing as well as new vocabulary. After the individual reading, the tutor asks the reader to write these words on flashcards. The reader may draw a picture that defines the word on the other side of the flashcard.

Games: The tutor concludes the session by engaging the reader in a number of games: for example, a memory game.

It is important to mention that peer tutors are not expected to be perfect. In an immersion setting, it is accepted that they may occasionally need to seek the help of the teacher coordinator and/or parent volunteers to clarify and explain vocabulary or points of grammar.

7.3.5. Resources

A wide selection of appealing, well-designed and colourful books reinforces the quality of the reading experience. In the programme, special effort is made to select books ranging from, for example absurd stories to interesting science or sports books that appeal particularly to boys. The combination of (1) working with peers who themselves clearly enjoy the experience, and (2) having access to compelling books makes reading fun, even for rather reluctant readers.

7.3.6. Feedback session

Three to four weeks after the start of a term, a feedback session takes place. The core team arranges for the feedback session to be held during class time. The feedback session is interactive and facilitated by the core team. Tutors are asked whether they have any questions or suggestions to improve tutoring and together they address specific areas of difficulty.

7.3.7. Research results: Evidence about the practice

The Peer Tutoring Literacy Program contains key elements that make it a distinctive and effective mechanism to improve primary school students' literacy, which also succeeds in acknowledging all members of the school community and positively reinforcing their relationships with one another and the school at large. The advantages are clearly seen. When comparing students in The Peer Tutoring Literacy Program with matched students in control schools not implementing the programme, the research reveals positive results for all programme participants. Readers most clearly benefit by showing improvement in various aspects of literacy: reading proficiency and decoding, reading comprehension and increased concentration while reading. Students' attitude toward reading and the pleasure they derive from it are enhanced as well (Bournot-Trites et al., 2003; Chipman & Roy, 2006). Further, these studies indicate that primary students with minor reading difficulties can achieve grade-level fluency after two to three terms of peer tutoring. Over time, classes appear to become more 'homogeneous' in terms of reading ability, with the result that they progress in a more dynamic fashion as compared to natural spontaneous improvement and development with time.

A survey using questionnaires with all stakeholders further indicated that parents of readers also benefit from the programme. Emotionally, they are comforted by the knowledge that the school is addressing the needs of their children. Once they see their child progress academically with the aid of peer tutoring, they are also more likely to keep them in immersion schools (Bournot-Trites, 2004).

Finally, also the older students benefit from the programme and from being in the role as tutor. More particularly, they gain organisational, teaching and leadership skills. Socially and emotionally tutors make gains in self-confidence and in their sense of importance in their own community. Beyond this, tutors themselves show some improvement in their own literacy skills. Explaining vocabulary and grammar forces tutors to learn the material in a more profound and complex manner. Classroom teachers are also very satisfied with the programme (Chipman & Roy, 2006).

7.4. Paired Maths, cross-age tutoring for primary and secondary education

Paired Maths was developed for primary and secondary education, aiming at consolidation and deepening of children's mathematical understanding and ability and at improving their motivation and confidence in doing maths by involving them in mathematical games (Topping & Bamford, 1998). Underneath, we present a description of the objectives, components, and typical features of the programme. Interested readers can consult more detailed information and reproducible resources in the *Paired Maths Handbook* of Topping and Bamford (1998) and at www.dundee.ac.uk/esw/research/resources/problemsolving.

7.4.1. Overview and main objectives

Paired Maths using games has characteristics in common with Duolog Maths (presented in Chapter 6) and aims to improve the mathematics learning of students. Both numeracy skills and attitudes to mathematics are focused on. The rationale behind the programme is that mathematics is useful and important throughout life. Poor numeracy skills are a major disadvantage in everyday life and for active and effective participation in the job market as well. By the end of the primary school years, children's attitude towards mathematics is unfortunately often becoming fixed into rejection and antagonism. Especially at the secondary school level, many parents see themselves as bad at mathematics and hated maths as a subject at school. Consequently, disliking mathematics can all too readily be construed as normal. In addition, gender stereotypes can be transmitted. There is a danger of parents and teachers modelling negative attitudes to mathematics, which are then adopted by children and become a self-fulfilling prophecy. Paired Maths is designed to help deal with this.

The concept of Paired Maths is to highlight the different methods or problem solving approaches that can be employed when doing maths for both the tutee and tutor. The inherent enjoyment and success can foster positive attitudes to the self and to mathematics as a subject. Paired Maths also aims to encourage turn-taking, cooperation, communication and other interpersonal skills.

7.4.2. Description

The Paired Maths template is multifaceted, highly flexible and adaptable. It offers a range of options for schools to plan, structure and design their specific and unique Paired Maths programme. It can be designed as a home-based or school-based intervention. The former involves parents or older children at home in the programme, while the latter involves peers in schools as tutors. Paired Maths is equally suitable for 'ordinary' children as for students with special needs – even including children with severe learning difficulties (see, for example, Chapter 7 of Topping and Bamford, 1998, for readers seeking inspiration concerning involving a special needs target group) – whether as tutees or tutors. This book mainly focuses on implementing peer tutoring in schools.

Paired Maths is a method of learning in maths in which discussion between two students (i.e., tutor and tutee) is used to solve math questions, which are rooted in math games. The role of the tutor is to provide support to the tutee and mediate the learning processes for the tutee. In order to do this, the tutor will try to ensure that the tutee considers the math question using a structured approach. It is the job of the tutee to do the actual mathematical working-out to arrive at an answer to the math question at hand.

Games are intentionally included in the Paired Maths programme, since they have the advantage that they are less threatening for students, promote active involvement, are intrinsically motivating, exciting and challenging, and are grounded in concrete meaningful experiences. Taking into account all these characteristics and benefits of working with games, Paired Maths requires children to think and do more mentally then they could record on paper (Topping & Bamford, 1998).

7.4.3. Grouping and matching pairs

Grouping: The Paired Maths programme can be planned as a cross-school cross-age peer tutoring project, which pairs students from secondary schools (e.g., in second year) as tutors with selected students in primary school (e.g., in second grade). More common, however, is cross-age peer tutoring within one school (Topping & Bamford, 1998). It can also be used on a same-age basis, but the present chapter focuses on the cross-age variant of the Paired Maths programme.

Matching pairs: A number of guidelines as to the matching of the student pairs are put forward. First, it is suggested that teachers should aim for heterogeneous maths ability in the pairing of students. Related to this, it is recommended that the tutor is about two years older than the tutee. In any case, all participants should find some cognitive challenge in their joint activities, and the teacher should ensure that one partner is a capable reader of instructions. Further, tutors in the programme should be prepared to take up their tutor role effectively. Additionally, teachers should consider whether to match pairs within or across gender and what the adverse effects of either might be, taking into account their specific class and school context, on the one hand, and the specific individualities of the students they are working with, on the other. As to the gender issue, it might be interesting to consider matching girls as tutors for boys in view of breaking the gender stereotype of girls being less able at maths. Alternatively, pair female tutors with female tutees in terms of the tutor functioning as a potential model to counter the negative effects of the gender stereotype threat.

Finally, it is recommended that teachers avoid matching children who are already good friends, as this can lead to much off-task behaviour. However, we must leave it to the teachers to take a well-considered decision in such a case, based on their knowledge of and experiences with the students (since friends can be good partners as well, as underlined in Chapter 4).

7.4.4. Activities

7.4.4.1. Structuring for peer interaction

Paired Maths projects run for six weeks after matching and training the involved student pairs. The programme consists of two sessions of 30 minutes each week. Paired Maths relies on a dialogue between two pupils about a mathematical question.

The interactions between tutors and tutees are structured in order for the tutor to help the tutee gain a clearer understanding of the solution and the path to this mathematical solution. More specifically, the peer tutors are required to employ tutoring strategies such as thinking out loud, praising, questioning and summarising, and generalising. Pairs of students work together solving maths questions in three main steps with the following strategies from the tutors:

1. Understanding the question: Read (i.e., in case tutees have trouble reading a word question), Identify (i.e., make sure that the tutee understands what the question is) and Listen (i.e., give the tutee time to think about the question and then ask them to explain how he/she might solve it).
2. Finding an answer to the question: Question (i.e., Ask helpful and intelligent questions that give clues, to stimulate and guide tutees thinking), Praise (i.e., give tutees praise and encouragement very often), and Think out loud (i.e., Give tutees thinking time before expecting an answer. Encourage them to tell what they are thinking all the time).
3. Finish the problem by having tutees ask themselves what have they done and how it links to things they have done in the past: Check (i.e., check that the tutee eventually gets the right answer), Sum-it-up (i.e., have the tutee summarise the key steps in doing the maths question), Link-it-up (i.e., talk about how the learning might be used to do another similar question or apply it in a wider context).

7.4.4.2. Scaffolds for peer interaction

The rules and materials of the math games provide strong scaffolding for the interaction between the peer tutor and his or her tutee. In Paired Maths, the games readily stimulate discussion of joint and purposeful, concrete activities, requiring children to use and understand words and phrases in a mathematical context.

7.4.5. Resources

The math games used in the programme should meet the following criteria: they should be enjoyable, allow equal competition, be easy to understand, be flexible, encourage discussion, not look like schoolwork, be physically attractive, be physically robust, be well packaged and easily kept together, be safe and be inexpensive (Topping & Bamford, 1998).

The first Paired Maths projects were aimed at children aged 5 to 7 (level 1), and over 40 different games were accumulated for this age group, grouped into six differentiated categories: matching, counting, conservation, shape, pattern and ordering. These six categories are related to a six-week project in which participants are asked to choose one game from a different category each week. Each game is accompanied with a list of activities to do with the materials, a list of words to be used and a diary or record sheet. The categories for the level 2 games, aiming at children aged 7 to 11, were somewhat different and focused on bonds, relations, shape, strategy and puzzles (included as examples of cross-area activities). The last level of games focused on students up to 14 years old, and included for example games focusing on number (e.g., arithmetic, probability), strategy games (e.g., requiring an algebraic understanding of mathematical principles involved) and so on.

7.4.6. Research results: Evidence about the practice

Research studying the effects of Paired Maths by comparing students' pre-test to post-test competence reveals significant increases in the use of mathematical words, strategic dialogue and praise between partners and a corresponding decline in procedural talk. The project appears to be largely successful in increasing self-esteem for both tutors and tutees, and in simultaneously increasing the quantity and the quality of the interactive discussion about mathematics between children, as well as generic social and communication behaviours in the tutors (Topping et al., 2003; Topping, Kearney, McGee & Pugh, 2004). During the sessions, a great deal of mathematical language use is evident and mathematical vocabulary is reinforced. Finally, improvements are observed in students' attention control (Topping et al., 2004).

7.5. Peer tutoring in physical education as a tool for inclusion

This section describes a quite specific and noteworthy focus of peer tutoring, namely the opportunities for peer tutoring in physical education in primary and secondary schools. In particular, the research literature specifically stresses the possibilities for inclusive education (e.g., Cervantes, Lieberman, Magnesio & Wood, 2013).

7.5.1. Overview and main objectives

The idea behind peer tutoring in physical education classes stems from the fact that schools have been identified as crucial health settings and should be encouraged to further develop physical education and physical activity programmes that are appropriate and motivating for all students. Peer tutoring in physical education can motivate students and improve physical activity in both primary and secondary school contexts. Within the peer tutoring activities, students are able to practice new skills or new components of a skill and receive immediate feedback on their performance; both factors are needed for the acquisition and maintenance of new skills.

In particular, peer tutoring can play an important role for inclusion in physical education. Inclusion is the idea that all students, with and without (physical or mental) disabilities or conduct disorders, should be educated within the same environment, while meeting each child's educational and social needs. More and more students with disabilities continue to be included in general education classes. Therefore, teachers should develop ways to meet the demands of the diversity that results from such inclusive environments. Cross-age peer tutoring can potentially solve the challenges of inclusion and associated heterogeneous grouping of students. The aim is to develop peer tutoring as a strategy for inclusively teaching students with disabilities in general physical education classes. Different types of peer tutoring for physical education are reported in the literature. However, this chapter focuses on the cross-age peer tutoring variant described below.

7.5.2. Description

7.5.2.1. Initial training or preparing learners

To realise true inclusive education, general physical education teachers must create an environment of trust and peer acceptance in which all members of the class are welcomed. To accomplish this, teachers must prepare their classes for the inclusion of students with disabilities before the implementation of peer tutoring activities. Disability awareness training, class discussions, role playing and potential guest speakers are some strategies that teachers may use to inform students without disabilities about the fact that their peers with disabilities are different, yet similar to themselves.

In addition to fostering this overall disability awareness, specific training of peer tutors is also critical for successful tutoring strategy implementation. Next to the physical education teacher, other members of a multidisciplinary team (e.g., para-educators or previous peer tutors) can help to set up and implement the training. As a way to start, it is advised to select a small group of students or a single class to pilot the programme. Importantly, it is recommended that only students who volunteer to become a tutor and who show the characteristics of a good tutor should be selected for tutor training and consequently for taking up the tutor role.

Some general steps to follow for training and for implementing peer tutoring are recommended:

1 Obtain permission from parents of tutors and tutees.
2 Develop an application procedure: create an application and give it to eligible students.
3 Conduct disability awareness activities: the training should include different types of disability awareness to ensure that the peer tutor understands his or her tutee's specific disability.
4 Develop communication techniques: during a physical education lesson, communication is extremely important. Terminology as well as how to communicate (e.g., using sign language, communication symbols) should be taught during the training.
5 Teach instructional techniques: techniques such as explaining, demonstrating and specific physical assistance should be taught, as well as positive general, positive specific and corrective feedback – and when to use each.
6 Use scenarios: utilise upcoming units of instruction as well as real life examples.
7 Use behaviour management programmes: if a student requires behaviour management, then it is important to teach the techniques that work for that child to the peer tutor.
8 Test for understanding: give each peer tutor a test on what you taught.

The time necessary for training the peer tutors will be based on the teacher's understanding of the students, the school and the community. The tutor training can take place on diverse occasions (e.g., before school, after school, during part of the physical education class, during recess). When possible, it is recommended to include the child with a disability in the training.

7.5.3. Grouping and matching pairs

Notwithstanding the fact that this chapter particularly focuses on (the benefits of) cross-age tutoring, two types of peer tutoring grouping are distinguished and occur in physical education tutoring, each with its own characteristics and advantages:

Unidirectional peer tutoring: The unidirectional and mainly – though not exclusively – cross-age physical education tutoring occurs when only one student is trained to serve as a peer tutor to a student with a disability. For instance, an older student would come into the class to help a particular student with disabilities. Utilising the unidirectional type of tutoring allows a student with a disability to receive additional support and attention from a student without disabilities. An advantage to using unidirectional peer tutoring is that both students know and stick to their assigned role. Further, a benefit of using cross-age peer tutoring in general physical education is that the older tutor is typically more experienced, reliable and responsible than same-age peers would be. With the cross-age tutor, the younger tutee might behave and perform better than with a same-age peer.

Reciprocal peer tutoring: This type of peer tutoring is mainly same-age in nature and involves two or more students who are grouped together, preferably in a pair consisting of a student with and one without a disability. It follows a format in which each student in the pair monitors and evaluates the other, which provides a sense of equal status among participants. The student with a disability has the opportunity to function both as tutor and tutee, reciprocally exchanging roles with the peer without a disability for each practiced motor skill.

The reciprocal strategy provides a way for all students to be partnered with one another. If peers without disabilities serve only in the tutor role, an imbalance in the relationship between peers and students with disabilities may result. This imbalanced relationship can lead students serving as tutors to believe that students with disabilities always need help and are inferior to students without disabilities. Further, these relationships can cause low self-esteem in students with disabilities.

It is important to take into account that reciprocal peer tutoring works best with students who have mild-to-moderate disabilities and who are able to work and/or follow instructions with minimal assistance.

Independent of the approach opted for, it appears important to train at least three peer tutors per each child with a disability. Then the peers can rotate and take turns each class.

7.5.4. Activities

Using task cards specifically illustrating motor skill analysis may benefit peers without disabilities when in the role of tutor.

7.5.5. Monitoring

In physical education classes, peer tutors and their tutees should be provided with feedback. They should be monitored and given feedback each lesson, but less and less as they become more efficient tutors. Teachers must ensure that the children with disabilities are having increased social interactions with their peers. This should happen as soon as the programme is implemented and be enhanced throughout the complete programme.

7.5.6. Research results: Evidence about the practice

There is evidence to support the benefits of peer tutoring in physical education for students with and without disabilities. The literature review of Cervantes et al. (2013) refers to different studies with diverse study designs, illustrating such benefits as increased academic learning time in physical education, increased moderate-to-vigorous physical activity levels, enhanced motor performance, improved social interaction and social skills development and motivation as well as gains in self-efficacy and performance (Cervantes et al., 2013).

Moreover, it appears that compared to untrained peer tutors, trained peer tutors tend to have a greater impact on the motor performance of students with disabilities – and in this case trained peer tutors may benefit most from the peer tutoring experience. Tutors must pay attention to the various demands of different components of the task, including the physical, instructional and social components. Inadequately trained tutors may be unable to manipulate the task cards or support materials, communicate the necessary information to execute the task or successfully manage personal interactions with the tutee (Cervantes et al., 2013).

7.6. Online peer tutoring in asynchronous discussion groups in higher education

The programme described here features online cross-age peer tutoring in asynchronous discussion groups. This implies tutoring in an online learning environment, which can be considered typical for learning in twenty-first-century higher education. The programme was implemented in university education, including first-year bachelor students as tutees and students in their second master year as tutors.

7.6.1. Overview and main objectives

The programme focuses on cross-age peer tutoring in the context of freshmen collaborating in asynchronous discussion groups in a higher education university context. The asynchronous task-based discussion groups are a particular formal component of a blended course (i.e., instructional sciences), which is part of the first-year bachelor's degree in the educational sciences curriculum.

The online discussion groups aim at stimulating freshmen to actively discuss the course content in thematic group assignments to get an in-depth grasp of the different theoretical concepts introduced in the course. The thematic group assignments are identical for all discussion groups and are open-ended tasks, implying no standard approach or single right answers. The different assignments throughout the semester are of more or less equal complexity and difficulty and relate to distinct themes in the course. The assignments are quite complex and extensive, in order to force group members to work collaboratively instead of solving tasks on their own.

As is the case in most higher education institutions, master's students in Educational Sciences at Ghent University (Flanders–Belgium) participate in an internship during their senior years, as a formal part of the curriculum. As part of their internship, they become tutor to one of the asynchronous discussion groups for freshmen in Educational Sciences mentioned above, during the first semester of the academic year.

The general task for the cross-age peer tutors involved in the programme is *e-moderating* (Salmon, 2000), which specifically means supplying online support including technical help for accessing the online learning environment, motivation, socialisation, academic advice or information-exchange, and cues for knowledge construction and personal development.

The first moderation stage 'access and motivation' centres on welcoming participants and offering them technical support to get online. At the second moderation stage 'online socialisation', getting to know each other, sharing empathy and having a clear sense of the 'discussion group audience' are the priorities. At this stage, the tutors or e-moderators help establishing a feeling of 'community'. At the third stage of 'information exchange', learning becomes the more prominent objective. Two typical kinds of interaction are pursued in this stage, namely individual interaction that reflects coping with the course content and social interaction with other participants, including the e-moderator. Central to the fourth stage of 'knowledge construction' are social negotiation and task-related engagement. The overall purpose at this stage is sharing meaning and building common understanding. At the fifth and final stage of 'development', participants reassess their own thinking and explore the social learning processes. The key ingredient at this stage of personal development is reflection and becoming responsible for one's own learning. In this respect, e-moderators need to challenge learners' thoughts; for example, by encouraging critical thinking.

7.6.2. Description

7.6.2.1. Initial training and preparing learners

To structure and enhance the online peer tutoring work and to meet the quality requirements for tutoring, an initial training for tutors is implemented. In general, the engaged peer tutors are initially trained in the theoretical basis of e-moderating. Further, the design of the tutor training is based on the specific purpose of the task-based asynchronous discussion groups, namely to stimulate freshmen to actively discuss the course content and relevant external sources to grasp the different theoretical concepts introduced in the course. In addition, an online peer tutor should also feel comfortable online. Therefore, the tutor training ends with a demonstration of the technical asynchronous discussion environment. Furthermore, a tutor website is made available to the tutors, summarising practical information, such as clarifying the aims of tutoring and the evaluation criteria. Finally, a specific guidebook with background information about the tutor training is distributed.

7.6.3. Grouping and matching pairs

Grouping: The peer tutoring activities are *cross-age* in nature, referring to older students tutoring younger students. Fourth-year students operate as online tutors to support freshmen in discussing cases and solving authentic problems. Tutors are each supporting one asynchronous discussion group of, on average, 12 freshmen students.

Matching pairs: Tutees are assigned randomly to the different discussion groups. Group composition is fixed and remains unchanged during the complete semester. Also the assignment of the tutors to the respective discussion groups occurs randomly.

7.6.4. Activities

Completing each discussion assignment lasts two weeks. After two weeks, the discussion is accessible on a read-only basis, and a new assignment is presented to the freshmen's discussion groups.

7.6.5. Role of the teacher and reflection periods

Throughout the complete semester, two faculty members are available for discussion and questions through e-mail. In addition, every two weeks focus groups for tutors are organised to discuss tutors' e-moderating behaviour and to improve their peer tutoring activities. These in-service, face-to-face and on-campus meetings are set up in small groups of approximately ten peer tutors.

7.6.6. Research results: Evidence about the practice

From the studies focusing on exploring tutors' peer tutoring activities in the context of the asynchronous discussion groups (De Smet, Van Keer & Valcke, 2008, 2009; De Smet, Van Keer, De Wever & Valcke, 2010), it appears that cross-age peer tutors in this particular higher education setting perform a blend of tutoring activities. The data show that very different e-moderating activities are being adopted over time: from fostering access and motivation, through encouraging socialisation, information exchange and knowledge construction, to stimulating personal development. This illustrates the broad variety of tutoring dimensions that can be found in the e-moderating model of Salmon (2000). Moreover, it has been shown that tutors alternate group support with individual support and modelling behaviour with coaching behaviour. However, a slight predominance of giving additional information, clarifying the learning task and planning activities can be seen in tutors' activities. Salmon (2000) would regard these activities as reflecting the third step of e-moderating, namely 'information-exchange'. Peer tutors, however, more rarely stimulate tutees' personal development, the fifth and highest step of e-moderating.

The research results further reveal peer tutoring behaviour as being tutor-dependent and reflecting a tutor's preferred tutor style or approach. In line with the work of Salmon (2000), the following tutor styles were distinguished: 'motivators', 'informers', and 'knowledge constructors'.

A study focusing on the evolution in tutors' actual tutoring behaviour showed that the nature of tutor contributions did not change radically over time. There was no significant evolution from introductory and social talk to contributions reflecting cognitive processing or stimulating tutees' knowledge construction. This might be due, however, to the fact that the group assignments in each consecutive discussion theme were completely new and not linked to the former assignments.

7.7. Cross-age peer tutoring in medical higher education

Here we describe a cross-age peer tutoring programme in Flemish medical education. More particularly, second-year masters medical sciences students are involved in the programme as tutees and tutored by students with skill-specific prior expertise from different years of training (Berghmans, Druine, Dochy & Struyven, 2012).

7.7.1. Overview and main objectives

The educational curriculum of the medical faculty of the University of Leuven (Flanders–Belgium) is characterised by rather traditional teaching methodologies. This is mainly due to practical reasons (e.g., staff restrictions, large student populations) also internationally acknowledged in medical school curricula. In this context, the challenge of implementing more student-centred learning environments has been placed high on the agenda. A primary goal is to stimulate future medical doctors to become self-regulating professionals in the workplace. After all, medical students need to be prepared to make decisions founded on a decisive and critical attitude, while taking into account diverse patient and context-related features.

As such, the medical faculty of the University of Leuven has introduced a peer tutoring programme into its clinical skills training (i.e., in view of the following skills: stitching, venipuncturing and intravenous catheterisation, injecting and bladder catheterisation). The objective of this programme is to prepare second-year masters medical students for their structured clinical examination. More specifically, the programme comprises different strategies that involve support, with the intent to help others achieve their learning goals (i.e., in both knowledge and skills).

7.7.2. Description

7.7.2.1. Initial training or preparing learners

In the programme, peer tutors are responsible for tutoring small groups of students who are practising diverse technical skills. All peer tutors receive two types of training. First, a medical training refreshes peer tutors' skill-related knowledge and introduces them to a set of course-related objectives that have to be dealt with during the tutoring sessions. Second, a three-hour didactical training is organised to prepare peer tutors for their specific role. The training sessions use video examples of good and bad practices, which are discussed in depth. A role play is also provided in which peer tutors practice their approach and receive feedback and coaching.

Since directive peer tutoring strategies often appear to predominate and not all peer tutors manage to adopt facilitative strategies spontaneously, these strategies are explicitly trained in the peer tutors. The latter is especially important, since peer tutors' facilitative strategies stimulate students to think more deeply about the content matter, as well as generating discussion within the student group. A facilitative approach aims to engage students in a more active and profound way (such as by questioning, hinting and prompting), which has proved to have added value in the context of peer tutoring. Moreover, a facilitative peer tutor addresses students' responsibility and initiative (i.e., active learning), while a directive peer tutor reduces the role of students to that of a rather passive participant in the learning process. Taking this into account, the tutor training in the programme is aimed at stimulating the development of a facilitative tutoring approach.

It is important to mention that not only the peer tutors but also the tutee-students are prepared and trained with regard to, on the one hand, their responsibilities within the tutor dialogue, and, on the other hand, with what they can and cannot expect from peer tutors.

7.7.3. Grouping and matching pairs

Selection: Students with skill-specific prior expertise are invited to act as peer tutors for fellow students. Students who have acquired extra skill-specific competencies during internships or volunteering work, for example, are recruited as peer tutors to support second-year master's students in the acquisition of diverse procedural skills. These peer tutors can come from different years of training.

Grouping: A small-group tutoring format with a tutor–tutee ratio of one tutor for approximately 12 tutees is generally implemented in the programme. Every tutor is responsible for six to eight one-hour peer tutoring sessions.

7.7.4. Monitoring: Role of the faculty staff

The first session of every peer tutor is observed by a member of the faculty staff, after which feedback is given. As such, tutor-specific feedback and coaching are guaranteed. During the other sessions, the presence of a staff member is guaranteed to provide support when needed and/or to answer tutor-related questions or to coach where necessary.

Additionally, all peer tutors receive a manual for the specific skill to be tutored and a list of course-related objectives that have to be dealt with during the sessions. This guarantees that every student is treated equally in terms of covered course content. Further, each peer tutor is also asked to reflect on his or her training approach by means of a logbook.

The training of the peer tutors does not stop after the first initial training. There is at least one follow-up meeting after peer tutors have some experience with tutoring and have already experienced some specific challenges. As peer tutors differ both in their approaches to tutoring and in their experience of challenges with their tutees, they can help one another to overcome weaknesses by sharing strengths and tips. Besides these follow-up meetings in which peer tutors can reflect on their experiences, observations of peers also can be helpful. In this respect, we also recommend experimenting with stimulated-recall techniques using video-observations, as this could support peer tutors' reflection on their actual performance and motives – and it challenges experience while tutoring.

7.7.5. Research results: Evidence about the practice

The shift towards student-centred education and the related role change of educators from a 'director' to a 'facilitator' of learning appears to be not always well received by medical students. However, if the development of deep-level learning competencies is actually high on the agenda of medical schools, they have to face the challenge of finding a balance between meeting students' preferences and stimulating more student centeredness or student activity in learning (Berghmans et al., 2012).

As to the results of peer tutoring itself, research has proven that peer tutoring is a valid and successful strategy in many higher educational settings, such as physics, medicine and engineering. In the context of clinical skills training in particular, tutors are challenged to differentiate and adapt their tutoring approach to the specific student group in terms of course-specific prior knowledge. Students with low levels of course-specific prior knowledge will especially benefit from facilitative tutoring – in comparison with more directive peer tutoring – in terms of gains in their clinical knowledge and understanding. Moreover, data on students' perceptions also reveal that facilitative trained students report more deep-level learning (Berghmans et al., 2012).

7.8. Concluding remark

Parallel to Chapter 6, this chapter describes the cross-age peer tutoring programmes which illustrate how diverse the settings are in which older and/or more experienced students can be engaged to collaborate with younger and/or more novice peers. More particularly, all educational levels and a broad variety of subjects and learning objectives lend themselves to the cross-age approach of peer tutoring, leading to positive effects both for tutors and tutees. As different age groups are involved in these types of programmes, it is however advisable to develop a school- or institution-wide and shared vision on the objectives of and the specific approach of the programme used to guarantee effectiveness.

Part IV

Conclusions and onward directions

Chapter 8

Advantages, problems, potential and challenges of peer learning

Part I introduced peer learning, describing mutual and directional peer interactions. Chapter 1 discussed mutual interactions, encompassing collaboration and cooperative learning. Chapter 2 discussed directional interactions, encompassing same-age peer tutoring and cross-age peer tutoring.

Part II explored more deeply the principles for structuring effective peer interaction, with chapters on preparing learners for constructive interactions and on organising peer interactions in academic tasks. Chapter 3 discussed positive frameworks for learning in interactions with mastery goals and the validation of social support and cooperative attitudes, training learners for appropriate use of cooperative skills, and group processing with feedback and reflection. Chapter 4 discussed grouping learners, positive interdependence, individual responsibility, scripts and scaffolds for peer interaction, monitoring and evaluating peer learning.

Part III gave many practical examples of peer interaction projects throughout the age range from primary school to university. Concrete exemplars of the principles described in Part II were highlighted. Chapter 5 explored how to structure peer interactions in symmetrical relationships (cooperative learning); Chapter 6 discussed how to structure interactions between learners from different levels inside the class (same-age tutoring); and Chapter 7 outlined the structure of interactions between learners from different levels from different classes (cross-age tutoring).

This final part and chapter consider what we have learned and how it will be useful. We synthesise advantages and benefits of the use of peer learning. We identify the main problems or barriers to put peer learning into practice. We give some advice about maximising advantages and reducing problems. Thus the challenges and the opportunities of peer learning are equally balanced.

8.1. Advantages and benefits of peer learning

You might wonder exactly why you as a teacher are (or will be) keen to emphasise peers as mediators of learning and to engage in fostering and optimising student peer interactions, when these are not generally encouraged in everyday class practice. Why invest in offering opportunities for students to work together instead of further pursuing individual and competitive learning? This obviously has to do with the advantages and benefits of peer interactions in learning – and this in diverse domains and for all educational levels, from kindergarten to higher education, including university students and adult education.

In this respect, statements such as *"to teach is to learn twice"* or *"explaining something in your own words to others is the best way to learn"* are often heard. Robert Heinlein, one of the most popular science fiction authors of the twentieth century, left us an analogous quote: "When one teaches, two learn".

There is scientific evidence that shows that teaching is a good way to learn (Duran, 2016). We are more engaged in learning content when we expect to have to teach it to others. When we explain something, we have more opportunities to understand it. The better opportunities for learning by teaching come when the person has to explain – transforming the information and questioning (Roscoe & Chi, 2007).

Taking into account the wide range of benefits, peer learning indeed seems worthwhile to engage in! So, let us summarise the advantages of the different relevant domains we've discussed:

- In the (meta)cognitive *domain*, peer learning leads to increased student performance and achievement in diverse subjects (e.g., language, maths, science), as well as to more higher-order thinking and deep-level learning. Additionally, peer learning gives rise to more meta-cognitively skilled and self-regulated learners, which is exceedingly relevant in view of lifelong learning and officially recommended in many curricula.
- In addition to the cognitive advantages of peer learning – and in our opinion not less valuable – are advantages in the social and communicative field, such as more positive social and intergroup relationships, better mutual concern, and more pro-social and communicative behaviour. Nowadays, cooperation is more important than ever. In the last century our society shifted from a mainly agricultural and manufacturing economy to a knowledge society, where people make a living by means of exchanging and processing information. Moreover, with political and economic changes encouraging migration, schools are characterised by highly heterogeneous populations. Successful intercultural interaction and cooperation skills therefore become core competencies for effective participation in our twenty-first-century knowledge society and globalised world.
- Further, benefits are recorded in the affective (i.e., motivational and emotional) domains, with for example better self-esteem, more self-confidence, and greater emotional growth for learners, but also a more positive attitude towards education in general and towards the subject domain under study during peer learning. Gains in self-concept (as self-efficacy and perceived competence) are likely to favour cognitive engagement, while the value devoted to school knowledge sustains perseverance.
- One of the crucial challenges in our twenty-first century is the increasing diversity in society and in our schools and classes, partly due to recommendations for becoming stronger regarding the inclusive school. In this respect, peer learning as an instructional strategy provides opportunities for differentiation and individualisation between learners with the intention of providing quality education for all (i.e., for students at risk or with special needs as well as for gifted and high-achieving students). Peer learning considers diversity, heterogeneity and differences between students as opportunities for learning. Therefore, it is not surprising that the positive effects referred to above also apply to students with difficulties, disabilities or other special needs. However, bear in mind that these positive effects may not be a reason for replacing or reducing inclusion supports from professional teachers. Obviously, these children are still entitled to receive special and customised support.

In addition to these well-documented advantages from the research literature and from personal educational experiences, proposing peer learning inside the classroom offers teachers wonderful opportunities to observe their students when they interact together. When teachers propose that their students work together, they have the chance to observe them closely while they are constructing their knowledge and to listen the way they discuss the content. To listen to how they think. Teachers can access student's naïve representations as well their understanding of the lesson, as well as the way they co-construct the content or conflict in their viewpoints.

Instead of accessing only the answers of the few students who agree to share their propositions thinking that their responses are good or at least acceptable, teachers can access all students' constructions. These observations represent a valuable source of information that helps in identifying both students' difficulties and their skills. Thanks to this information, teachers can offer interactive regulation during peer work and can regulate their teaching. This observation and the subsequent regulation is positive for the whole class and gives the opportunity to make all students' contributions valuable – it is a way to integrate and value all students.

8.2. Problems or barriers to peer learning

Research on peer interaction convincingly leads to learning. This we know and it was elaborated on and illustrated in previous sections. Notwithstanding the convincing benefits, however, barriers in implementing peer learning are also sometimes found. Importantly, teachers and schools should be aware of these and be able to overcome them consciously. An effective implementation of cooperative learning is complex (Jolliffe, 2015) and requires a major reorganisation of the teaching-learning situation (Gillies, 2008) and the definition of a new contract with students (Y. Sharan, 2010b). As mentioned by Cooper (2002), "Peer learning represents a major shift in focus from what is being taught to what is being learned, and transfers great responsibility for knowledge acquisition, organization, and application from the teacher to the student" (p. 54).

Implementation barriers can be found on the level of the teacher, the class, the school, and the wider school community (e.g., parents).

As to the teacher level, barriers for implementation often have to do with teachers' opinions and beliefs regarding peer learning (for example, viewing teaching as transmission, Y. Sharan, 2010b); teachers' beliefs about the purpose of schooling and the process of knowledge acquisition (Rich, 1990) and especially regarding the time and preparation required to create the conditions for effective peer learning (Buchs & Volpé, 2015; Jolliffe, 2015).

As you have read above, learners should be well prepared in order to guarantee true student engagement and constructive interaction. Further, consistently structuring peer interactions and teacher monitoring, coaching and evaluation is needed as well. Investing time and energy in this – when the ordinary curriculum is already thought overloaded – might be considered a burden for teachers or at least an important barrier to start implementing peer interaction for learning in class. Especially since peer learning requires effort first without necessarily having immediate results.

Secondly, teachers' perception of their competence (or assumed incompetence) in implementing and supporting peer learning in their class is important. If teachers feel insecure or that they lack crucial practical and realistic information, it will be difficult for them to put peer learning into practise.

According to Abrami, Poulsen and Chambers (2004), expectancies of success (teachers' beliefs that they can succeed in implementing an innovation in their own context) are the most important predictors for implementing cooperative learning. Teacher preparation is therefore important (Y. Sharan, 2010b). In line with these propositions, a recent survey (Filippou, Pulfrey & Buchs, 2016) involving more than 200 primary teachers indicated that self-transcendence and cooperative learning knowledge predicted self-efficacy beliefs regarding peer learning, especially for those lower in self-transcendence values. In turn self-efficacy as well as knowledge predicted the reported frequency of cooperative learning implementation. We hope that the previous chapters have helped to prepare you and make you feel that you can successfully introduce peer learning in your own context.

Peer learning is coherent with current and modern ways to understanding learning and teaching based on a socio-constructivism and sociocultural perspectives – in which learning, even if it is individual, is built from social interactions with someone more skilful. This perspective implies understanding that students can develop into the role of mediators (teachers) of their peers. When students work in pairs or in groups, the classroom becomes a community of learners where students learn not only from teacher assistance but from the peer's assistance too. But to make this happen, the teacher must share the ability to teach with their students. This implies trust in the students, stimulating situations in which they can provide mutual assistance to each other.

Regarding the class level, one main problem experienced by teachers relates to behaviour management (for example ensuring that students stay on task; see Jolliffe, 2015). Moreover, students' age, the class size, the presence of students with learning difficulties or nonnative speakers – these are often referred to as barriers to implementation. Classes are often felt to be too large or too diverse, the children too young or too immature to be engaged in peer learning practices. From research and in practice, however, we learn that it is the diversity between learners that makes all the difference and actually provides opportunities for learning, that peer learning offers chances for differentiation and individualisation also in large class groups, and that all age groups benefit. Cooperative learning favours changes in practices regarding diversity and sustains social inclusion of all students in classroom activities (Y. Sharan, 2010a, 2014).

It could be useful to know what are the main mistakes made when teachers start using cooperative learning in their classrooms (Grisham & Molinelli, 2001). They tend to

- make oversized and over-homogeneous teams,
- give little explicit instruction,
- give insufficient time for interaction,
- leave too much physical distance between team members,
- use a low-structured activity (with little interdependence),
- change teams before resolving the problems,
- give little or no time or guidelines for team self-assessment,
- ignore what doesn't work,
- use teams infrequently and
- evaluate complex cooperative work too soon.

It is obvious that if we are promoting students' working in teams, talking, reading aloud and discussing, we will have noisy classes. Maybe we need to change the old conception that suggests silence is synonymous with learning. But we can reduce noise just helping students to develop their "library voice", sitting members of teams as close as possible and creating a role in each team to control it (Jacobs et al., 2002).

When students are engaged in teamwork, it can be difficult to stop them. In order to manage cooperative learning classes is important to establish a quit signal, not requiring teachers to raise their voice to gain control. One of the most common is that the teacher raises a hand and says nothing, looking at students and waiting for them to quiet down (Jolliffe, 2007).

Finally, and especially in higher education, another important aspect to consider is the physical setup of the classroom: the arrangement of tables and chairs. Clearly, tables and chairs need moving to pair or group situations according to the nature of the peer interaction.

Barriers at the school level often have to do with the fact that a clear and shared vision on peer learning is lacking in schools. Further, a school culture fostering collaboration among teachers is often reported as an important stimulating condition for successfully implementing peer learning (Johnson & Johnson, 1994). Especially in the case of cross-age peer tutoring, which inherently assumes collaboration between teachers of different grades, this is indispensable. This evidently implies that the school organisation (e.g., timetables, teaching materials, space for placing groups of learners in a relatively quiet learning environment) is attuned as well.

Maybe there is no better way to teach students about the importance of cooperation than showing them their teachers cooperating. Co-teaching or two teachers sharing their responsibilities for teaching a class (Nevin, Thousand & Villa, 2009) is not only a good mechanism for responding to the students' needs, but also is a mechanism for peer learning between teachers (Beaten & Simons, 2014). Sharing knowledge and skills offers to the teachers great opportunities for peer learning, based on mutual understanding of the context, reflection and dialog on the shared practice (Rytivaara & Kershner, 2012).

Finally, as to the broader school community, parental expectations and opinions regarding teaching and learning (which are often in favour of individual or competitive learning or with a sole focus on performance, based on the parents' own experiences and on what they are accustomed to) might give rise to problems or reactions when teachers and schools consistently opt for the implementation of peer learning programmes.

8.3. Advice on maximising advantages and reducing problems

As mentioned above, teachers might think investing time and energy in student training and in organising peer interaction is a burden or drawback of this instructional strategy. One should know, however, that well-considered design of the peer learning programme, including training and continued support of students, and introducing principles for organising and realising true peer interactions pay off in terms of learning outcomes. Just putting students together and expecting the best is not what we are hoping for. Taking into account our previous discussions, we put forward the following guidelines and principles:

- Design and assign tasks actually and truly eliciting interaction and collaboration, instead of assignments that can be accomplished easily individually (i.e., by one student in a cooperative learning group or by the tutee in case of peer tutoring).
- Compose relatively small groups of students, to enable the comfortable, active and more or less equal, or at least harmonious, participation of all. Take into account students'

experience with peer learning, but also their age and developmental level. In the case of secondary and higher education students somewhat larger groups are manageable than for primary school learners, where working one-on-one in the case of same-age or cross-age peer tutoring or in group sizes of up to four students in the case of cooperative learning seems advisable.
- When composing groups for cooperative learning, carefully consider whether you opt for teams formed by yourself as a teacher, by learners or for random grouping. You can base your decision on your objectives, the class culture, or the students' characteristics. But remember that, at least at the beginning, it could be good to control the group composition in order to guarantee that teams can work.
- Ensure role differences between the students involved in peer tutoring to make sure that tutors can successfully take up their supportive role for their tutees. Especially in the case of (reciprocal) same-age peer tutors, this has to be taken into account explicitly, for example by providing tutors with additional information or resources. Cross-age peer tutoring already implies an inherent difference between tutors and tutees. However, in this case also take into account the guideline of at least two years of age difference between involved students and reflect on tutors' and tutees' achievement level and temperament when composing cross-age tutoring groups.
- Install positive interdependence. Goal interdependence is essential and may be reinforced by other dimensions like reward interdependence. Interdependence should be related to means to make students feel like sharing a common group goal in cooperative learning (e.g., through group recognition, division of resources, or complementary roles). This concretely shows that the success of each member is connected to the rest of the team and vice versa.
- Install individual accountability and mutual responsibility in the group (e.g., through individual assessment of personal work or progress, appointing a random choice of spokesperson), to make students feel like taking up personal responsibility in accomplishing cooperative learning assignments. This implies concretely that the contribution of each student is necessary and has to be visible.
- Ensure that the responsibilities devoted to students in cooperative learning is explicitly described and understood, so each student knows what to do and what to expect from others.
- Ensure supportive and simultaneous social interactions and mutually helpful behaviour between learners in both symmetrical and more directional peer interactions, which requires the following:
  - A focus on achievement goals oriented toward mastery goals that motivate students to learn and progress. This motivation allows students to perceive their classmates as informational support on which they can rely to improve their competence.
  - The installation of cooperative values and norms in the class (e.g., respect, motivation and engagement, genuine assistance, trust), for example through explicit instruction or teacher modelling.
  - The development of positive interpersonal relationships, which can be promoted stepwise from introducing activities to get to know each other, through creating positive relationships in teams, to introducing norms for supporting the quality of peer interaction.
  - The development of appropriate use of cooperative and interpersonal skills, such as giving and receiving help, managing group processes, providing frequent and immediate feedback and reinforcement.

In view of these guidelines, deliberately prepare students for the expected cooperative and communicative skills by means of preliminary training, including both instruction and practice. Along with the abovementioned constructive social interaction, ensure high-quality and in-depth interaction related to the content of the assignment, leading to the promotion of effective learning. This especially implies the following:

- Summarising, which facilitates the understanding and acquisition of information
- Regular and thought-provoking questioning and knowledge-building elaborative explanations, promoting co-construction through active and reciprocal discussions of all team members
- Argumentation and reasoning, forcing learners to justify their understanding and positions for others
- Disagreement, confrontation and socio-cognitive conflicts, supporting conceptual change and learning in individual learners through the expression of different opinions or viewpoints

Consequently, these aspects should also be part of students' preliminary training:

- Incorporate continuous supervision and support for the students throughout the programme, since only relying on an introductory training is unlikely to be sufficient. This support aims at further optimising all important and trained aspects of both the cooperative and content-related interaction during peer learning and consequently leads to improved future collaboration. Take into account that this support can take the form of providing students with scripts and scaffolds for effective peer interaction (e.g., in view of fostering the peer dialogue, the processing of information, joint construction of knowledge, and problem solving).
- Install individual and group reflection on and evaluation of the group process after each session. Unfortunately, this reflection moment is often overlooked, because time went too fast, the teacher wants to start the next lesson, students are already expected in another room, it is lunch time already.... Reasons enough we hear for skipping this important component of peer learning. However, involving students in reflection on whether or not the group goals were achieved, as well as on their learning and interaction processes and on their mutual relationships, improves the upcoming sessions.

As a teacher, you should also be well aware of the fact that providing students with responsibility for their own learning through working together with peers does not absolve you from offering the necessary coaching and guiding. This is already referred to in the guideline concerning the need for continuous supervision and support, but teacher monitoring and assessment deserves special attention as well. Observing and monitoring cooperative groups or peer tutoring pairs in action and providing them with genuine feedback during and after task execution is absolutely necessary. Bear in mind, however, that finding a balance between observing (i.e., letting students have their say and offering them time and space to learn from each other) and intervening (with your feedback, advice and/or modelling) is not always that easy and might need time. However, from our own experience, we know that practice makes perfect here.

As to the evaluation part, think of bringing in the assessment of both the academic and cooperative goals aimed at in peer learning, and reflect on how the interdependence between students will be mirrored in the evaluation. What aspects will be considered in the individual evaluation, and what for the collective or group evaluation? Further, consider blending teacher evaluations with self-evaluations and peer evaluations. This can help students develop ownership not only for their learning, but also for 'evaluating' their learning, giving rise to the development of self-regulated learners.

In addition to preparing students and structuring their interactions, informing other possible stakeholders of the programme can reduce implementation problems and maximise the advantages of peer learning. Talk to parents first. Providing them with all the available information on the objectives, timeline, procedures, and expected outcomes for all students (i.e., regardless of their achievement level or role in the case of cross-age and same-age tutoring) is mandatory before the onset of the implementation. Further, also present them with evidence of the diverse benefits of peer learning and do this in an accessible and illustrative way. You can base this information on the research findings this book presents, but also on your experiences with peer learning in your educational practice. Of course, also inviting parents and families to visit the class while the students are working together is possible in view of informing them about the programme. Even more far-reaching, some programmes also explicitly incorporate parental involvement in the peer learning activities. In this respect, it may be also necessary to train parents to ensure that all supervisors or facilitators are on the same wavelength.

8.4. A final word

Yes, peer learning is more complicated than you had realised. But doing anything well always is. However, there is no need to try to absorb the whole of *Effective Peer Learning* at one sitting, and then enact a perfect peer learning project. Teachers tend not to just learn by absorbing information, but by actually doing. So start off by trying to implement what seem to you to be some of the most important principles. Observe the effects closely and reflect upon them. Then implement a further project embodying some more of the principles. Go on blending your learning from this book with your learning from what you see in front of you as you implement successive peer learning projects. Try to involve other teachers. Reflect on the projects together and learn from each other. Peer learning not only works for students! Progressively, your projects will become better and better as you become more experienced and more expert. Eventually much of what now seems complicated will become second nature and automatic – it won't seem to be complicated anymore, just common sense. Then you will know you are a peer learning expert.

References

Abbott, M., Greenwood, C. R., Buzhardt, J. & Tapia, Y. (2006). Using technology-based teacher support tools to scale up the classwide peer tutoring program. *Reading & Writing Quarterly*, *22*(1), 47–64. doi: http://dx.doi.org/10.1080/10573560500203525.

Abrami, P. C., Chambers, B., Poulsen, C., De Simone, C., d'Apollonia, S. & Howden, J. (1995). *Classroom connections: Understanding and using cooperative learning.* Toronto: Harcourt-Brace.

Abrami, P. C., Poulsen, C. & Chambers, B. (2004). Teacher motivation to implement an educational innovation: Factors differentiating users and non-users of cooperative learning. *Educational Psychology*, *24*(2), 201–216.

Ames, C. (1992). Classrooms: Goals, structures, and student motivation. *Journal of Educational Psychology*, *84*(3), 261–271.

Ames, G. J. & Murray, F. B. (1982). When two wrongs make a right: Promoting cognitive change by social conflict. *Developmental Psychology*, *18*, 894–897.

Annis, L. F. (1983). The processes and effects of peer tutoring. *Human Learning*, *2*(1), 39–47.

Archer-Kath, J., Johnson, D. W. & Johnson, R. T. (1994). Individual versus group feedback in cooperative groups. *Journal of Social Psychology*, *134*(5), 681–694.

Aronson, E. (1978). *The jigsaw classroom.* Beverly Hills, CA: Sage.

Aronson, E. & Patnoe, S. (2011). *Cooperation in the classroom. The jigsaw method* (2nd ed.). London: Pinter & Martin.

Arreaga-Mayer, C., Terry, B. J. & Greenwood, C. R. (1998). Classwide peer tutoring. In K. Topping & S. Ehly, *Peer-Assisted Learning*. Mahwah, NJ: Lawrence Erlbaum Associates, Inc.

Ashman, A. F. & Gillies, R. M. (1997). Children's cooperative behavior and interactions in trained and untrained work groups in regular classrooms. *Journal of School Psychology*, *35*(3), 261–279.

Ashwin, P. (2003). Peer support: Relations between the context, process, and outcomes for the students who are supported. *Instructional Science*, *31*, 159–173.

Azevedo, R. & Hadwin, A. F. (2005). Scaffolding self-regulated learning and metacognition: Implications for the design of computer-based scaffolds. *Instructional Science*, *33*, 367–379.

Baer, J. (2003). Grouping and achievement in cooperative learning. *College Teaching*, *51*(4), 169–174.

Baines, E., Rubie-Davies, C. & Blatchford, P. (2009). Improving pupil group work interaction and dialogue in primary classrooms: Results from a year-long intervention study. *Cambridge Journal of Education*, *39*(1), 95–117. doi:10.1080/03057640802701960.

Bargh, J. & Schul, Y. (1980). On the cognitive benefits of teaching. *Journal of Educational Psychology*, *72*, 593–604.

Barkley, E. F., Cross, K. P. & Major, C. H. (2005). *Collaborative learning techniques: A handbook for college faculty.* San Francisco, CA: Jossey-Bass.

Beaten, M. & Simons, M. (2014). Student teacher's team teaching: Models, effects, and conditions for implementation. *Teaching and Teacher Education*, *41*, 92–110.

Bell, N., Grossen, M. & Perret-Clermont, A.-N. (1985). Sociocognitive conflict and intellectual growth. In M. W. Berkowitz (Ed.), *Peer conflict and psychological growth* (pp. 41–54). San Francisco: Jossey-Bass.

Bennett, B., Rolheiser, C. & Stevahn, L. (1991). *Cooperative learning: Where hearts meets mind*. Ontario: Educational Connections.

Bentz, J. L. & Fuchs, L. S. (1996). Improving peers' helping behavior to students with learning disabilities during mathematics peer tutoring. *Learning Disability Quarterly, 19*, 202–215.

Berghmans, I., Druine, N., Dochy, F. & Struyven, K. (2012). A facilitative versus directive approach in training clinical skills? Investigating students' clinical performance and perceptions. *Perspectives on Medical Education, 1*, 104–118.

Bertucci, A., Conte, S., Johnson, D. W. & Johnson, R. T. (2010). The impact of size of cooperative group on achievement, social support, and self-esteem. *Journal of General Psychology, 137*(3), 256–272.

Bertucci, A., Johnson, D. W., Johnson, R. T. & Conte, S. (2012). Influence of group processing on achievement and perception of social and academic support in elementary inexperienced cooperative learning groups. *The Journal of Educational Research, 105*(5), 329–335.

Blanch, S., Corcelles, M., Duran, D., Dekhinet, R. & Topping, K. J. (2014). La escritura y corrección de textos a través de tutoría entre iguales, recíproca y virtual, para la mejora en inglés y español. *Revista de Educación, 363*, 309–333.

Blanch, S., Duran, D., Valdevenito, V. & Flores, M. (2013). The effects and characteristics of family involvement on a peer tutoring programme to improve the reading comprehension competence. *European Journal of Psychology Education, 28*, 101–119.

Blaney, N. T., Stephan, C., Rosenfield, R., Aronson, E. & Sikes, J. (1977). Interdependence in the classroom: A field study. *Journal of Educational Psychology, 69*, 121–128.

Blatchford, P., Baines, E., Rubie-Davies, C., Bassett, P. & Chowne, A. (2006). The effect of a new approach to group work on pupil-pupil and teacher-pupil interactions. *Journal of Educational Psychology, 98*(4), 750–765. doi:10.1037/0022-0663.98.4.750.

Blatchford, P., Kutnick, P., Baines, E. & Galton, M. (2003). Toward a social pedagogy of classroom group work. *International Journal of Educational Research, 39*(1–2), 153–172. doi.org/10.1016/S0883-0355(03)00078-8.

Bournot-Trites, M. (2004). Peer tutoring: A parent–school initiative to improve reading in French immersion primary grades. In *The state of French second language education in Canada 2004* (pp. 56–57). Ottawa, Ontario: Canadian Parents for French.

Bournot-Trites, M., Lee, E. & Séror, J. (2003). Tutorat par les pairs en lecture: une collaboration parents-école en milieu d'immersion française. *La Revue des Sciences de l'Éducation, 29*, 195–210.

Bowen, C. W. (2000). A quantitative literature review of cooperative learning effects on high school and college chemistry achievement. *Journal of Chemical Education, 77*, 116–119.

Bowman-Perrott, L., Davis, H., Vannest, K., Williams, L., Greenwood, C. & Parker, R. (2013). Academic benefits of peer tutoring: A meta-analytic review of single-case research. *School Psychology Review, 42*, 39–55.

Box, J. A. & Little, D. C. (2003). Cooperative small-group instruction combined with advanced organizers and their relationship to self-concept and social studies achievement of elementary school students. *Journal of Instructional Psychology, 30*(4), 285–287.

Brandenburguer, A. & Nalebuff, B. (1998). *Co-opetition*. New York: Currecy Doubleday.

Brody, C. M. (2009). Cooperative learning and collaborative learning: Is there a difference? *IASCE Newsletter, 28*(1), 7–9.

Brody, C. & Davidson, N. (Eds.) (1998). *Professional development for cooperative learning: Issues and approaches*. Albany, NY: Sunny Press.

Brooks, G. (2013). *What works for children and young people with literacy difficulties? The effectiveness of intervention schemes*. (4th ed.). Bracknell: The Dyslexia-SpLD Trust. Retrieved 26 October 2014 from www.interventionsforliteracy.org.uk/widgets_GregBrooks/What_works_for_children_fourth_ed.pdf. Fifth edition retrieved 23 November 2016 from www.interventionsforliteracy.org.uk/assets/What-Works-5th-edition.pdf.

Bruffee, K. A. (1995). Sharing our toys: Cooperative versus collaborative learning. *Change, 27*, 12–18.

Buchs, C. (2015). *Positive resource interdependence for young students: A nudge for cooperation but a pitfall for learning*. Geneva: University of Geneva.

Buchs, C. & Butera, F. (2004). Socio-cognitive conflict and the role of student interaction in learning. *New Review of Social Psychology*, *3*, 80–87.

Buchs, C. & Butera, F. (2009). Is a partner's competence threatening during dyadic cooperative work? It depends on resource interdependence. *European Journal of Psychology of Education*, *24*, 145–154.

Buchs, C. & Butera, F. (2015). Cooperative learning and social skills development. In R. Gillies (Ed.), *Collaborative learning: Developments in research and practice* (pp. 201–217). New York: Nova Science.

Buchs, C., Butera, F. & Mugny, G. (2004). Resource interdependence, student interactions and performance in cooperative learning. *Educational Psychology*, *24*, 291–314. doi:10.1080/0144341042000211661.

Buchs, C., Butera, F., Mugny, G. & Darnon, C. (2004). Conflict elaboration and cognitive outcomes. *Theory Into Practice*, *43*(1), 23–30.

Buchs, C., Gilles, I., Antonietti, J. P. & Butera, F. (2016). Why students need training to cooperate: A test in statistics learning at university. *Educational Psychology*, *36*(5), 956–974. http://dx.doi.org/10.1080/01443410.2015.1075963.

Buchs, C., Lehraus, K. & Crahay, M. (2012). Coopération & apprentissage. In M. Crahay (Ed.), *L'école peut-elle être juste et efficace* (pp. 421–454). Bruxelles: De Boeck.

Buchs, C., Pulfrey, C., Gabarrot, F. & Butera, F. (2010). Competitive conflict regulation and informational dependence in peer learning. *European Journal of Social Psychology*, *40*(3), 418–435. doi: 10.1002/ejsp.631

Buchs, C. & Volpé, Y. (2015). *How elementary teachers implement cooperative learning after a short training*. Paper presented at the International Association for the Study of Cooperation in Education, Odense Denmark, October 2015.

Buchs, C., Wiederkehr, V., Filippou, D., Sommet, N. & Darnon, C. (2015). Structured cooperative learning as a mean to improve average-achievers' mathematic learning in fractions. *Teaching Innovation*, *25*, 15–35.

Butera, F., Darnon, C. & Mugny, G. (2010). Learning from conflict. In J. Jetten & M. Hornsey (Eds.), *Rebels in groups: Dissent, deviance, difference and defiance* (pp. 36–52). Oxford: Oxford University Press.

Carette, V., Content, A., Rey, B., Coché, F., & Gabriel, F. (2009). Etude de l'apprentissage des nombres rationnels et des fractions dans une approche par compétences à l'école primaire. Final report 126/07. Retrieved 23 November 2016 from www.ulb.ac.be/facs/sse/img/fractions.pdf.

Cervantes, C. M., Lieberman, L. J., Magnesio, B. & Wood, J. (2013). Peer tutoring: Meeting the demands of inclusion in physical education today. *Journal of Physical Education, Recreation & Dance*, *84*(3), 43–48.

Chan, C., Burtis, J. & Bereiter, C. (1997). Knowledge building as a mediator of conflict in conceptual change. *Cognition and Instruction*, *15*(1), 1–40.

Cheng, Y. C. & Ku, H. Y. (2009). An investigation of the effects of reciprocal peer tutoring. *Computers in Human Behavior*, *25*, 40–49.

Chi, M., Siler, S., Jeong, H., Yamauchi, T. & Hausmann, R. (2001). Learning from human tutoring. *Cognitive Science*, *25*, 471–533.

Chipman, M. & Roy, N. (2006). *Peer Tutoring Literacy Program. The bridge: From research to practice*. Retrieved 15 May 2016 from http://carla.umn.edu/immersion/acie/vol10/nov2006_research_tutoring.html.

Chun, C. C. & Winter, S. (1999). Classwide Peer Tutoring with or without reinforcement: Effects on academic responding, content coverage, achievement, intrinsic interest and reported project experiences. *Educational Psychology*, *19*(2), 191–205. doi: http://dx.doi.org/10.1080/0144341990190206.

Clarke, J., Wideman, R. & Eadie, S. (1990). *Together we learn*. Toronto: Prentice-Hall.

Cohen, B. P. & Cohen, E. G. (1991). From groupwork among children to R&D teams: Interdependence, interaction and productivity. *Advances in Group Processes*, *8*, 205–225.

Cohen, E. G. (1994). *Designing groupwork: Strategies for the heterogeneous classroom* (2nd ed.). New York: Teachers College Press.

Cohen, P. A., Kulik, J. A. & Kulik, C. C. (1982). Educational outcomes of tutoring: A meta-analysis of findings. *American Educational Research Journal, 19*, 237–248.

Colvin, J.W. (2007). Peer tutoring and social dynamics in higher education. *Mentoring and Tutoring, 15*, 165–181.

Cook, S. B., Scruggs, T. E., Mastropieri, M. A. & Casto, G. C. (1985). Handicapped students as tutors. *The Journal of Special Education, 19*, 483–492.

Cooper, S. M. A. (2002). Classroom choices for enabling peer learning. *Theory into Practice, 41*(1), 53.

Cuseo, J. (1992). Collaborative & cooperative learning in higher education: A proposed taxonomy. *Cooperative Learning and College Teaching, 2*(2), 2–4.

Cuseo, J. (2002). *Igniting student involvement, peer interaction and teamwork: A taxonomy of specific cooperative learning structures and collaborative learning strategies*. Stillwater, OK: New Forums Press.

Damon, W. & Phelps, E. (1989). Critical distinctions among three approaches to peer education. *International Journal of Educational Research, 13*(1), 9–19.

Dansereau, D. F. (1988). Cooperative learning strategies. In C. E. Weinstein, E. T. Goetz & P. A. Alexander (Eds.), *Learning and study strategies, issues in assessment, instruction and evaluation* (pp. 103–119). San Diego: Academic Press.

Darnon, C., Buchs, C. & Butera, F. (2002). Epistemic and relational conflicts in sharing identical vs complementary information during cooperative learning. *Swiss Journal of Psychology Zeitschrift fur Psychologie Revue Suisse de Psychologie, 61*(3), 139–151.

Darnon, C., Butera, F. & Harackiewicz, J. (2007). Achievement goals in social interactions: Learning with mastery vs. performance goals. *Motivation and Emotion, 31*, 61–70.

Darnon, C., Doll, S. & Butera, F. (2007). Dealing with a disagreeing partner: Relational and epistemic conflict elaboration. *European Journal of Psychology of Education, 22*, 227–242.

Darnon, C., Muller, D., Schrager, S. M., Pannuzzo, N. & Butera, F. (2006). Mastery and performance goals predict epistemic and relational conflict regulation. *Journal of Educational Psychology, 98*, 766–776.

Davidson, N. (1994). Cooperative and collaborative learning. In J. S. Thousand, R. A. Villa & A. Nevin (Eds.), *Creative and collaborative learning*. Baltimore: Paul H. Brookes Publishing Company.

Davidson, N. & Major, C. H. (2014). Boundary crossings: Cooperative learning, collaborative learning, and problem-based learning. *Journal on Excellence in College Teaching, 25*(3 & 4), 7–55.

De Backer, L., Van Keer, H., Moerkerke, B. & Valcke, M. (2015). Examining evolutions in the adoption of metacognitive regulation in reciprocal peer tutoring groups. *Metacognition and Learning, 11*, 187–213.

De Backer, L., Van Keer, H. & Valcke, M. (2012). Exploring the potential impact of reciprocal peer tutoring on higher education students' metacognitive knowledge and metacognitive regulation. *Instructional Science, 40*, 559–588.

De Backer, L., Van Keer, H. & Valcke, M. (2015a). Socially shared metacognitive regulation during reciprocal peer tutoring: Identifying its relationship with students' content processing and transactive discussions. *Instructional Science, 43*, 323–344.

De Backer, L., Van Keer, H. & Valcke, M. (2015b). Promoting university students' metacognitive regulation through reciprocal peer tutoring. *Higher Education, 70*, 469–486.

De Backer, L., Van Keer, H. & Valcke, M. (2015c). Exploring evolutions in reciprocal peer tutoring groups' socially shared metacognitive regulation and identifying its metacognitive correlates. *Learning and Instruction, 38*, 63–78.

De Backer, L., Van Keer, H & Valcke, M. (2016). Eliciting reciprocal peer tutoring groups' metacognitive regulation through structuring and problematising scaffolds. *The Journal of Experimental Education, 84*, 804–828.

Dekhinet, R.; Topping, K. J.; Duran, D. & Blanch. S. (2008). Let me learn with my peers online!: Foreign language learning through reciprocal peer tutoring. *Innovate. Journal of Online Education, 4*, 3.

Deseco (2002). *Definition and selection of competences: Theoretical and conceptual foundations*. Retrieved 11 April 2014 from www.deseco.admin.ch.

De Smet, M., Van Keer, H. & Valcke, M. (2008). Blending asynchronous discussion groups and peer tutoring in higher education: An exploratory study of online peer tutoring behaviour. *Computers and Education*, *50*, 207–223.

De Smet, M., Van Keer, H. & Valcke, M. (2009). Cross-age peer tutors in asynchronous discussion groups: A study of the evolution in tutor support. *Instructional Science*, *37*, 87–105.

De Smet, M., Van Keer, H., De Wever, B. & Valcke, M. (2010). Cross-age peer tutors in asynchronous discussion groups: Exploring the impact of three types of tutor training on patterns in tutor support and on tutor characteristics. *Computers and Education*, *54*, 1167–1181.

Deutsch, M. (1949). A theory of cooperation and competition. *Human Relations*, *2*, 129–152.

Deutsch, M. (1962). Cooperation and trust: Some theoretical notes. In M. R. Jones (Ed.), *Nebraska symposium on motivation* (pp. 275–319). Lincoln: University of Nebraska Press.

DeVries, D. & Edwards, K. (1973). Learning games and student teams: The effects on classroom process. *American Education Research Journal*, *10*, 307–318.

DeVries, D. & Slavin, R. (1978). Teams Games Tournament: A research review. *Journal of Research and development in Education*, *12*, 28–38.

De Wever, B., Van Keer, H., Schellens, T., & Valcke, M. (2009). Structuring asynchronous discussion groups: The impact of role assignment and self-assessment on students' levels of knowledge construction through social negotiation. *Journal of Computer Assisted Learning*, *25(2)*, 177–188.

Dillenbourg, P. (1999). What do you mean by "collaborative learning"? In P. Dillenbourg (Ed.), *Collaborative learning: Cognitive and computational approaches* (pp. 1–16). Amsterdam, NL: Pergamon, Elsevier Science.

Dillenbourg, P., Baker, M., Blaye, A. & O' Malley, C. (1996). The evolution of research on collaborative learning. In P. Reiman & H. Spada (Eds), *Learning in humans and machines: Towards an interdisciplinary learning science* (pp.189–211). Oxford: Elsevier.

Doise, W. & Mugny, G. (1984). *The social development of the intellect*. Oxford: Pergamon Press.

Duran, D. (2009). Aprender a cooperar. Del grupo al equipo. In J. I. Pozo & M. del P. Pérez, *La Psicología del aprendizaje universitario: la formación en competencias* (pp. 182–195). Madrid: Ediciones Morata.

Duran, D. (2016). Learning-by-teaching. Evidence and implications as a pedagogical mechanism. *Innovations in Education and Teaching International*, first online 11 March 2016. DOI: 10.1080/14703297.2016.1156011.

Duran, D., Blanch. S., Dekhinet, R. & Topping, K. J. (2010). Una experiencia de tutoría entre iguales virtual para el aprendizaje del castellano y el inglés. *Textos de Didáctica de la Lengua y la Literatura*, *53*, 89–101.

Duran, D., Blanch. S., Thurston. A. & Topping, K. J. (2010). Tutoría entre iguales recíproca y virtual para la mejora de habilidades lingüísticas en español e inglés. *Infancia y Aprendizaje*, *33(2)*, 209–222.

Duran, D. & Flores, M. (2015). Prácticas de tutoría entre iguales en universidades del Estado Español y de Iberoamérica. *Revista Iberoamericana sobre Calidad, Eficacia y Cambio en Educación*, *13*(1), 5–17.

Duran, D., Flores, M., Oller, M., Thomson-Garay, L. & Vera, I. (2016). *Reading in pairs. Peer tutoring for reading and speaking in English as a foreign language*. Barcelona: Horsori.

Duran, D. & Huerta, V. (2008). Una experiencia de tutoría entre iguales en la Universidad mexicana de Oaxaca. *Revista Iberoamericana de Educación*, *48*, 1–12.

Duran, D. & Monereo, C. (2005). Styles and sequences of collaborative learning in fixed and reciprocal peer tutoring. *Learning and Instruction*, *15*, 179–199.

Duran, D. & Monereo, C. (2012). *Entramado. Métodos de aprendizaje cooperativo y colaborativo*. Barcelona: Horsori.

Duran, D. & Utset, M. (2014). *Reading in pairs* network: A training model based on peer learning (pairs of teachers and school networks) for the sustainability of educational innovation. *Cultura y Educación*, *26*(2), 377–384.

Elbaum, B. E., Schumm, J. S. & Vaughn, S. (1997). Urban middle-elementary students' perceptions of grouping formats for reading instruction. *The Elementary School Journal*, *97*(5), 475–500.

Falchikov, N. (2001). *Learning together. Peer tutoring in higher education*. London: Routledge Falmer.

Fantuzzo, J. W., King, J. A. & Heller, L. R. (1992). Effects of reciprocal peer tutoring on mathematics and school adjustment. *Journal of Educational Psychology, 84*, 331–339.

Fantuzzo, J. W., Riggio, R. E., Connelly, S. & Dimeff, L. A. (1989). Effects of reciprocal peer tutoring on academic achievement and psychological adjustment: A component analysis. *Journal of Educational Psychology, 81*, 173–177.

Filippou, D., Pulfrey, C. & Buchs, C. (2016). Predicting cooperative learning in primary school: The role of teachers' self-transcendence values, their cooperative learning knowledge, and their perceived self-efficacy. Paper submitted for publication.

Fitz-Gibbon, C. T. (1988). Peer tutoring as a teaching strategy. *Educational Management and Administration, 16*, 217–229.

Flores, M. & Duran, D. (2013). Effects of peer tutoring on reading self-concept. *International Journal of Educational Psychology, 2*(3), 297–324.

Flores, M. & Duran, D. (2016). Influence of a Catalan peer tutoring programme on reading comprehension and self-concept as a reader. *Journal of Research in Reading, 39*(3), 330–346. doi: 10.1111/1467-9817.12044.

Foot, H. & Howe, C. (1998). The psycho-educational basis of peer-assisted learning. In K. Topping & S. Ehly (Eds.), *Peer-assisted learning* (pp. 27–44). Mahwah, NJ: Lawrence Erlbaum Associates.

Fuchs, D., Fuchs, L. S. & Burish, P. (2000). Peer assisted learning strategies: An evidence based practice to promote reading achievement. *Learning Disabilities Research & Practice, 15*, 85–91.

Fuchs, L. S., Fuchs, D., Hamlett, C. L. & Karns, K. (1998). High-achieving students' interactions and performance on complex mathematical tasks as a function of homogeneous and heterogeneous pairings. *American Educational Research Journal, 35*(2), 227–267.

Fuchs, L. S., Fuchs, D., Hamlett, C. L., Phillips, N. B., Karns, K. & Dutka, S. (1997). Enhancing students' helping behavior during peer-mediated instruction with conceptual mathematical explanations. *Elementary School Journal, 97*(3), 223–249.

Fuchs, L. S., Fuchs, D., Kazdan, S. & Allen, S. (1999). Effects of peer-assisted learning strategies in reading with and without training in elaborated help giving. *Elementary School Journal, 99*(3), 201–219.

Fuchs, L. S., Fuchs, D., Kazdan, S. A., Karns, K., Calhoon, M. B., Hamlett, C. L. & Hewlitt, S. E. (2000). Effects of workgroup structure and size on student productivity during collaborative work on complex tasks. *Elementary School Journal, 100*(3), 183–212.

Gaudet, D., Jacques, D., Lachance, B., Lebossé, C., Morelli, C., Pagé, M., Robert, G., Thomas-Petit, M. & Walenta, T (1998). *La coopération en classe: Guide pratique appliqué à l'enseignement quotidien*. Montréal: Chenelière/McGraw-Hill.

Gillies, R. M. (1999). Maintenance of cooperative and helping behaviors in reconstituted groups. *Journal of Educational Research, 92*(6), 357–363.

Gillies, R. M. (2000). The maintenance of cooperative and helping behaviours in cooperative groups. *British Journal of Educational Psychology, 70*(1), 97–111. doi:10.1348/000709900157994.

Gillies, R. M. (2002). The residual effects of cooperative-learning experiences: A two-year follow up. *Journal of Educational Research, 96*(1), 15–20.

Gillies, R. M. (2007). *Cooperative learning: Integrating theory and practice*. Thousand Oaks: Sage Publications.

Gillies, R. M. (2008). The effects of cooperative learning on junior high school students' behaviours, discourse and learning during a science-based learning activity. *School Psychology International, 29*(3), 328–347. doi:10.1177/0143034308093673.

Gillies, R. M. (2015a). Academic talk in the collaborative classroom. In R. M. Gillies (Ed.), *Collaborative learning: Developments in research and practice* (pp. 141–156). New York: Nova Science.

Gillies, R. M. (Ed.) (2015b). *Collaborative learning: Developments in research and practice*. New York: Nova Science.

Gillies, R. M. & Ashman, A. F. (1996). Teaching collaborative skills to primary school children in classroom-based work groups. *Learning and Instruction, 6*(3), 187–200.

Gillies, R. M. & Ashman, A. F. (1998). Behavior and interactions of children in cooperative groups in lower and middle elementary grades. *Journal of Educational Psychology, 90*(4), 746–757.

Gillies, R. M., Ashman, A. & Terwel, J. (Eds.). (2008). *Structuring group interaction to promote thinking and learning during small group learning in high school settings.* New York: Springer.

Ginsburg-Block, M. D. & Fantuzzo, J. W. (1997). Reciprocal peer tutoring: An analysis of "teacher" and "student" interactions as a function of training and experience. *School Psychology Quarterly, 12*, 134–149.

Ginsburg-Block, M., Rohrbeck, C. & Fantuzzo, J. W. (2006). A meta-analytic review of social, self-concept, and behavioral outcomes of peer-assisted learning. *Journal of Educational Psychology, 98*, 732–749.

Golub, M. (2011). *Le travail sur les habiletés coopératives, lors d'une séquence de groupe structurée, en vue d'augmenter les bénéfices de la coopération pour les élèves.* Masters thesis in Educational Sciences, Université de Genève.

Golub, M. & Buchs, C. (2014). Preparing pupils to cooperate during cooperative controversy in grade 6: A way to increase positive interactions and learning? *European Journal of Psychology of Education*, 453–466.

Good, T. L. & Brophy, J. E. (1997). *Looking in classrooms.* New York: Addison Wesley Longman.

Goodlad, S. & Hirst, B. (1989). *Peer tutoring. A guide to learning by teaching.* London: Kogan Page.

Graesser, A. C. & Person, N. (1994). Question asking during tutoring. *American Educational Research Journal, 31*, 104–137.

Graesser, A., Person, N. & Magliano, J. (1995). Collaborative dialogue patterns in naturalistic one-to-one tutoring. *Applied Cognitive Psychology, 9*, 495–522.

Greenwood, C. R., Carta, J. C. & Hall, R. V. (1988). The use of peer tutoring strategies in classroom management and educational instruction. *School Psychology Review, 17*, 258–275.

Greenwood, C. R., Carta, J. J. & Kamps, D. (1990). Teacher-mediated versus peer-mediated instruction: A review of educational advantages and disadvantages. In H. C. Foot, M. J. Morgan, and R. H. Shute (Eds.), *Children helping children* (pp. 177–205). New York: John Wiley & Sons.

Griffin, M. M. & Griffin, B. W. (1998). An investigation of the effect of reciprocal peer tutoring on achievement, self-efficacy, and test anxiety. *Contemporary Educational Psychology, 23*, 298–311.

Grisham, D. & Molinelli, P. (2001). *Cooperative learning. Professional's guide.* Westminster, CA: Teacher Created Materials, Inc.

Gruber, H. E. (2000). Creativity and conflict resolution: The role of point of view. In M. Deutsch & P. T. Coleman (Eds.), *The handbook of conflict resolution: Theory and practice* (pp. 345–354). San Francisco, CA: Jossey-Bass.

Hänze, M. & Berger, R. (2007). Cooperative learning, motivational effects, and student characteristics: An experimental study comparing cooperative learning and direct instruction in 12th grade physics classes. *Learning and Instruction, 17*(1), 29–41. doi:10.1016/j.learninstruc.2006.11.004.

Harackiewicz, J. M., Barron, K. E. & Elliot, A. J. (1998). Rethinking achievement goals: When are they adaptive for college students and why? *Educational Psychologist, 33*, 1–21.

Hattie, J. (2006). Cross-age tutoring and the reading together program. *Studies in Educational Evaluation, 32*, 100–124.

Hooper, S. & Hannafin, M. J. (1988). Cooperative cbi: The effects of heterogeneous versus homogeneous grouping on the learning of progressively complex concepts. *Journal of Educational Computing Research, 4*(4), 413–424.

Hooper, S. & Hannafin, M. J. (1991). The effects of group composition on achievement, interaction, and learning efficiency during computer-based cooperative instruction. *Educational Technology Research and Development, 39*(3), 27–40.

Howden, J. & Kopiec, M. (1999). *Structurer le succès: Un calendrier d'implantation de la coopération.* Montréal: La Chenelière.

Howden, J. & Kopiec, M. (2000). *Ajouter aux compétences: Enseigner, coopérer et apprendre au post-secondaire.* Montréal: La Chenelière.

References

Howe, C. (2015). *Dialogue and knowledge transformation: Towards a socio-cultural theory of cognitive growth*. Paper presented at EARLI conference, Limassol, Cyprus, 3–5 August.

Howe, C., Tolmie, A., Thurston, A., Topping, K., Christie, D., Livingston, K., Jessiman, E. & Donaldson, C. (2007). Group work in elementary science: Towards organisational principles for supporting pupil learning. *Learning & Instruction, 17*, 549–563.

Jacobs, G. (2015). Collaborative learning or cooperative learning? The name is not important; flexibility is. *Beyond Words, 3*(1), 32–52.

Jacobs, G. M., Power, M. A. & Inn, L. W. (2002). *The teacher's sourcebook for cooperative learning*. Thousand Oaks, CA: Corwin Press.

Järvelä, S. (2011). How does help seeking help? New prospects in a variety of contexts. *Learning and Instruction, 21*(2), 297–299. doi:10.1016/j.learninstruc.2010.07.006.

Jenkins, J. & O'Connor, R. E. (2003). Cooperative learning for students with learning disabilities: Evidence from experiments, observations, and interviews. In H. L. Swanson, K. R. Harris & S. Graham (Eds.), *Handbook of learning disabilities* (pp. 417–430). New York: Guilford Press.

Johnson, D. W. & Johnson, R. T. (1989). *Cooperation and competition: Theory and research*. Edina, MN: Interaction Books.

Johnson, D. W. & Johnson, R. T. (1991). *Learning together and alone. Cooperative, competitive, and individualistic learning* (1st ed.). Boston: Allyn & Bacon.

Johnson, D. W. & Johnson, R. T. (1994). *Leading the cooperative school* (2nd ed.). Edina, MN: Interaction Book Company.

Johnson, D. W. & Johnson, R. T. (1999). Making cooperative learning work. *Theory into Practice, 38*, 67–73.

Johnson, D. W. & Johnson, R. T. (2002). Cooperative learning methods: A meta-analysis. *Journal of Research in Education, 12*(1), 5–24.

Johnson, D. W. & Johnson, F. P. (2006). *Joining together. Group theory and group skills* (9th ed.). Boston: Allyn & Bacon.

Johnson, D. W. & Johnson, R. T. (2007). *Creative controversy: Intellectual challenge in the classroom* (4th ed.). Edina, MN: Interaction Book Company.

Johnson, D. W. & Johnson, R. T. (2009a). Energizing learning: The instructional power of conflict. *Educational Researcher, 38*(1), 37–51.

Johnson, D. W. & Johnson, R. T. (2009b). An educational psychology success story: Social interdependence theory and cooperative learning. *Educational Researcher, 38*(365), 365–379. doi: 10.3102/0013189X09339057.

Johnson, D. W. & Johnson, R. T. (2014). Cooperative learning in the 21st century. *Anales de psicología, 30*(3), 841–851.

Johnson, D. W. & Johnson, R. T. (2015). Theoretical approches to cooperative learning. In R. M. Gillies (Ed.), *Collaborative learning: Developments in research and practice* (pp. 17–46). New York: Nova Science.

Johnson, D. W., Johnson, R. T. & Holubec, E. (1998). *Advanced cooperative learning* (3rd ed.). Minneapolis: Interaction Book Company.

Johnson, D. W., Johnson, R. T. & Holubec, E. J. (2002). *Circles of learning: Cooperation in the classroom* (5th ed.). Edina, MN: Interaction Book Company.

Johnson, D. W., Johnson, R. T. & Holubec, E. (2008). *Cooperation in the classroom* (8th ed.). Edina, MN: Interaction Book Company.

Johnson, D. W., Johnson, R. T. & Holubec, E. J. (2013). *Cooperation in the classroom* (9th ed.). Edina, MN: Interaction Book Company.

Johnson, D. W., Johnson, R. T., Roy, P. & Zaidman, B. (1985). Oral interaction in cooperative learning groups: Speaking, listening, and the nature of statements made by high-, medium-, and low-achieving students. *Journal of Psychology, 119*(4), 303–321.

Johnson, D. W., Johnson, R. T. & Smith, K. A. (1998). *Active learning: Cooperation in the college classroom*. Edina, MN: Interaction Book Company.

Johnson, D. W., Johnson, R. T., Stanne, M. B., & Garibaldi, A. (1990). Impact of group processing on achievement in cooperative groups. *Journal of Social Psychology, 130*(4), 507–516.

Johnson, D. W., Maruyama, G., Johnson, R., Nelson, D. & Skon, L. (1981). Effects of cooperative, competitive, and individualistic goal structures on achievement: A meta-analysis. *Psychological Bulletin, 89*, 47–62.

Jolliffe, W. (2007). *Cooperative learning in the classroom: Putting it into practice*. Thousand Oaks, CA: Paul Chapman Publishing.

Jolliffe, W. (2015). Developing cooperative learning pedagogy in initial teacher education. In R. Gillies (Ed.), *Collaborative learning: Developments in research and practice* (pp. 175–200). New York: Nova Science.

Kagan, S. (1992). *Cooperative learning*. San Juan Capistrano, CA: Resources for Teachers, Inc.

Kagan, S. (2013). *Kagan cooperative learning structures*. San Clemente, CA: Kagan.

Kagan, M. & Kagan, S. (2000). *Advanced cooperative learning*. San Clemente, CA: Kagan.

Kagan, S. & Kagan, M. (1999). The structural approach: Six keys to cooperative learning. In S. Sharan (Ed.), *Handbook of cooperative learning methods* (pp. 115–133). Westport, CT: Greenwood.

Kagan, S. & Kagan, M. (2009). *Kagan cooperative learning*. San Clemente, CA: Kagan.

Kagan, M., Kagan, L. & Kagan, S. (2012). *Classbuilding: Cooperative learning structures*. San Clemente, CA: Kagan.

Kasser, T., Cohn, S., Kanner, A. D. & Ryan, R. M. (2007). Some costs of American corporate capitalism: A psychological exploration of value and goal conflicts. *Psychological Inquiry, 18*(1), 1–22.

King, A. (1989). Verbal interaction and problem-solving within computer-assisted cooperative learning groups. *Journal of Educational Computing Research, 5*(1), 1–15.

King, A. (1994). Guiding knowledge construction in the classroom: Effects of teaching children how to question and how to explain. *American Educational Research Journal, 31*(2), 338–368. doi:10.2307/1163313.

King, A. (1998). Transactive peer tutoring: Distributing cognition and metacognition. *Educational Psychology Review, 10*, 57–74.

King, A. (1999). Discourse patterns for mediating peer learning. In A. M. O'Donnell & A. King (Eds.), *Cognitive perspectives on peer learning* (pp. 87–115). Mahwah, NJ: Lawrence Erlbaum Associates.

King, A. (2002). Structuring peer interaction to promote high-level cognitive processing. *Theory Into Practice, 41*(1), 33–39.

King, A. (2007). Beyond literal comprehension: A strategy to promote deep understanding of text. In D. S. McNamara (Ed.), *Reading comprehension strategies: Theories, interventions, and technologies* (pp. 267–290). Mahwah, NJ: Lawrence Erlbaum Associates.

King, A. & Rosenshine, B. (1993). Effects of guided cooperative questioning on children's knowledge construction. *Journal of Experimental Education, 61*(2), 127–148.

King, A., Staffieri, A. & Adelgais, A. (1998). Mutual peer tutoring: Effect of structuring tutorial interaction to scaffold peer learning. *Journal of Educational Psychology, 90*, 134–152.

Klingner, J. K. & Vaughn, S. (1996). Reciprocal teaching of reading comprehension strategies for students with learning disabilities who use English as a second language. *Elementary School Journal, 96*, 275–293.

Kneser, C. & Ploetzner, R. (2001). Collaboration on the basis of complementary domain knowledge: Observed dialogue structures and their relation to learning success. *Learning and Instruction, 11*, 53–83.

Kutnick, P. & Kington, A. (2005). Children's friendships and learning in school: Cognitive enhancement through social interaction? *British Journal of Educational Psychology, 75*(4), 521–538.

Kutnick, P., Ota, C. & Berdondini, L. (2008). Improving the effects of group working in classrooms with young school-aged children: Facilitating attainment, interaction and classroom activity. *Learning and Instruction, 18*(1), 83–95. doi:10.1016/j.learninstruc.2006.12.002.

Kyndt, E., Raes, E., Lismont, B., Timmers, F., Cascallar, E. & Dochy, F. (2013). A meta-analysis of the effects of face-to-face cooperative learning. Do recent studies falsify or verify earlier findings? *Educational Research Review, 10*, 133–149.

Lambiotte, J. G., Dansereau, D. F., O'Donnell, A. M., Young, M. D., Skaggs, L. P., Hall, R. H. & Rocklin, T. R. (1987). Manipulating cooperative scripts for teaching and learning. *Journal of Educational Psychology, 79*(4), 424–430.

Lambiotte, J. G., Dansereau, D. F., O'Donnell, A. M., Young, M. D., Skaggs, L. & Hall, R. (1988). Effects of cooperative script manipulations on initial learning and transfer. *Cognition and Instruction, 5*(2), 103–121.

Lambiotte, J. G., Dansereau, D. F., Rocklin, T. R., Fletcher, B., Hythecker, V. I., Larson, C. O. & O'Donnell, A. M. (1987). Cooperative learning and test taking: Transfer of skills. *Contemporary Educational Psychology, 12*(1), 52–61.

Larson, C. O., Dansereau, D. F., O'Donnell, A. M., Hythecker, V. I., Lambiotte, J. G. & Rocklin, T. R. (1985). Effects of metacognitive and elaborative activity on cooperative learning and transfer. *Contemporary Educational Psychology, 10*(4), 342–348.

Lazarowitz, R., Baird, J. H., Hertz-Lararowitz, R. & Jenkins, J. (1985). The effects of modified jigsaw on achievement, classroom social climate, and self-esteem in high school science classes. In R. E. Slavin, S. Sharan, S. Kagan, R. Hertz-Lazarowitz, C. Webb & R. Schmuk (Eds.), *Learning to cooperate, cooperating to learn* (pp. 231–253). New York: Plenum Press.

Leung, K. C. (2015). Preliminary empirical model of crucial determinants of best practice for peer tutoring on academic achievement. *Journal of Educational Psychology, 107*, 558–579.

Levine, J. M., Resnick, L. B. & Higgins, E. T. (1993). Social foundations of cognition. *Annual Review of Psychology, 44*, 585–612.

Lew, M., Mesch, D., Johnson, D. W. & Johnson, R. T. (1986a). Components of cooperative learning: Effects of collaborative skills and academic group contingencies on achievement and main streaming. *Contemporary Educational Psychology, 11*(3), 229–239.

Lew, M., Mesch, D., Johnson, D. W. & Johnson, R. T. (1986b). Positive interdependence, academic and collaborative-skills group contingencies, and isolated students. *American Educational Research Journal, 23*(3), 476–488.

Lin, C. P., Wenli, C., Lin, C. C., Su, Y. T. & Xie, W. (2014). Group scribbles to support "fraction" collaborative learning in a primary school. *Research and Practice in Technology Enhanced Learning, 9*(3), 461–473.

Lindauer, P. & Petrie, G. (1997). A review of cooperative learning: An alternative to everyday instructional strategies. *Journal of Instructional Psychology, 24*(3), 183–187.

Loke, A. & Chow, F. (2007). Learning partnership. The experience of peer tutoring among nursing students: A qualitative study. *International Journal of Nursing Studies, 44*, 237–244.

Lou, Y., Abrami, P. C., Spence, J. C., Poulson, C., Chambers, B. & d'Apollonia, S. (1996). Within-class grouping: A meta-analysis. *Review of Educational Research, 66*(4), 423–458. doi:10.3102/00346543066004423.

Lyman, F. T. (1992). Think-Pair-Share, Thinktrix, Thinklinks, and Weird Facts: An interactive system for cooperative thinking. In D. David & T. Worsham (Eds.), *Enhancing thinking through cooperative learning* (pp. 169–181). New York: Teachers College Press.

Madden, N., Slavin, R. & Stevens, R. (1986). *Cooperative Integrated Reading and Comprehension: Teacher's manual*. Baltimore: Johns Hopkins University, Center for Research on Elementary and Middle Schools.

Maehr, M. L. & Midgley, C. (1991). Enhancing student motivation: A schoolwide approach. *Educational Psychologist, 26*, 399–427.

Mahenthiran, S. & Rouse, P. J. (2000). The impact of group selection on student performance and satisfaction. *International Journal of Educational Management, 14*(6), 255–264.

Marr, M. B. (1997). Cooperative learning: A brief review. *Reading & Writing Quarterly: Overcoming Learning Difficulties, 13*(1), 7–20.

Martin, W. G. & Strutchens, M. E. (Ed.). (2007). *The learning of mathematics (69th yearbook)*. Reston, VA: National Council of Teachers of Mathematics.

Mastropieri, M., Scruggs, T., Mohler, L., Beranek, M., Spencer, V., Boon, R. T. & Talbott, E. (2001). Can middle school students with serious reading difficulties help each other learn anything? *Learning Disabilities Research and Practice, 16,* 18–27.

Mathes, P. G. & Fuchs, L. S. (1994). The efficacy of peer tutoring in reading for students with mild disabilities: A best-evidence synthesis. *School Psychology Review, 23,* 59–80.

McDonald, B. A., Larson, C. O., Dansereau, D. F. & Spurlin, J. E. (1985). Cooperative dyads: Impact on text learning and transfer. *Contemporary Educational Psychology, 10,* 369–377.

McLuckie, J. & Topping, K. J. (2004). Transferable skills for online peer learning. *Assessment and Evaluation in Higher Education, 29,* 563–584.

McMaster, K. N. & Fuchs, D. (2002). Effects of cooperative learning on the academic achievement of students with learning disabilities: An update of Tateyama-Sniezek's review. *Learning Disabilities Research & Practice, 17*(2), 107–117.

McWhaw, K., Schnackenberg, H., Sclater, J. & Abrami, P. C. (2003). From co-operation to collaboration: Helping students become collaborative learners. In R. M. Gillies & A. F. Ashman (Eds.), *Co-operative learning: The social and intellectual outcomes of learning in groups* (pp. 69–86). New York: Routledge.

Meece, J. L., Anderman, E. M. & Anderman, L. H. (2006). Classroom goal structure, student motivation, and academic achievement. *Annual Review of Psychology, 57,* 487–503. doi:10.1146/annurev.psych.56.091103.070258.

Melero, M. A. & Fernández, P. (1995). El aprendizaje entre iguales: El estado de la cuestión en Estados Unidos. In P. Fernández & M. A. Melero (Comps.), *La interacción social en contextos educativos* (pp. 35–98). Madrid: Siglo XXI.

Mercer, N. (1996). The quality of talk in children's collaborative activity in the classroom. *Learning and Instruction, 6*(4), 359–377.

Mercer, N., Wegerif, R. & Dawes, L. (1999). Children's talk and the development of reasoning in the classroom. *British Educational Research Journal, 25*(1), 95–111.

Miller, S. R. & Miller P. F. (1995). Cross-age peer tutoring. A strategy for promoting self-determination in students with severe emotional disabilities/behavior disorders. *Preventing School Failure, 39,* 32–38.

Miller, D., Topping, K. J. & Thurston, A. (2010). Peer tutoring in reading: The effects of role and organization on two dimensions of self-esteem. *British Journal of Educational Psychology, 80*(3), 417–433.

Millis, B. & Cottell, P. G. J. (1998). *Cooperative learning for higher education faculty.* Phoenix: Oryx Press.

Mitchell, S. N., Reilly, R., Bramwell, F. G., Solnosky, A. & Lilly, F. (2004). Friendship and choosing groupmates: Preferences for teacher-selected vs. student-selected groupings in high school science classes. *Journal of Instructional Psychology, 31*(1), 20–32.

Moliner, L., Flores, M. & Duran, D. (2011). Efectos sobre la mejora de las competencias lingüísticas y la autoimagen lectora a través de un programa de tutoría entre iguales. *Revista de Investigación en Educación, 9*(2), 209–222.

Moskowitz, J. M., Malvin, J. H., Schaeffer, G. A. & Schaps, E. (1985). Evaluation of jigsaw, a cooperative learning technique. *Contemporary Educational Psychology, 10*(2), 104–112.

Muller Mirza, N. & Perret-Clermont, A.-N. (Eds.). (2009). *Argumentation and education. Theoretical foundations and practices.* New York: Springer.

Nastasi, B. K. & Clements, D. H. (1991). Research on cooperative learning: Implications for practice. *School Psychology Review, 20*(1), 110–131.

Neber, H., Finsterwald, M. & Urban, N. (2001). Cooperative learning with gifted and high-achieving students: A review and meta-analyses of 12 studies. *High Ability Studies, 12*(2), 199–214.

Nevin, A. I., Thousand, J. S. & Villa, R. A. (2009). Collaborative teaching for teacher educators – what does the research say? *Teaching and Teacher Education, 25,* 569–574.

Newmann, F. & Thompson, J. A. (1987). *Effects of cooperative learning on achievement in secondary schools: A summary of research*. Madison, WI: University of Wisconsin–Madison.

Nota, L., Soresi, S. & Zimmerman, B. J. (2004). Self-regulation and academic achievement: A longitudinal study. *International Journal of Educational Research, 41*, 198–215.

Oddo, M., Barnett, D. W., Hawkins, R. O. & Musti-Rao, S. (2010). Reciprocal peer tutoring and repeated reading: Increasing practicality using student groups. *Psychology in the Schools, 47*, 842–858.

O'Donnell, A. M. (1999). Structuring dyadic interaction through scripted cooperation. In A. M. O'Donnell & A. King (Eds.), *Cognitive perspectives on peer learning. The Rutgers invitational symposium on education series* (pp. 179–196). Mahwah, NJ: Lawrence Erlbaum Associates.

O'Donnell, A. M., Dansereau, D., Hall, R. & Rocklin, T. (1987). Cognitive, social/affective, and metacognitive outcomes of scripted cooperative learning. *Journal of Educational Psychology, 79*(4), 431–437.

O'Donnell, A. M. & Dansereau, D. F. (1995). Scripted cooperation in student dyads: A method for analyzing and enhancing academic learning and performance. In R. Hertz-Lazarowitz & N. Miller (Eds.), *Interaction in cooperative groups: The theoretical anatomy of group learning* (pp. 120–143). New York: Cambridge University Press.

O'Donnell, A. M. & King, A. (Eds.). (1999). *Cognitive perspectives on peer learning*. Mahwah, NJ: Lawrence Erlbaum.

Okilwa, N. S. A. & Shelby, L. (2010). The effects of peer tutoring on academic performance of students with disabilities in grades 6 through 12: A synthesis of the literature. *Remedial and Special Education, 31*, 450–463.

Olivier, F. (2013). *Mise en place d'une séquence d'apprentissage coopératif en mathématiques dans une classe de 6P Harmos*. Masters thesis in primary teaching. Geneva: Université de Genève.

Palincsar, A. & Brown, A. (1984). Reciprocal teaching of comprehension-fostering and metacognitive strategies. *Cognition and Instruction, 1*, 117–175.

Panitz, T. (1999). Collaborative versus cooperative learning: A comparison of the two concepts which will help us understand the underlying nature of interactive learning. Retrieved 15 May 2015 from http://files.eric.ed.gov/fulltext/ED448443.pdf.

Perrenoud, P. (2001). The key to social fields: Competencies of an autonomous actor. In D. S. Rychen & L. H. Salganik (Eds.), *Defining and selecting key competences*. Göttingen: Hogrefe & Huber.

Piaget, J. (1928). Logique génétique et sociologie. *Revue Philosophique de La France et de l'Etranger, 105*(1 & 2), 168–205.

Piaget, J. (1932). *Le jugement moral chez l'enfant*. Paris: Presses Universitaires de France.

Pianta, R. C., Belsky, J., Houts, R. & Morrison, F. (2007). Opportunities to learn in America's elementary classrooms. *Science, 315*, 1795–1796. doi:10.1126/science.1139719.

Poortvliet, P. M. & Darnon, C. (2010). Toward a more social understanding of achievement goals: The interpersonal effects of mastery and performance goals. *Current Directions in Psychological Science, 19*, 324–328.

Poortvliet, P. M. & Darnon, C. (2014). Understanding positive attitudes toward helping peers: The role of mastery goals and academic self-efficacy. *Self and Identity, 13*(3), 345–363.

Prichard, J. S., Bizo, L. A. & Stratford, R. J. (2006). The educational impact of team-skills training: Preparing students to work in groups. *British Journal of Educational Psychology, 76*(1), 119–140. doi:10.1348/000709904X24564.

Prichard, J. S., Bizo, L. A. & Stratford, R. J. (2011). Evaluating the effects of team-skills training on subjective workload. *Learning and Instruction, 21*(3), 429–440.

Prichard, J. S., Stratford, R. J. & Bizo, L. A. (2006). Team-skills training enhances collaborative learning. *Learning and Instruction, 16*(3), 256–265.

Proulx, J. (1999). *Le travail en équipe*. Sainte Foy: Presses de l'Unviversité du Québec.

Puntambekar, S. (2006). Analyzing collaborative interactions: divergence, shared understanding, and construction of knowledge. *Computers & Education, 47*, 332–351.

Qin, Z., Johnson, D. W. & Johnson, R. T. (1995). Cooperative versus competitive efforts and problem solving. *Review of Educational Research, 65*, 129–143.

Quiamzade, A. & Mugny, G. (2001). Social influence dynamics in aptitude tasks. *Social Psychology of Education*, *4*(3–4), 311–334.

Reiser, B. J. (2004). Scaffolding complex learning: The mechanisms of structuring and problematizing student work. *Journal of the Learning Sciences*, *13*, 273–304.

Rich, Y. (1990). Ideological impediments to instructional innovation: The case of cooperative learning. *Teaching & Teacher Education*, *6*, 81–91.

Ritschoff, K. A. & Griffin, B. W. (2001). Reciprocal peer tutoring: Re-examining the value of a co-operative learning technique to college students and instructors. *Educational Psychology*, *21*, 313–331.

Robinson, D., Schofield, J. & Steers-Wentzell, K. (2005). Peer and cross-age tutoring in math: Outcomes and their design implications. *Educational Psychology Review*, *17*, 327–362.

Rodríguez, L. M., Fernández, C., Escudero, T. & Sabirón, F. (2000). La investigación sobre el aprendizaje colaborativo: enfoques, métodos y resultados. *Anuario de Pedagogía*, *2*, 305–338.

Rohrbeck, C. A., Ginsburg-Block, M. D., Fantuzzo, J. W. & Miller, T. R. (2003). Peer-assisted learning interventions with elementary school students: A meta-analytic review. *Journal of Educational Psychology*, *95*, 240–257.

Romero, C. C. (2010). Cooperative learning instruction and science achievement for secondary and early post-secondary students: A systematic review. *Dissertation Abstracts International Section A: Humanities and Social Sciences*, *Vol 70*(8-A), 2010, 2943.

Roschelle, J. & Teasley, S. (1995). The construction of shared knowledge in collaborative problem solving. In C. E. O'Malley (Ed.), *Computer supported collaborative learning*. Heidelberg: Springer-Verlag.

Roscoe, R. D. (2014). Self-monitoring and knowledge building in learning by teaching. *Instructional Science*, *42*, 327–351.

Roscoe, R. D. & Chi, M. (2007). Understanding tutor learning: Knowledge-building and knowledge-telling in peer tutors' explanations and questions. *Review of Educational Research*, *77*, 534–574.

Roscoe, R. D. & Chi, M. (2008). Tutor learning: The role of explaining and responding to questions. *Instructional Science*, *36*, 321–350.

Roseth, C., Johnson, D. & Johnson, R. (2008). Promoting early adolescents' achievement and peer relationships: The effects of cooperative, competitive, and individualistic goal structures. *Psychological Bulletin*, *134*, 223–246.

Ross, S. M. & DiVesta, F. J. (1976). Oral summary as a review strategy enhancing recall of textual material. *Journal of Educational Psychology*, *68*, 689–687.

Rouiller, Y. & Howden, J. (2010). *La pédagogie coopérative: Reflets de pratiques et approfondissements*. Montreal: Chenelière Education.

Rytivaara, A. & Kershner, R. (2012). Co-teaching as a context for teachers' professional learning and joint knowledge construction. *Teaching and Teacher Education*, *28*, 999–1008.

Sabourin, M., Bernard, L., Duchesneau, M.-F., Fugère, O. & Ladouceur, S. (2002). *Coopérer pour réussir (préscolaire et 1er cycle): Scénarios d'activités coopératives pour développer des compétences*. Montréal: Chenelière/McGraw-Hill.

Saleh, M., Lazonder, A. W. & De Jong, T. (2005). Effects of within-class ability grouping on social interaction, achievement, and motivation. *Instructional Science*, *33*(2), 105–119. doi:10.1007/s11251-004-6405-z.

Saleh, M., Lazonder, A. W. & De Jong, T. (2007). Structuring collaboration in mixed-ability groups to promote verbal interaction, learning, and motivation of average-ability students. *Contemporary Educational Psychology*, *32*(3), 314–331.

Salmon, G. (2000). *A model for CMC in education and training. E-moderating. The key to teaching and learning online*. London: Kogan Page.

Schellens, T., Van Keer, H., De Wever, B. & Valcke, M. (2007). Scripting by assigning roles: Does it improve knowledge construction in asynchronous discussion groups? *International Journal of Computer-Supported Collaborative Learning*, *2*(2–3), 225–246.

Schraw, G., Crippen, K. J. & Hartley, K. (2006). Promoting self-regulation in science education: Metacognition as part of a broader perspective on learning. *Research in Science Education, 36*, 111–139.

Schwartz, S. H. (1996). Value priorities and behavior: Applying a theory of integrated value systems. In C. Seligman, J. M. Olson & M. P. Zanna (Eds.), *The psychology of values: The Ontario symposium* (Vol. 8, pp. 1–24). Hillsdale, NJ: Erlbaum.

Shamir, A. & Tzuriel, D. (2004). Children's meditational teaching style as a function of intervention for cross-age peer mediation. *School Psychology International, 25*, 59–78.

Shamir, A., Zion, M. & Spector-Levi, O. (2008). Peer tutoring, metacognitive processes, and multimedia problem-based learning: The effect of mediation training on critical thinking. *Journal of Science Education and Technology, 17*, 384–398.

Sharan, S. (Ed.). (1999). *Handbook of cooperative learning methods*. Westport, CT: Greenwood.

Sharan, S. (2002). Differentiating methods of cooperative learning in research and practice, *Asia Pacific Journal of Education, 22*, 106–116.

Sharan, S. & Sharan, Y. (1992). *Expanding cooperative learning through group investigation*. New York: Teacher's College Press, Columbia University.

Sharan, Y. & Sharan, S. (1999). Group investigation in the cooperative classroom. In S. Sharan (Ed.), *Handbook of cooperative learning methods* (pp. 97–114). Westport, CT: Greenwood.

Sharan, Y. (2010a). Cooperative learning: A diversified pedagogy for diverse classrooms. *Intercultural Education, 21*(3), 195–203.

Sharan, Y. (2010b). Cooperative learning for academic and social gains: Valued pedagogy, problematic practice. *European Journal of Education, 45*(2), 300–310.

Sharan, Y. (2014). Editorial. *Intercultural Education, 25*(3), 175–178.

Sharan, Y. (2015). Meaningful learning in the cooperative classroom. *Education, 3–13, 43*, 1, 83–94.

Silberman, M. (1996). The use of pairs in cooperative learning. *Cooperative Learning and College Teaching, 7*(1), 2–12.

Slavin, R. (1978). *Using student team learning*. Baltimore: Center for Social Organization of Schools. The Johns Hopkins University.

Slavin, R. (1980). Cooperative learning. *Review of Educational Research, 50*(2), 315–342.

Slavin, R. (1983). When does cooperative learning increase student achievement? *Psychological Bulletin, 94*, 429–445.

Slavin, R. E. (1995). *Cooperative learning: Theory, research, and practice*. Boston: Allyn and Bacon.

Slavin, R. E. (1996). Research for the future. Research on cooperative learning and achievement: What we know, what we need to know. *Contemporary Educational Psychology, 21*, 43–69.

Slavin, R. E. (2000). *Educational psychology: Theory and practice* (6th ed.). New Jersey: Allyn & Bacon.

Slavin, R. E, Leavey, M. & Madden, N. (1984). Effects of cooperative learning and individualized instruction on mainstreamed students. *Elementary School Journal, 84*, 409–422.

Sommet, N., Darnon, C., Mugny, G., Quiamzade, A., Pulfrey, C., Dompnier, B. & Butera, F. (2014). Performance goals in conflictual social interactions: Toward the distinction between two modes of relational conflict regulation. *British Journal of Social Psychology, 53*, 134–153.

Souvignier, E. & Kronenberger, J. (2007). Cooperative learning in third graders' jigsaw groups for mathematics and science with and without questioning training. *British Journal of Educational Psychology, 77*(4), 755–771.

Spencer, V. G. & Balboni, G. (2003). Can students with mental retardation teach their peers? *Education and Training in Mental Retardation and Developmental Disabilities, 38*, 32–61.

Springer, L., Stanne, M. E. & Donovan, S. S. (1999). Effects of small-group learning on undergraduates in science, mathematics, engineering and technology: A meta-analysis. *Review of Educational Research, 69*, 21–52.

Spurlin, J. E., Dansereau, D. F., Larson, C. O. & Brooks, L. W. (1984). Cooperative learning strategies in processing descriptive text: Effects of role and activity level of the learner. *Cognition and Instruction*, *1*(1), 451–463.

Stainback, S. & Stainback, W. (1999). *Curriculum consideration in inclusive classrooms*. Baltimore: Paul H. Brookes.

Staquet, C. (2001). *Le livre du moi: developper une image positive de soi*. Lyon: Chronique sociale.

Staquet, C. (2007). *Une classe qui coopère. Pourquoi? Comment?* Lyon: Chronique sociale.

Stipek, D. & MacIver, D. (1989). Developmental change in children's assessment of intellectual competence. *Child Development*, *60*(3), 521–538.

Sutherland, K. S., Wehby, J. H. & Gunter, P. L. (2000). The effectiveness of cooperative learning with students with emotional and behavioral disorders: A literature review. *Behavioral Disorders*, *25*(3), 225–238.

Tateyama-Sniezek, K. M. (1990). Cooperative learning: Does it improve the academic achievement of students with handicaps? *Exceptional Children*, *56*(5), 426–437.

Thanh, P. T. H., Gillies, R. & Renshaw, P. (2008). Cooperative learning and academic achievement of Asian students: A true story. *International Education Studies*, *1*, 83–88.

Thurston. A., Duran, D., Cunningham, E., Blanch, S. & Topping, K. J. (2009). International on-line reciprocal peer tutoring to promote modern language development in primary schools. *Computers & Education*, *53*, 462–472.

Tjosvold, D. & Johnson, D. W. (1978). Controversy and cognitive perspective taking. Paper presented at The American Educational Research Association, Toronto Canada, March 1978.

Tolmie, A. K., Topping, K. J., Christie, D., Donaldson, C., Howe, C., Jessiman, E., Livingston, K. & Thurston, A. (2010). Social effects of collaborative learning in primary schools. *Learning and Instruction*, *20*(3), 177–191. doi:10.1016/j.learninstruc.2009.01.005.

Tomasetto, C., Matteucci, M. C., Carugati, F. & Selleri, P. (2009). Effect of task presentation on students' performances in introductory courses. *Social Psychology of Education*, *12*, 191–211. doi: 10.1007/s11218-008-9081-z.

Topping, K. J. (1995). *Paired reading, spelling and writing: The handbook for teachers and parents*. London & New York: Cassell.

Topping, K. J. (1996). Effective peer tutoring in further and higher education: A typology and review of the literature. *Higher Education*, *32*, 321–345.

Topping, K. J. (2001). *Thinking reading writing. A practical guide to paired learning with peers, parents and volunteers*. London: Continuum.

Topping, K. J. (2005a). Trends in peer learning. *Educational Psychology*, *25(6)*, 631–645.

Topping, K. J. (2005b). Problem-solving evaluation. Retrieved December 10, 2015 from www.dundee.ac.uk/esw/research/resources/problemsolving/.

Topping, K. J. & Bamford, J. (1998). *The paired maths handbook: Parental involvement and peer tutoring in mathematics*. London: Fulton.

Topping, K. J. & Bryce, A. (2004). Cross-age peer tutoring of reading and thinking: Influence on thinking skills. *Educational Psychology*, *24*, 595–621.

Topping, K. J., Campbell, J., Douglas, W. & Smith, A. (2003). Cross-age peer tutoring in mathematics with seven- and 11-year-olds: Influence on mathematical vocabulary, strategic dialogue and self-concept. *Educational Research*, *45(3)*, 287–308.

Topping, K. J., Dehkinet, R., Blanch, S., Corcelles, M. & Duran, D. (2013). Paradoxical effects of feedback in international online reciprocal peer tutoring. *Computers & Education*, *61*, 225–231.

Topping, K. J., Duran, D. & Van Keer, H. (2016). *Using peer tutoring to improve reading skills: A practical guide for teachers*. London & New York: Routledge.

Topping, K. & Ehly, S. (2001). Peer assisted learning: A framework for consultation. *Journal of Educational and Psychological Consultation*, *12*, 113–132.

Topping, K. J., Kearney, M., McGee, E. & Pugh, J. (2004). Tutoring in mathematics: a generic method. *Mentoring & Tutoring: Partnership in Learning*, *12*, 353–370.

Topping, K. J. & Lindsay, G. A. (1992). Paired Reading: A review of the literature. *Research Papers in Education*, *7*(3), 199–246.
Topping, K. J., Miller, D., Murray, P., Henderson, S., Fortuna, C. & Conlin, N. (2011). Outcomes in a randomised controlled trial of mathematics tutoring. *Educational Research*, *53*(1), 51–63. DOI: 10.1080/00131881.2011.552239.
Topping, K. J., Miller, D., Murray, P. & Conlin, N. (2011). Implementation integrity in peer tutoring of mathematics, *Educational Psychology*, *31*(5), 575–593.
Topping, K. J., Thurston, A., McGavock, K. & Conlin, N. (2012). Outcomes and process in reading tutoring. *Educational Research*, *54*(3), 239–258.
Tymms, P., Merrell, C., Andor, J., Topping, K. J. & Thurston, A. (2011). Improving attainment across a whole district: Peer tutoring in a randomised controlled trial. *School Effectiveness and School Improvement*, *22*(3), 265–289.
UNESCO (1996). *Learning: The treasure within*. Report to UNESCO of the International Commission on Education for the Twenty-First Century. Paris: UNESCO.
Urdan, T. C. (1997). Achievement goal theory: Past results, future directions. In P. Pintrich (Ed.), *Advances in motivation and achievement* (Vol. 10, pp. 99–141). Greenwich, CT: JAI.
Van Keer, H. (2002). Een boek voor twee. *Strategieën voor begrijpend lezen via peer tutoring*. [One book for two. Strategies for reading comprehension by means of peer tutoring.] Antwerpen: Garant.
Van Keer, H. (2004). Fostering reading comprehension in fifth grade by explicit instruction in reading strategies and peer tutoring. *British Journal of Educational Psychology*, *74*, 37–70.
Van Keer, H. & Vanderlinde, R. (2008). *Nog een boek voor twee. Strategieën voor begrijpend lezen via peer tutoring*. [Another book for two. Strategies for reading comprehension by means of peer tutoring.] Antwerpen: Garant.
Van Keer, H. & Vanderlinde, R. (2010). The impact of cross-age peer tutoring on third and sixth graders' reading strategy awareness, reading strategy use, and reading comprehension. *Middle Grades Research Journal*, *5*, 33–46.
Van Keer, H. & Verhaeghe, J. P. (2005). Effects of explicit reading strategies instruction and peer tutoring in second and fifth graders' reading comprehension and self-efficacy perceptions. *Journal of Experimental Education*, *73*, 291–329.
Vermette, P., Harper, L. & DiMillo, S. (2004). Cooperative & collaborative learning with 4–8 year olds: How does research support teachers' practice? *Journal of Instructional Psychology*, *31*(2), 130–134.
Villa, R., Thousand, J. & Nevin, A. (2013). *A guide to co-teaching: New lessons and strategies to facilitate student learning* (3rd ed.). Thousand Oaks, CA: Corwin Press.
Vygotsky, L. (1978). *Mind in society: The development of higher psychological processes*. Cambridge, MA: Harvard University Press.
Webb, N. M. (1985). Student interaction and learning in small groups. A research summary. In R. E. Slavin, S. Sharan, S. Kagan, R. Hertz-Lazarowitz, C. Webb & R. Schmuk (Eds.), *Learning to cooperate, cooperating to learn* (pp. 147–172). New York: Plenum Press.
Webb, N. M. (1991). Task related verbal interaction and mathematics learning in small groups. *Journal for Research in Mathematics Education*, *22*(5), 366–389.
Webb, N. M. (2009). The teacher's role in promoting collaborative dialogue in the classroom. *British Journal of Educational Psychology*, *79*(1), 1–28. doi:10.1348/000709908x380772.
Webb, N. M., Farivar, S. H. & Mastergeorge, A. M. (2002). Productive helping in cooperative groups. *Theory Into Practice*, *41*(1), 13–20.
Webb, N. M., Franke, M. L., Ing, M., Turrou, A. C. & Johnson, N. C. (2015). Student participation, teacher instructional practices, and the development of mathematical understanding in the elementary classroom. In R. M. Gillies (Ed.), *Collaborative learning: Developments in research and practice* (pp. 47–68). New York: Nova Science.
Webb, N. M., Ing, M., Kersting, N. & Nemer, K. M. (2006). Help seeking in cooperative learning groups. In S. A. Karabenick & R. S. Newman (Eds.), *Help seeking in academic settings: Goals, groups, and context* (pp. 45–88). Mahwah, NJ: Laurence Erlbaum Associates.

Webb, N. M. & Palincsar, A. S. (1996). Group processes in the classroom. In D. C. Berliner & R. C. Calfee (Eds.), *Handbook of educational psychology* (pp. 841–873). New York: Macmillan.

Webb, N. M., Troper, J. D. & Fall, R. (1995). Constructive activity and learning in collaborative small groups. *Journal of Educational Psychology, 87*(3), 406–423.

Wells, G. (1999). *Dialogic inquiry*. Cambridge: The Press Syndicate of the University of Cambridge.

Wentzel, K. (1991). Social competence at school: Relation between social responsability and academic achievement. *Review of Educational Research, 61*(1), 1–24.

Wheldall, K. & Colmar, S. (1990). Peer tutoring in low-progress readers using pause, prompt and praise. In H. Foot, M. Morgan & R. Shute (Eds.), *Children helping children* (pp. 117–134). Chichester: John Wiley & Sons.

Winne, P. H. (2011). A cognitive and metacognitive analysis of self-regulated learning. In B. J. Zimmerman & D. H. Schunk (Eds), *Handbook of self-regulation of learning and performance* (pp. 15–32). New York: Routledge.

Yager, S., Johnson, R. T., Johnson, D. W. & Snider, B. (1986). The impact of group processing on achievement in cooperative learning groups. *The Journal of Social Psychology, 126*, 389–397.

Zajac, R. J. & Hartup, W. W. (1997). Friends as coworkers: Research review and classroom implications. *Elementary School Journal, 98*(1), 3–13.

Zimmerman, B. J. (2002). Becoming a self-regulated learner: An overview. *Theory into Practice, 41*, 64–70.

Index

Abrami 38, 44, 63, 162
academic tasks 57
Active Knowledge Sharing 74
argumentation and reasoning 30
Aronson 12, 68
ASK TO THINK procedure 49–50
asynchronous discussion groups 152
authority 40

basic academic skills 123
Buchs 33, 90, 106
Butera 33, 90

Chi 19, 29, 35
ClassWide Peer Tutoring 123
co-construction of knowledge 9
cognitive benefits 21
Cohen 13, 77
collaboration 6
collaborative learning 6
collaborative versus cooperative learning 5–6
competitive and individualistic learning 14
complementary expertise 80, 100
Complex Instruction 13
Constructive Controversy 11
constructive feedback 52
cooperation 6–12
Cooperative Integrated Reading and Composition 12–13
cooperative learning 2–7; methods 11–12; principles 10; research 14; structures 11; techniques 11; values, norms and attitudes 37
Cooperative Note-Taking Pairs 74
cooperative skills 44–51; *coopetition* 9; development 46; evidences 50; explaining 53; group processing 54; interpersonal and small group skills 51; questioning 51; type 44

Damon 2, 17
Dansereau 83, 86
Darnon 32
De Backer 18, 22, 133

degree of structuring 3
directional peer learning 2
dissipation of responsibilities 7
Duolog Math 113–16
Duran 119, 123, 160
dyadic cooperative controversy 94–5

effective learning 165
English as a foreign language 123
equality 3
E-tutoring 120
evaluation 42, 77, 165
explaining and co-construction 30

Falchikov 25, 135
family involvement 43, 166
five finger test 114
focus on learning 40–1
foreign language learning 116–19
formal education 8
French immersion 141
Fuchs 23, 50, 57

generations of research 14
Gillies 5, 7, 48
Graesser 18, 24, 28, 30, 48
Group Investigation 13
group processing 11, 56
group work 7
grouping 40; group formation 58; size 57

Hattie 137
higher education *see* university
high-need and at-risk students 23

inclusive education 149
individual accountability 34, 68

Jigsaw 12
Johnson 10, 12, 15, 36, 45, 62, 68
Jolliffe 162

Index

Kagan 34, 38, 74
King 30, 50

learning by teaching 160
learning to cooperate 7
Learning Together 11

mathematics 100, 104, 116
medical education 153
Mercer 30–2, 39
metacognitive benefits 22
metacognitive regulation 133
monitoring 76
monitoring and assessment 75
mutual peer learning 2
mutual responsibility 70
mutuality 3

Numbered Heads Together 75

O'Donnell 28, 74, 83, 86–7
One Book for Two 138–41
oral expression 123

pair thinking-aloud problem solving 75
Paired Maths 145–8
Paired Reading 109–13
Palincsar 13
Pause, Prompt, Praise 122
peer collaboration 2
peer interaction 1; constructive 28; scripts 73
peer learning 1–3, 16–8, 27–34, 77, 159–63; advantages and benefits 159; dimensions 3; guidelines 163; problems or barriers 161
peer tutoring 2, 16–20; concept 17; cross-age 19, 136, 142, 146, 154; equality and mutuality 18; fixed 20; online 120, 152; reciprocal 19, 131, 134; research 22; roles 17; same-age 19
The Peer Tutoring Literacy Program 142
physical education 149
Piaget 2, 31
positive interdependence 11, 34, 62–3; goal interdependence 64; resource interdependence 67; reward interdependence 65; role interdependence 66; task interdependence 67
positive interpersonal relationships 39
practices 79–81
primary education 100, 142, 146, 148
promotive interactions 11

questioning 28–9

Read On 41, 109
reading 111
reading comprehension 123, 138
Reading in Pairs 41, 119–23
Reading Together 135–7
Reciprocal Teaching 13
recognition 40
Role Playing 75
Roscoe 17, 19, 22, 24, 28–30, 160

scaffold 73
school *see* primary education
Scripted Cooperation 74, 83–90
scripts 73–5
secondary education 146, 148
send a problem 75
Sharan 8, 11, 162
Slavin 11, 12, 14, 66, 70
social, affective, and motivational benefits 22
social skills 11
socio-cognitive conflict 31
socio-constructivism 162
statistics learning 91
structure of the interactions 7
structured responsibilities 103
Student Teams–Achievement Division 12
studying texts 84
summarising 28

Talking Chips 74
task 42
teacher education 126
team 8
Team Assisted Individualisation 12
Teammates Consult 74
Team-pair-solo 75
Teams-Games-Tournaments 12
TEL WHY 50
Think-Pair-Share 74
Three-Step Interview 74
Topping 22, 109, 116, 146

university 83, 87, 90

van Keer 132, 138, 153
Vygotsky 2, 8

Webb 30, 35

Taylor & Francis eBooks

Helping you to choose the right eBooks for your Library

Add Routledge titles to your library's digital collection today. Taylor and Francis ebooks contains over 50,000 titles in the Humanities, Social Sciences, Behavioural Sciences, Built Environment and Law.

Choose from a range of subject packages or create your own!

Benefits for you
- Free MARC records
- COUNTER-compliant usage statistics
- Flexible purchase and pricing options
- All titles DRM-free.

Benefits for your user
- Off-site, anytime access via Athens or referring URL
- Print or copy pages or chapters
- Full content search
- Bookmark, highlight and annotate text
- Access to thousands of pages of quality research at the click of a button.

REQUEST YOUR FREE INSTITUTIONAL TRIAL TODAY | **Free Trials Available** We offer free trials to qualifying academic, corporate and government customers.

eCollections – Choose from over 30 subject eCollections, including:

Archaeology	Language Learning
Architecture	Law
Asian Studies	Literature
Business & Management	Media & Communication
Classical Studies	Middle East Studies
Construction	Music
Creative & Media Arts	Philosophy
Criminology & Criminal Justice	Planning
Economics	Politics
Education	Psychology & Mental Health
Energy	Religion
Engineering	Security
English Language & Linguistics	Social Work
Environment & Sustainability	Sociology
Geography	Sport
Health Studies	Theatre & Performance
History	Tourism, Hospitality & Events

For more information, pricing enquiries or to order a free trial, please contact your local sales team:
www.tandfebooks.com/page/sales

Routledge — Taylor & Francis Group | The home of Routledge books | **www.tandfebooks.com**